Library of
Davidson College

Outstanding Studies in
Early American History

EDITED BY
John Murrin
Princeton University

A Garland Series

Political Institutions in Virginia, 1619–1660

Jon Kukla

Garland Publishing, Inc.
NEW YORK & LONDON 1989

Copyright © 1989 by Jon Kukla
All Rights Reserved

Library of Congress Cataloging-in-Publication Data

Kukla, Jon
        Political institutions in Virginia, 1619–1660 / Jon Kukla.
      p. cm. — (Outstanding studies in early American history)
  Thesis (Ph.D.)—University of Toronto, 1979.
        Bibliography: p.
        Includes index.
        ISBN 0-8240-6188-8 (alk. paper)
        1. Virginia—Politics and government—Colonial period, ca. 1600–1775. I. Title. II. Series.
F229.K87   1989
306.2'09755'09032—dc20   89-32412

Printed on acid-free, 250-year-life paper

MANUFACTURED IN THE UNITED STATES OF AMERICA

To Jeanette

Take heed of small beginnings, . . .
for the disease and alteration of a
Common-wealth, doth not happen all at
once, but grows by degrees, which
every common wit cannot discern, but
men expert in POLICIE.
>   Sir Walter Raleigh,
>   *Maxims of State*

CONTENTS

Preface to the Garland Edition	v
Acknowledgments	viii
Preface: Historiographical Note	x

Introduction
    Settlement and the Beginning
    of Politics, 1607-1660
	1

The Founding of the General Assembly
    The Governor, the Council of State, and
    the Assembly of 1619
	40

The Founding of the House of Burgesses
    The Dissolution of the Virginia Company,
    Uncertainty and Coup d'Etat, and
    Reform, 1624-1643
	65

A Well-Tempered Cavalier
    Sir William Berkeley and Institutional
    Maturation during the Civil War, 1643-1652
	123

The Burgesses Ascendant 1652-1660	158
Epilogue The Restoration, and After	205
Short Titles and Abbreviations	217
Notes	220
Selected Bibliography	251
Index	258

PREFACE TO THE GARLAND EDITION

The inception and completion of this dissertation in the 1970s coincided with the season of quantified Chesapeake social history as a fashionable subfield of early American history. Political and institutional history were out of vogue, and few historians thought intellectual history possible from seventeenth-century southern colonial sources. Steeped by William H. Nelson in the scholarship of Perry Miller as well as that on the transatlantic civic republican tradition, until 1973 I had intended to study Virginia in the era of the ratification of the United States Constitution.[1] Seventeenth-century Virginia was then as unfamiliar to me as it remains to many historians today, and I was astonished when an assignment to identify some "missing" early Virginia officials led me to seldom-used sources and novel conclusions. At one level, this fresh examination of early Virginia political institutions was something that simply needed to be done, for the existing monographs had serious shortcomings. Compared especially to the late-nineteenth- and early-twentieth-century studies of politics and institutions on which scholars had relied for so long, Political Institutions in Virginia, 1619-1660 attempted to delineate an economic, social,

---

1. "A Spectrum of Sentiments: Virginia's Federalists, Antifederalists, and 'Federalists Who Are For Amendments,' 1787-1788," Virginia Magazine of History and Biography 96 (1988): 277-296.

and intellectual context for political events and institutional change.

At another level, however, Arthur Lovejoy was right that "the more you press in towards the heart of a narrowly bounded historical problem, the more likely you are to encounter in the problem itself a pressure which drives you beyond those bounds"--and the quotation of Lovejoy's observation in my acknowledgments was meant to signal the possibility that meaningful chapters in American intellectual history might be written from seventeenth-century Virginia sources. A subsequent decade of research and discovery has convinced me of that reality. Some recondite suggestions have been exhibited in "Order and Chaos in Early America: Political and Social Stability in Pre-Restoration Virginia" in the April 1985 number of the American Historical

---

2. For some of these matters see also my prefaces to the second editions of H. R. McIlwaine, ed., Legislative Journals of the Council of Colonial Virginia (2d ed., Richmond, 1979) and H. R. McIlwaine, ed., Minutes of the Council and General Court of Colonial Virginia, (2d ed., Richmond, 1979); my introductions to Cynthia Miller Leonard, comp., The General Assembly of Virginia, July 30, 1619-January 11, 1978: A Bicentennial Register of Members (Richmond, 1978) and the Guide-Index to the Scholarly Resources Microform Edition of The Journals of the House of Burgesses of Virginia (Wilmington, Del., 1984); and my "Robert Beverley Assailed: Appellate Jurisdiction and the Problem of Bicameralism in Seventeenth-Century Virginia," Virginia Magazine of History and Biography 88 (1980): 415-429; "Some Acts Not in Hening's "Statutes": The Acts of Assembly, October 1660," ibid., 83 (1975): 77-97; Speakers and Clerks of the Virginia House of Burgesses, 1643-1776 (Richmond, 1981); "Kentish Agues and American Distempers: The Transmission of Malaria from England to Virginia in the Seventeenth Century," Southern Studies 25 (1986): 135-147; and "The Founding of Virginia Counties-1634?" Magazine of Virginia Genealogy 22, no. 3 (August 1984): 3-6.

Review and at professional meetings. The index for this Garland edition identifies some concepts (such as "popular sovereignty," "policy," or "conquest") that will, in time, be explicated.

Finally, to echo Perry Miller and thereby "bring into conjunction a minute event in the history of historiography with a great one," the example of Miller's own career and dissertation, published as Orthodoxy in Massachusetts, 1630-1650 (Cambridge, Mass., 1933), bolstered my decision to link intellectual and institutional history in Political Institutions in Virginia, 1619-1660. Whether the Aristotelian temperament of colonial Virginia can be shown as analogous to the Augustinian Strain of Piety in colonial New England remains to be seen.

Richmond, Virginia
The Feast Day of St.   Jon Kukla
Augustine of Hippo, 1988

---

3. For example in the paper "Recipes and Rights: The Transmission of Anglo-American Political Ideas as Reflected in Manuscript Commonplace Books from Seventeenth- and Eighteenth-Century Virginia" (Citadel Conference on the South, Charleston, S.C., April 1985); and as a conference participant at "The Glorious Revolution in America--Three Hundred Years After" (University of Maryland, College Park, Md., 30 April 1988).

ACKNOWLEDGMENTS

As a younger man, having come to Richmond, Virginia, to write a dissertation about the Virginia opponents to ratification of the United States Constitution, I found a job at the Virginia State Library doing some research, some compiling, and a great deal of typing at the initial stages of what would become <u>The General Assembly of Virginia, July 30, 1619-January 11, 1978: A Bicentennial Register of Members</u> (Richmond, 1978).

In December 1973 I set out to complete one of my assignments in that job, to find the names of unknown Speakers of the House of Burgesses between 1619 and 1643. Enthusiastically, eight hours a day for a month, I read Public Record Office documents on microfilm, determined to discover the missing Speakers or know the reason why. In the end, the "missing" Speakers proved not elusive but nonexistent; this study tells why, and my biographical findings about the others became <u>Speakers and Clerks of the Virginia House of Burgesses, 1643-1776</u> (Richmond, 1981).

Although my curiosity about seventeenth-century Virginia had been sparked by a quite unfashionable and seemingly simple problem, between 1973 and 1976 as I conducted my research and formulated my hypotheses I felt the truth of Arthur Lovejoy's observation that "the more you press in towards the heart of a narrowly bounded historical problem, the more likely you are to encounter in the problem itself a pressure which drives you beyond those bounds."

In various ways my efforts to understand early Virginia

have been assisted by counsel from Warren M. Billings, Jane Carson, Wesley Frank Craven, John W. Dudley, J. Frederick Fausz, George S. Reese, William M. E. Rachal, Edward M. Riley, and Waverly K. Winfree. Brent Tarter read or listened to more drafts and false starts than either of us cares to remember. At the University of Toronto, John M. Beattie and Michael G. Finlayson criticized the manuscript and sharpened my thinking or expression in many places. I am especially indebted to William H. Nelson, who directed my study, for probing questions that helped me to face the implications of the story that I had uncovered. I am also grateful to Gerald M. Craig, with whom I studied briefly in Canadian history, for sharpening my awareness of Toronto's contributions to economic history, especially in the work of Harold Innis and Donald Creighton, and to C. B. Macpherson, of Toronto, and W. W. Abbot, of the University of Virginia, who joined the pleasant conversation that constituted my formal defense of this dissertation.

The intellectual debt I owe to the late Nelson Peter Ross, my undergraduate mentor at Carthage College, is profound. Would that Peter had lived to see it acknowledged here. Far deeper is the appreciation I offer to my parents and to Jeanette.

Richmond, Virginia   Jon Kukla
All Saints' Day, 1979

PREFACE

Historiographical Note

The modern American historian's tendency to neglect Virginia history in the years that separate John Smith from George Washington has been reversed in the aftermath of the three-hundred-fiftieth anniversary in 1957 of the founding of Jamestown in 1607. To be sure, a number of historians wrote about seventeenth- and early-eighteenth-century Virginia well before the 1960s. Philip Alexander Bruce, Henry Read McIlwaine, and Thomas Jefferson Wertenbaker began in the decades about 1910. Wesley Frank Craven is the most eminent of a group--including Susie M. Ames, Charles McLean Andrews, Richard Beale Davis, Jack P. Greene, Richard L. Morton, Wilcomb E. Washburn, and Louis B. Wright--whose valuable studies of Virginia were undertaken while the New England puritans dominated most of their colleagues' research in early American history.[1]

Renewed interest in the seventeenth- and early-eighteenth-century Chesapeake colonies also has been fostered by other historiographical inquiries. Virginia and Maryland are being studied by historians whose heavily quantified demographic approach to human society propels them in an ever-expanding comparative study of different places and times. Such able social historians as Lois Green Carr and Russell

R. Menard are the Chesapeake vanguard of a legion whose advance might be traced, through New England and the British Isles, to post-World War II France, and ultimately to the Annales school of Marc Bloch and Lucien Febvre.[2] Another impulse propels historians of American slavery and race relations, who have pressed into seventeenth-century Virginia to discover how the famous "20. and odd Negroes" brought to Jamestown in 1619 became the slave gangs of the Old South, or how twentieth-century social attitudes emerged from those of Elizabethan Englishmen.[3] Third, and most recently, interest in the American Indian has turned many a scholar's eye toward Jamestown.

Whatever the historian's reason for investigating Virginia history between the age of discovery and the age of revolution, the overall enterprise is made possible by the increased availability of the primary sources from which Virginia's colonial history can be written or rewritten. Despite tragic losses of records--most notably, but not exclusively, by fire in 1865--two sorts of material now are readily available for research: Virginia county records and Virginia-related records from British archives. Agents of the Church of Jesus Christ of Latterday Saints microfilmed many county records after World War II, and in the post-war years Martha Woodroof Hiden personally gathered and transported volumes of county records to the Virginia State Library for preservation. The result of these and other efforts is that researchers can consult Virginia's antebellum local records both in the reading rooms of the State Library and at microfilm readers throughout the world. Similarly, as a result of the Virginia Colonial Records Project (the most significant legacy of the 1957 celebration of the founding of Jamestown) research in Great Britain is no longer the only way one can consult the essential documents preserved in the Public Record Office, the British Library, and other repositories. Much important information, of course, is lost forever.[4]

Despite the advances made on other fronts, with few exceptions the study of Virginia's political culture and institutional structure between 1607 and 1660 has remained --as Craven observed three decades ago--fixed within the parameters set by Philip Alexander Bruce in 1910. Appraised in light of the sources available to him, Bruce's scholarship was superb, and generally he can be trusted on points of detail. But, except for the statutes, Bruce had limited evidence for the period from 1620 to 1680; the pertinent extant journals of the Council and burgesses were not published until after Bruce's books had appeared.[5]

No assistance is to be had in the many books on colonial Virginia by Thomas Jefferson Wertenbaker, who carried into the middle of the twentieth century the romantic notion of history (and of historical research) that gave life to the works of Macaulay (whom Wertenbaker greatly admired), Bancroft,

Parkman, Prescott, and Motley. Wertenbaker brought his theme to his sources, finding there the incident and detail from which to fashion, at least in his later books, stirring narrative. His dissertation (published privately in 1910) is especially revealing: faulting Bruce for paying "little attention . . . to generalization and for arriving at conclusions by induction rather than by deduction" (whatever that may have been intended to mean), he praised John Fiske's work, which "like Macaulay's History of England holds the interest of the reader from beginning to end." Wertenbaker expressed "deepest regret that the journals from 1619 to 1680 are missing, for they leave a gap in Virginia history that it is impossible to fill," but that did not prevent him from formulating the story that he told, scarcely altered, until the 1950s.[6]

Unable to rely on Bruce or Wertenbaker, a scholar might turn to Henry Read McIlwaine, who edited most of the journals essential to an account of Virginia's colonial institutions. In his prefaces, McIlwaine briefly described the institutions --the General Assembly, the Council, the General Court, and the House of Burgesses--whose records he published. Like Bruce's, McIlwaine's writing is often useful on points of detail, but his commentary about seventeenth-century institutions often is confused. He wrote from incomplete evidence and presumed that Virginia's government always had been organized in discrete legislative, executive, and judicial branches. By the 1930s, McIlwaine had seen enough fresh evidence to modify some of his earlier statements--which he did--but it was too late for the evidence seriously to alter the pattern he had prescribed for it.[7]

A student of early American political institutions may safely ignore the conclusions and formulations of the late-nineteenth-century predecessors of Bruce and McIlwaine, for, as Thomas Nelson Page observed, Virginia suffered from "a deluge of orators and a dearth of historians." The stale old debates about Captain John Smith's veracity, which were inflamed by Civil War-era sectionalism, have been resolved (generally in Smith's favor) by the scholarship of Philip Barbour and Laura Polanyi Striker. Partisan depictions of the military regime under the <u>Lawes Divine</u>, <u>Morall and Martiall</u>, which passed for scholarship in the nineteenth century and lingered in twentieth-century popular accounts, have been laid to rest by Darrett B. Rutman. The introductory chapter of Wesley Frank Craven's <u>Dissolution of the Virginia Company</u> shows that writers had found not the final bankruptcy of an insolvent corporation, but rather the defeat of Sir Edwin Sandys and a "Patriot party" at the hands, variously, of "King James and his successors, Captain Smith and his supporters, American publishers and Yankee reviewers." A few phrases in Craven's review of this textbook reading of Virginia Company history have the Progressive-Era historians' special emphasis on "economic factors," but after forty-seven years Craven's scholarship stands impeccable, his writing fresh, and his judgment balanced, precise, and convincing. The same virtues characterize the useful discussion of the historiography of Virginia's early General Assembly that was Craven's 1969 address to the Virginia Historical Society. Finally, although Bacon's Rebellion fell well after the period under consideration here, the so-called democratic myth (in which Nathaniel Bacon, Jr., plays John the Baptist to Thomas Jefferson) cast its shadow back across the middle decades of the century. Historians continue to debate the precise nature of the rebellion, but Wilcomb E. Washburn and Jane Carson have dispelled the myth.[8]

Both Craven, in his Southern Colonies in the Seventeenth Century, and Jack P. Greene, in the introductory passages of his The Quest for Power, have treated Virginia's political institutions from the demise of the company to the Glorious Revolution with clarity and precision, giving details when they were certain of them, and making only general comments when they were not. Both accounts remain useful, and of course Greene's study is a starting point for students of eighteenth-century colonial politics.[9]

Charles McLean Andrews's Colonial Period of American History remains essential reading for students of Virginia history before the mid-1620s; thereafter the narrative is spotty. Seriously misled by McIlwaine's anachronistic use of the word convention to describe the assembly of 1625, Andrews's account of post-1625 developments is not always trustworthy. His chronological narrative ends with a chapter entitled "Virginia in 1641." Andrews's choice of the year seems prescient, for important institutional changes occurred in the two following. For the early history of the empire, the student of early Virginia should supplement Andrews's fourth volume with George Louis Beer's Origins of the British Colonial System, 1578-1660 (New York, 1908).

Richard L. Morton's two-volume Colonial Virginia is helpful and balanced, although politics and institutions are not treated in a detailed or comprehensive way. Morton's succinct assessments of the individuals who people his history, his brief characterizations of Yeardley, Wyatt, Harvey, Berkeley, and dozens of others, are especially valuable and reliable. His account of the Thrusting Out of Governor Harvey in 1635 is useful, especially for the personalities involved, although J. Mills Thornton's article on the subject is the best narrative treatment. Neither Morton or Thornton addressed the question of the powers that Harvey enjoyed by virtue of the king's commission, and neither recognized the full implications of the mercantile connections between Harvey's opponents. Wilcomb E. Washburn's 1957 pamphlet about Virginia from 1625 to 1660 had much to say about the incident, although in his enthusiasm to dispel "democratic myth," Washburn became Harvey's advocate. His assertion that Harvey returned to Virginia in 1637 with enhanced powers, will not hold.[11]

Warren M. Billings's studies of the seventeenth-century county courts are important, although probably power gained by the county benches did not always come at the expense of Jamestown authorities. The authority of the county courts and vestries did increase, but procedural reforms and administrative streamlining can enhance central authority, and the delegation of bothersome or routine details to the counties or vestries can strengthen effective central control of larger matters. While Billings stresses the extreme fragility of seventeenth-century social and political life, there was an emerging sense of order and stability in society and government evident in the later 1630s and increasingly evident thereafter.[12]

This may be a matter of emphasis, but the coming of a measure of stability (and the questions of when and how it came to Virginia) is an important matter. In an important 1969 pamphlet, J. R. Pole linked the emergence of sophisticated and complex institutions to the increasing socio-economic differentiation of a maturing society. "The development of bicameralism in native American legislatures," Pole wrote, "may be taken both as a token of the increasing sophistication of procedures and of the sense of actual difference of purpose between elected assemblymen and appointed councillors." With this insight, suddenly the narrow focus of an institutional monograph expands one's comprehension of broader social development. Conclusions about Virginia's transformation from an outpost to a society, advanced in the 1950s by Sigmund Diamond and Wilcomb E. Washburn and in 1975 by Edmund S. Morgan, correspond to the hypothesis that the General Assembly of Virginia became bicameral in 1643: "Virginians during the second quarter of the seventeenth century," Morgan concluded, "at last began to look upon their raw new land as a home rather than a temporary stopping place." Although Morgan's is not the last word on colonial Virginia, this perception of an increasingly complex pattern of social organization and of an increasingly mature society at mid-century rings true.[13]

The political and institutional implications of Sigmund Diamond's 1958 recognition of an emerging society in mid-seventeenth-century Virginia, however, had been preempted by the contrasting view advanced by Bernard Bailyn in a brilliant, highly influential 1957 essay with broad implications for the general shape of early American history, "Politics and Social Structure in Virginia." Idealistic visions of the glories of colonization failed to survive the first generation of Virginia leaders, Bailyn argued, and the pursuit of profit obsessed the prominent second-generation men, whose positions "rested on their ability to wring material gain from the wilderness," and for whom learning and even literacy were incidental to the main chance. Real society began to develop about 1655, when "ambitious younger sons of middle-class families who knew well enough what gentility was and sought it as a specific objective," began to succeed Virginia's second-generation of self-made men. These newcomers--Burwells, Carters, Lees, and others--founded Virginia's great eighteenth-century families, which gained control of the counties, the legislature, and provincial society. After 1689 they adopted the temper and terminology of the English country, or opposition, whigs, and a century later they carried Virginia to republicanism, revolution, and the Republic.[14]

Bailyn's depiction of Virginia's second-generation leadership and of mid-century politics and society stands on doubtful legs. One is the assumption that because Virginia lacked families of the English sort, which Sir Lewis Namier described as having blood, name, and estate (the last "the most important of the three"), Virginia therefore lacked "stable parties or factions" and was "a veritable anarchy." The other is a falsely vivid contrast between the rough-hewn aspirations of the second-generation elite and the more genteel hopes of the first- and third-generation leaders; in both cases Bailyn mistook the paucity of printed biographies of second-generation Virginians for "a political void."[15]

In fact, people with attributes Bailyn found later in the century (men "just close enough to establishment in gentility to feel the pangs of deprivation most acutely" and driven by "the pent-up ambitions of the gentleman manqué,") were present earlier in significant numbers, and a pattern in Virginia politics was clear by the 1630s. Insistence upon <u>landed</u> family dynasties as the precondition of social and political stability may be misleading. The first evidence of political alignments is found among the merchants who managed Virginia's tobacco economy. From the second generation onward, colonial Virginia's leading planters were colonial Virginia's leading merchants. Within human limits, they defined objectives and pursued them in conventional ways, using both governmental and non-governmental tools. Their mid-seventeenth-century province was not Namier's England, but neither was it Hobbes's Nature. [16]

Although a fresh look at Virginia's early political institutions does not require a complete reexamination of seventeenth-century society, the social situation in Virginia on the eve of Sir William Berkeley's arrival in 1642 is important. Politics and political institutions are the productions of conscious human volition; they cannot be understood apart from the reasons, and context in which, people acted as they did. Yet, in any human transaction, the observer must extrapolate motive from imperfect evidence, and also recognize that professions of motive, if made, must also be subjected to careful scrutiny. There is no clear contemporary comment, no diary, tract, or letter, about the beginning of bicameralism in Virginia. Important and sometimes very revealing fragments of evidence about the

General Assembly's internal procedures and organization survive from the decades between 1620 and 1680, and from the extant evidence it seems clear that Virginia's elected burgesses organized themselves as a lower house of assembly for the first time in March 1643. Especially for the 1640s, then, the social context of institutional change is important. But since English officials were not particularly attentive to details of Virginia politics during the 1640s, and since no surviving public or private reports say much about the machinery of Virginia government and politics, the description of political circumstances requires a mental reconstruction of the configuration of political groups and interests as seen by the governor, the councillors, and the burgesses. The historian's challenge remains, as Hobbes wrote of Thucydides, to make "his Auditor a Spectator" but not to "enter into men's hearts further than the Actions themselves evidently guide him." Some readers will agree that this attribution of possible motive based on the seventeenth-century Virginians' probable perceptions of the political landscape and its underlying socio-economic topography is an exercise in historical thinking of the sort that R. G. Collingwood described, and that this account of politics and society seems best to fit the extant evidence. [17]

In addition to its challenge to the prevailing "chaotic" depiction of early American politics, this study may also suggest some modification in the prevailing understanding

of the early development of American political thought.
Especially in its moral certitude, sense of mission, and
Ramistic either/or categories, American political theory
was molded by the New England mind and fired by the American
Revolution. From a puritan or eighteenth-century republican
viewpoint, faction or party was seen—in a way that lingers
in American politics—as

> the sign of division and disaffection, a sign of
> lapse of government itself. Politics was not,
> as in modern liberal culture, an integral part
> of constitutional government; it was its antithesis. The idea that government was a prize to
> be fought for by contentious groups was opposed
> to the purposes for which government was established. Government was the embodiment as well
> as the servant of society. Its chief end was
> the promotion of the common good. . . .
>
> Particularism was opposed to the general
> good. . . . Party and faction were a blight.
> Outside government, they fomented discord; inside,
> corruption and tyranny. The well-ordered polity
> was free from "party spirit."

Perhaps, however, from early Virginia's rhetorical silence,
Americans can learn that a not-quite-cynical attitude toward
government as the process of governing in an imperfect world,
rather than the means of redeeming that world, as well as a
recognition much like Aristotle's that division is endemic

to human affairs and should be expected, were ancient parts of American colonial practice--whether or not they were proclaimed from New England pulpits on election days. Division, and tolerance of it, horrified the theoretician in John Winthrop as the diabolical work of "Matchiavell and the Jesuits," but for Sir William Berkeley and countless other practicing politicians it had its value. And perhaps it is not coincidence that a Virginian wrote *Federalist* number ten, the document that accepted faction and party within the language of American political theory. More recently, in a chapter that opened with a discussion of Madison and faction, Reinhold Niebuhr observed that "one of the greatest problems of democratic civilization is how to integrate the life of its various subordinate, ethnic, religious and economic groups in the community in such a way that the richness and harmony of the whole community will be enhanced and not destroyed by them," and also that our greatest "internal peril lies in the conflict of various schools and classes of idealists, who profess different ideals but exhibit a common conviction that their own ideals are perfect." Possibly, in the absence of exalted rhetoric among the founders of Virginia is to be found the origin of an in-bred resistance to the strains of illusory innocence and virtue that so frequently plague American politics.[18]

* * *

The main question, though, is why intelligent late-twentieth-century men and women should care to know what may have happened in a small English settlement on the banks of the James River nearly four centuries ago. Certainly for those curious about America, a pilgrimage to Jamestown, where it began, is essential. Or, if historical inquiry has general utility (whether defined in terms of philosophy, or religion, or as a liberating art), then Jamestown probably is as useful a location to pursue truth (or possibly even Truth) as Rome, Chartres, or Petrograd. But above all, Jamestown between 1607 and 1660 was a small stage on which a few thousand men and women confronted the American wilderness and the awful void at the center of modern Western existence. A critical era in the creation of today's world, an era marked by what some European historians call "the general crisis of the seventeenth century," played Jamestown, too.[20] Our fellow citizens in the post-medieval West, Sir Francis Wyatt and Sir William Berkeley and their Virginia contemporaries command our attention and respect.

INTRODUCTION

Settlement and the Beginning of Politics, 1607-1660

And forasmuch as of all humane Artes Political government is the chiefest, there must be a speciall care in the Magistrate how to carry himselfe in his place and order: for herein consists the verie maine matter of the successe of this businesse."

-Robert Gray
A Good Speed to Virginia, 1609

When the Reverend Robert Gray described government as "the verie maine matter" upon which the success of the Virginia colony depended, the problem of organization loomed in the minds of the Virginia Company of London's investors, leaders, and colonists. Already failures in the colony's first experiment in governance had brought disaster. Their attempt to "make habitacion, plantacion and to deduce a colonie" in the New World was novel, indeed, the word colony used in this now familiar sense was only a few decades old. Englishmen, having only recently decided what to call places like Virginia, could not have been expected to know how best to govern them. [1]

Aristotle, whose Politics informed contemporary political wisdom, would not have been surprised by anything that happened in early Virginia, but until they had blundered through two unsuccessful experiments, the leaders of the Virginia Company of London seem not to have used political wisdom to inform their plans. Despite the fact that the nature and disposition of political authority concerned all seventeenth-century Europeans (as is evident from the place their best thinkers occupy in the history of political theory, or the places their treatments of legitimate authority hold in the literature of the Elizabethan and Jacobean stage), politics did not concern the English colonizers until too late. Perhaps the Reverend Mr. Gray's notion--which smacks of the parson's study--that "men by nature . . . easily yielde to discipline and government upon any reasonable shewe of bettering their fortunes" was widely shared by company leaders.[2]

Such political naivete, which flourished amid the exuberant hopes for the New World, probably owes to the two impulses that had shaped England's first colonial program. First, since the early 1580s Sir Walter Raleigh, Sir Humphrey Gilbert, Sir Francis Drake, and others had advocated the creation of a military stronghold in North America to serve as a base for privateers to prey upon Spanish ships carrying American gold through the Carribean to Spain. Raleigh's Roanoke Island settlements in the 1580s had established the

Chesapeake Bay area (which was convenient to the Carribean sea lanes but distant enough to be safe from overland attack from Spanish Florida) as the site for a self-sustaining English military base. Of course, the governance of a military outpost posed no special problems.[3]

At the same time that some Englishmen planned for a military outpost in the New World, many others, hungry for lands and titles, discovered Ireland. Displacing the native Irish population with legal and ideological arguments that became fixed weapons in the rationale of overseas colonization, they sought to make Ireland a province of English landed society. Here developed the idea of reproducing English society in the New World, but the Irish plantations offered no special clue for the governance of a civilian New World population. In the hands of Sir Humphrey Gilbert and dozens of others, the two impulses were joined to form the program of overseas colonization that led to Jamestown. But when the Virginia Company leaders chose not to make Jamestown an outright military settlement, they found that they lacked realistic plans for civilian government.[4]

By letters patent issued in April (the First Charter) and November 1606 (instructions), James I established the Virginia Companies of London and Plymouth, granting each "licence to make habitacion, plantacion and to deduce a colonie of our people into that parte of America commonly called Virginia," and power "to give directions . . . for the good government of the people to be planted in those parts . . . as near to the Common Lawes of England and the equity thereof as may be." Under three successive charters, of 1606, 1609, and 1612, the Virginia Company of London became a joint-stock company capable of supplying capital for the expensive adventure of English colonization in North America between 41° and 34° north latitude. (The Plymouth Company had more northerly limits.) The company's primary objective was always, as it had to be, businesslike: to secure financial reward and a profit for its investors. But the glorious project of colonization was both a privately sponsored business venture and a great national enterprise. Few doubted that the noble undertaking would convert the heathen to the true faith, increase English trade, provide homes for England's excess population, and--if well managed --turn a profit.[5]

Between its founding in 1606 and its dissolution in 1624, the Virginia Company tried three approaches toward its goal of establishing a profitable colony. None was successful, and none saved the company from bankruptcy. The first experiment was government by a resident council under the First Charter. It failed completely; the company began to abandon conciliar government even before full reports of the disaster had been received. The second experiment was a military regime under an absolute governor. It brought order to the colony, but no profit to the company and its investors because unless accompanied by other measures no mere alteration in government could have made the company financially successful. The company's third experiment shaped the course of Virginia's, and America's, history for centuries after the Virginia Company of London collapsed.

From the outset the leaders of the Virginia Company were more concerned with business than with statesmanship. They were familiar with Aristotle's lessons--that monarchy promised unity but threatened tyranny, that aristocracy offered wise leadership at the risk of faction, and that democracy could preserve liberty or lose it in tumult-- but they simply did not take them into account in their planning for Virginia. Company leaders knew that Captain Christopher Newport needed "sole charge and Command" while the first ships carried colonists to Virginia, for no ship's captain would have sailed with less. Accordingly, they named the members of the Council of State in "several instruments Close Sealed," which remained unopened until the colonists were ashore. But after they had reached Virginia and opened the documents that named the councillors, only the company's earnest plea that councillors be "all of one mind for the Good of your Country and your own" stood against debilitating faction and division.[6]

The Susan Constant, Godspeed, and Discovery carried some one hundred forty colonists into Chesapeake Bay on Sunday, 26 April 1607. That evening, aboard ship, the

sealed instructions naming seven councillors were opened
and read, and several days later the colonists came
ashore at the penisula now known as Jamestown. On 13 May
the councillors swore their oaths of office and elected a
president. Aristotle could have foretold the rest:
immediately the Council of State, and the colony, was
plunged into division. John Smith came ashore a prisoner
charged with conspiracy. Bartholomew Gosnold soon died.
President Edward Maria Wingfield, accused of favoritism
in the distribution of provisions, was expelled from the
Council. George Kendall was tried for conspiracy, condemned
by a jury, and shot. Gabriel Archer and John Ratcliffe
nearly had Smith hanged in January 1608, but by September,
of the seven original councillors, only John Smith was
still in Virginia. Newport, Wingfield, Archer, and John
Martin had returned to England; the others were dead.

Smith imposed strict discipline and enforced the
dictum "He that will not worke, shall not eate." He
forced the colonists to accomplish the tasks necessary
for their survival. Then he left the colony in the hands
of George Percy, who was less able, and after the Starving
Time of 1609-1610 only sixty-five colonists were alive.
Ravaged by hunger and the Indians, on 10 June 1610 they
abandoned the settlement and sailed down the James to
intercept the fishing fleets off Newfoundland and return

with them to England. By sheer chance they met Lord De La Warr before they reached Hampton Roads.[8]

Meanwhile, former president Wingfield was in England reporting the councillors' divisions. He explained his own inadequacy with recollections of the "hard beginnings" and "intestine garboils" that had troubled Moses, Aaron, Romulus, and Remus, and he hoped that company leaders would "applie medicines accordinglie." Well before they heard Wingfield's version of events, however, the company leaders knew that counciliar government had failed. Along with important administrative changes in the company itself, the Second Charter, signed on 23 May 1609, abandoned the dangerous experiment. Government-by-council had been specified in the First Charter. The Second Charter allowed the company freedom to manage the colony as it saw fit. It chose to put "one *able* and *absolute* governor" in charge of a regimented, semimilitary colony, and it chose to recruit its soldier-governors from among those English officers who had fought in Ireland and the Netherlands.[9]

Late in 1608 the States General of the Netherlands gave leave to Sir Thomas Gates, a company captain and a patentee of the Virginia Company's First Charter who had served with Essex in Ireland, "to command . . . in the country of Virginia." Early in 1609 the company engaged Thomas West, baron De La Warr, whose credentials were more

impressive: Oxford educated, he had served in Parliament
and on the Privy Council under Elizabeth I and James I,
had fought in Essex's Irish expedition and in the Netherlands, and had been named to the company's ruling council
in the Second Charter. Sir Thomas Dale, the company's
third new officer, was a professional soldier who had
served in a 1594 Irish expedition, in France, with Essex
in Ireland, and finally with Gates as captain of an English
company in the Netherlands. The Reverend Mr. Gray's
humane art of political government waited the outcome of
military science, for Gates, De La Warr, and Dale represented a martial solution, modeled on English experience
in Ireland and the Low Countries, to the problem of securing
order in Virginia. [10]

The military regime established in Virginia under the
Second Charter was continued under the Third Charter,
signed 12 March 1612. During the military regime, which
lasted until 1618, the office of governor was created and
given its most important, lasting characteristics. Martial
leadership, a recognized attribute of the seventeenth-
century ruler, figured prominently in Virginia governors'
careers throughout the century, as they directed forces
against the Indians, using councillors and militia leaders
to organize both offensive and defensive strategies. In
turn, prominent planters commanded military expeditions,

and militia leaders exercised authority in civil affairs. Militia commanders during the decade prior to the establishment of county courts in 1634, for example, became "Conservators of the peace and had care of the militia" through the vehicle of local monthly courts held in the precincts, hundreds, and necks. This intermingling of civilian and military officeholding was common throughout Virginia's early history: a 1697 report to the Board of Trade described the governor as "his Majesty's Lieutenant-General and Commander in Chief" and the councillors as "the Colonels or Commanders in chief of the several Counties, in the Nature of the Lords Lieutenants in England."[11]

Whether soldier or civilian, however, the principal attribute of a successful governor was his personal authority, his power of command, the quality that Machiavelli called lo stato. "Great Actions are carryed with best success," a group of Virginia investors and planters wrote in a 1620 petition, "by such Commanders, who have personall Aucthoritye and greatness, Sithence itt is nott easye to swaye a vulgar and serville Nature, by vulgar and serville Spiritts." The governor charged with "raising of soe happy a State, as is hoped in the Plantation of Virginia," they continued, must be one "whereunto by Nature everye man subordinate is ready to yeild a willing submission." Of the men who governed Virginia before 1660, two soldiers, Smith and De La Warr, and two civilians, Wyatt and Berkeley, had the "personall Aucthoritye" that brought success.[12]

De La Warr's arrival at Jamestown on 10 June 1610 shows in highest relief the personal presence without which order could not have been impressed or maintained. Gates earlier had arrived at Jamestown and found "misery and misgovernment." Accepting George Percy's commission and the Council's seal, he had proclaimed the famous <u>Lawes Divine</u>, <u>Morall</u> <u>and</u> <u>Martiall</u>. After two weeks he had determined to abandon the colony, when, with Jamestown scarcely out of sight, on 8 June the colonists had met a skiff headed upriver. De La Warr, who had shipwrecked on Bermuda, had reached Point Comfort, learned of their plans, and sent orders to return.[13]

Two days later William Strachey recorded in careful detail the scene he witnessed as Governor De La Warr came ashore. Gathering men-in-arms "to stand in order and make a guard," Gates entrusted his banner to Strachey. As the colonists all watched, De La Warr came ashore near the river gate of the palisade, "fell upon his knees and before us all made a long and silent prayer to himself, and after marched up into the town, where at the gate I bowed with the colors and let them fall at his Lordship's feet." The colonists followed their new governor into the chapel to

hear a sermon by the Reverend Richard Buck, after which
De La Warr "caused a gentleman, one of his followers,
Master Anthony Scot, his ancient, to read his commission,
which entitled him lord governor and captain general
during his life of the colony and plantation in Virginia
(Sir Thomas Gates, our governor hitherto, being now
styled lieutenent general)." Gates surrendered his
commission, the council seal, and "both patents" (presumably his own instructions and a document Percy had
given him less than a month earlier). Then De La Warr
addressed the colonists, "Laying many blames upon them
for many vanities and their idleness." Two days later
De La Warr announced that he had chosen Gates, Strachey,
and four others as his advisory council. He administered
oaths of allegiance to each, and soon thereafter to "every
particular member of the colony."[14]

  Each Sunday De La Warr used ceremony to uphold
social rank and political order in Jamestown. Surrounded
by councillors, officers, and "a guard of halberdiers
in His Lordship's livery, fair red cloaks, to the number
of fifty," De La Warr progressed to worship, where, high
above the colonists on their wooden benches, he sat "in
the choir, in a green velvet chair . . . with a velvet
cushion spread on a table before him on which he kneeleth."

Around the governor sat the councillors, captains, and officers, each--said Strachey in a phrase weighted with the age's hope that this was comforting evidence of certainty and stability in the face of the crisis-- "each in their place." Each was a collective pronoun, agreeing with their not his, for Strachey was not listing individually assigned seats in a church, but ranks assigned their places in a well-ordered society and cosmos.[15]

Whether in civil or military affairs, Virginia's institutions of government rested on the legal authority of the governor. Although the nature and extent of this legal authority was radically altered in 1618 (when the able and absolute governorship was limited and De La Warr's successors were constituted primus inter pares, first among equals, in the Council of State), focussing on the authorities granted by commission can be misleading. A cage tells much about an animal, but we seek the beast itself: the most important description of the propulsive force-- that was restrained, not supplied, in the commission--was the word itself.[16]

Many of the specialized meanings that governor had in the seventeenth century have been obscured by its now familiar twentieth-century political sense. The word had entered English usage in the fourteenth century, when its most ancient definition suggested the metaphor inherent

in its subsequent application to affairs of the ship of
state: a steersman, pilot, captain of a vessel. A
second fourteenth-century meaning referred specifically
to the commander of a military or naval company (a usage
that was, significantly, current in the English garrisons
in the Low Countries, just as <u>governor-general</u> and <u>governor
and captain general</u>, respectively, were titles associated
with Leicester in Ireland and Sir Frances Vere in the
Netherlands). One etymological consequence of colonization
was the obsolescence of these maritime and garrison usages
of <u>governor</u> after 1625. Henceforth the cluster of political meanings, which also dated from the fourteenth century,
came to the fore: in the general political sense of the
term a governor was the ruler of subjects (and by the 1380s
the word had gained currency as the title either of the
head of an institution such as a board of regents, or of
one who governed a province, country, or town).[17]

An important dimension of this general political
meaning of <u>governor</u> was communicated in the favorite
sixteenth- and seventeenth-century term <u>vicegerent</u>. The
governor was to the king as the king was to God. He
sustained the divinely established order of society ("each
in their place," Strachey said) by fact of appointment
to an office named <u>governor</u>, rather than by any enumeration
of specific authorities; the governor of Virginia was

vicegerent to his king and his God.[18]

To suggest that vital energy was communicated in the term *governor* does not, of course, mean that the specific provisions of commissions were without significance. Clearly they were, especially after 1618 when the powers De La Warr and his lieutenant- and deputy-governors enjoyed during the military regime were severely restricted. In De La Warr's commission, which was the legal basis of all political authority in Virginia from his arrival in 1610 to his death in 1618, the Virginia Company did as much as, and perhaps more than, legally it could to grant him extensive powers. He had office for life, authority to exercise martial law, and power to choose as councillors advisors who had no power to restrain him. The commission suggested that he follow the company's instructions, but readily allowed him to "rule and governe by his owne discretion." Then, as if to emphasize the extent to which it wished to delegate authority to him, the company assigned De La Warr "as full and absolute power" as it "by virtue of his Majesties said Letters Patents have power to derive and graunt," and somehow promised to enlarge that authority "if it shall hereafter apeare to his Lordship that it shall be meet." The company's reaction against the lassitude of counciliar government

is nowhere more evident than in this desperate eagerness
to entrust the colony to a capable, unfettered leader
so that stability might bring growth, trade, and profit.[19]

Company instructions to Gates were more explicit:
Martial law was "of most dispatch and terror and fittest
for this government." He was to act "rather uppon . . .
equity then upon the nicenes and lettre of the lawe
which perplexeth in this tender body," and to dispatch
justice in "a summary and arbitrary way . . . discreetly
mingled" with an expeditious respect for the forms of
magistracy. Under the Second and Third Charters the three
veterans of the wars in the Low Countries were to reorganize the ailing and unprofitable colony as a semimilitary
post. Even "the basest and worst men," the Reverend
William Cranshaw said on the eve of De La Warr's departure
from England, "trained up in severe discipline, under
sharpe lawes, a hard life, and much labor, do prove good
members of a Commonwealth." [20]

The dramaturgical reading of De La Warr's commission
and all the ceremony witnessing to the transmission of
royal authority--the prayers, the bowing of banners, the
oath-taking--were critically important. Good, effective
government depended on the governor's personal authority,
and red-garbed halberdiers parading at the edge of the

great, green North American continent were to proclaim--
indeed to convince--that the agent of order had arrived
and was to be obeyed.[21]

To William Strachey, civilization itself seemed less
tenuous on the Thames than on the James, for "we know well
how short our memories are often-times, and unwilling to
give sto[w]age to the better things, and such things as
limit and bound mankind in their necessariest duties." The
familiar metaphor about the colonists' intellectual baggage was no cliché to those who asked whether the better
things had been packed, or forgotten. Among a newly transported, predominantly male, outpost population, estranged
by distance from traditional sanctions, De La Warr and his
immediate successors sustained social and political order
through self-conscious acts of will.[22]

Englishmen, of course, had written a substantial amount
of advice and exhortation to guide those who held the
important vocation of prince or governor. In this literature, according to Tim Breen, five prerequisites of the good
governor stood preeminent: wealth, piety, moderation,
justice, and wisdom. Wealth implied social status and
financial independence, characteristics that the Virginians
themselves recommended--"sufficient men, as well of birth
and quallyty." Piety was essential so that, in the words of
a typical governor's commission, "in the first place . . .
Almighty God may be duly and daily served . . . , which may
draw down a blessing on all your endeavors." Moderation

was especially noticed when absent; in Virginia, Harvey's temper, the aging Berkeley's vengeance after Bacon's Rebellion, Culpeper's greed, and Nicholson's whole second administration stand as testimony to the need to be able to temper one's ambition and restrain one's temper. Then, as now, a magistrate who saw justice "equallie administered to all his Majesties subjects" was highly respected. And finally, a good governor had wisdom--the capacity to judge rightly in matters of life and conduct.[23]

As laudable as these traits are, however, they were distinctly public characteristics. George Wyatt might counsel his son the governor "to shine in al partes of vertue and vertuous example," but unsullied virtue had to be moderated by wisdom, and writers distinguished between wisdom derived from fear of the Lord and that which "descendeth not from above, but is earthly, sensual, devilish." With varying degrees of candor they recognized that the ideal governor was both saintly and shrewd, and in what might be called advice-to-courtiers literature--as distinct from political sermons--the emphasis tended more toward the shrewd than the saintly.[24]

No Englishman wrote The Prince, and all claimed to be disgusted by Machiavelli's "politick religion"; nevertheless while decrying craft they lauded wisdom and policy. Policy and its synonyms became euphemisms for the wilier aspects of political wisdom. Before a government could be good it had to be effective: as a mariner tacking in the face of changing winds "still holdeth his purpose of getting in to the harbrough: so should Statesmen, upon every new occasion alter their sailes, and veere another way, still making their course to the Port of publike good and safetie." There could be no effective government without that quality that Machiavelli called lo stato: the ruler's personal authority to command obedience from those he governed. Neither a governor's "maturity of judgement to undertake, nor his alacritie of spirit to execute," one English maxim averred, "availe in the perfecting of his intended and resolved enterprise, where hee hath not a powerfull majesty to command, and his Officers an awefull readiness to doe as they are commanded."[25]

William Capps feared that Governor Wyatt might prove too "good so carefull mild, Religious, just honest," and Wyatt's father reminded his son that "art in a Commander is his proper worthe and vertue," and that if authority were not immediately established it would require "more force to raise it up when declined, then to keepe it up when it is yet standinge right at the first." The Virginia Company, too, had recommended that Gates and De La Warr use all available means, including "the attendance of a guarde uppon [the governor's] person," to win "more regard and respect of your place, to begett reverence to your authority."[26]

Wealth, piety, moderation, justice, and wisdom--
the public characteristics of a good ruler as defined in
sermons and public exhortations--were also qualities
admirable in a citizen, a nation, or a civilization. Lo
stato, however, was the peculiar concern of magistrates,
kings, governors, and courtiers. Generally it escapes
public definition. It is that inscrutable quality which
is the heart of leadership: the capacity to command obedience.
Consider again the events of 10 June 1610. Unquestionably
De La Warr was wealthy, pious, moderate, just, and wise.
But, above all, his person commanded obedience. His own
presence was authority. The dipping of Gates's banner, the
surrender of commissions and seals, the taking of oaths,
the red-liveried halberdiers, and the green velvet kneeler
were elements of a social drama in which this great truth
was proclaimed and confirmed. Thus began the military
regime, which brought order to Virginia, and which lasted
until 1618.

The tobacco economy

During the military regime a new land policy emerged,
as settlers who had worked the land in common and received
supplies from the common store were assigned small plots
to grow food. During these same years, Pocahontas, the
favorite daughter of Chief Powhatan, had been kidnapped by
Samuel Argall and brought to Jamestown where she and John
Rolfe had fallen in love. Conveniently, their marriage in

April 1614 brought eight years of peace; without it, had the Indians launched a devastating attack in 1614 as they did eight years later, the whole as-yet-unprofitable colonial venture might simply have collapsed. Finally, John Rolfe gave Virginia a staple, Nicotiana tobacum, a South American smoking tobacco more palatable than the harsh Nicotiana rustica of North America. Rolfe imported seed from Trinidad and found that it grew well in Virginia. Of these three important developments during the military regime, land and tobacco are the keys to understanding why the colony survived. [27]

Although modifications in the colony's collective labor system were made as early as 1609 to remedy the colonists' dependence on supply ships or Indians for food, significant change began in 1614 when the first of the company's indentured servants completed their seven-year obligations. Each man received three acres of land, twelve if he had a family, on which he was to raise his own food and two barrels and one half of corn for the company. By the end of 1614 the colony had eighty-one free farmers. [28]

November 1616 brought the end of another, more critical, seven-year term: the term after which the Virginia Company of London was to divide the profits earned by investors in the 1609 joint stock. Lacking funds even to pay the administrative cost of such a division, the company took

two important decisions: to audit its officers' accounts
and to offer as dividend its only resource, Virginia land.
The first decision was the seed of bitterness between Sir
Edwin Sandys and Treasurer Sir Thomas Smythe (and their respective associates) that blossomed after 1619. From the second
came a policy of private landowning: any member of the company--indeed anyone, so bad had things become--who paid
twelve pounds ten shillings got title to fifty acres in
Virginia. The colony began a decade-long period of "mixed
economy," as Irene Hecht described it in her important study,
"in which the Company and private sectors operated side by
side." Saddled by debt and an inflexible commitment to the
development of diversified commodities (few of which could
be produced in Virginia, transported to Europe, and sold at
anything but a loss), the company eventually went bankrupt.
Contrary to the lessons of countless schoolbooks, however,
the mere introduction of private enterprise did not save
Virginia. Tobacco saved Virginia.[29]

It long has been known that Rolfe's successful introduction of <u>Nicotiana tabacum</u> was a momentous event in the
history of Virginia, yet only as a result of Irene Hecht's
inquiry are the important implications of the tobacco economy recognizable. Three facts about the emerging tobacco
economy are important. First, tobacco production skyrocketed
during the mixed economy decade, for which Hecht supplied

these production figures:

Year	Pounds produced	Price/ pound
1616	2,300	-
1618	41,728	3 s.
1620	40 - 50,000	1 - 4 s.
1622	60,000	11 d.—1 s. 8 d.
1624	202,962	-
1626	260,254	3 d.

Second, based on papers of a particular plantation founded in 1619 by a group of private investors (the only body of such papers known to be extant), Hecht found that with a low production cost and exceedingly favorable English market, investors in Berkeley Hundred realized a minimum annual profit of 22 to 35 percent from their importation of Virginia-grown tobacco. Third, based on reasonable estimates that with a capital investment of twenty pounds a colonist might earn fifty or sixty pounds per year raising tobacco, Hecht concluded that tobacco culture promised an immediate return of 250 to 300 percent on a colonist's investment. In the long run, of course, as the production increased to more nearly equal demand, this remarkable market changed and the extraordinary profit margin disappeared. But, for as long as the boom market held, there were fortunes to be made.[30]

Tobacco renewed English hopes for the Virginia colony. It was a loathsome weed and a vicious habit, but the stuff sold, and it was better for Englishmen to buy it from their own colony than from Spain. Post-1617 investments, however --and this is the important point--largely went to support private ventures like Berkeley Hundred. The company, its leaders clinging steadfastly to the vision of a diversified economy and the production of things more useful than smoke, benefitted only temporarily from this renewed interest and ultimately failed.

In Virginia, only fur and tobacco enjoyed the unusually high margin between the cost of production and shipping and the price in the metropolitan market; the company's efforts to produce silk, flax, wheat, or glass were doomed. Nevertheless, company leaders thought otherwise, and hope proved sufficient incentive for a third experiment in the management of the colony. The hope of profit united Smith's and Sandys's associates in the support of one last try: the reform of 1618, which expanded the colony's political institutions by replacing De La Warr, whose life term had ended with his death on 7 June 1618, with a governor and Council, periodically augmented by elected burgesses meeting in a General Assembly.[31]

To reduce "the rigour of Martiall Law," the governor was bound to the majority will of his Council in most matters. Yet, the relative powers of the governor and the councillors never clearly were delineated. The governor no longer was absolute, but the unwritten characteristics of leadership implied in the word <u>governor</u> remained critically important.

With the death of their trusted governor, and after two unsuccessful attempts to make Virginia profitable, the Virginia Company of London began to treat political problems in recognizably political terms: they sought for the colony "a laudable form of government by Majestracy."[32]

At its quarterly meeting of November 1618 the Virginia Company determined to make the colony profitable by increasing its population and diversifying its economy. Although tobacco was the only profitable commodity Virginia produced, company leaders espoused economic diversification to the very end. In order to attract immigrants the company ended martial law, reformed the land tenure system, introduced English common law, and provided for a General Assembly. The assembly's principal value, of course, was as a vehicle through which the company's leaders might better secure the colonists' approbation and compliance to company policies.[33]

In 1619 Governor Yeardley arrived at Jamestown with instructions that required him to summon a General Assembly composed of councillors and elected burgesses and directed him to settle the colony's population in "cities or borroughs," in addition to the existing plantations and hundreds. It took centuries for genuinely urban areas to rise on the banks of the James River, but from the Virginia Company's choice of words came county names such as James City and Charles City, as well as the term burgesses--the designation of those members of the House of Commons who represented English boroughs.[34]

On Friday morning, 30 July 1619, two burgesses from each of eleven settlements met with the governor and councillors as a unicameral body in the choir of the church at Jamestown. The assembly remained in session only five days, but it followed parliamentary procedure under the guidance of Secretary John Pory, who had served in Parliament and had organized the assembly's working papers. Pory, secretary and a member of the Council of State, described himself as Speaker of the assembly of 1619, but he and Governor Yeardley shared the responsibilities of presiding.

Two other assemblies, in 1621 and 1624, met before Virginia became a royal colony when the Virginia Company of London formally was dissolved on 24 May 1624. Another assembly met in 1625, and although the status of the General Assembly remained uncertain for longer than a decade thereafter, the assembly met regularly throughout the 1620s and 1630s. Incontrovertible evidence exists of tacit royal recognition of the assembly during these years, but well-founded doubts about the continued existence of representative institutions also lingered throughout the seventeenth century. Historians generally accept Charles I's 1639 instruction authorizing the governor to summon annual meetings of the assembly as the formal confirmation of the General Assembly's continued existence. Contemporaries could not have been certain. Not only was the future as enigmatic to the Vir-

ginia colonists as it is to any generation, throughout
Western Europe the powers of diets and parlements were
declining as the power of monarchs increased. "In all
Christian kingdoms," Sir Dudley Carleton said in 1626,
"you know that parliaments were in use anciently, until
the monarchs began to know their own strength, and, seeing
the turbulent nature of their parliaments, at length little
by little began to stand upon their prerogatives, and at
last overthrew the parliaments throughout Christendom,
except here only with us." Virginia's assembly thrived
because the king was more interested in the colony's
tobacco than its institutions, and because the governors
were not strong enough to do without it.[35]

At the distance of three centuries, all this seems
to have been predictable, but the mood of Virginia colonists
throughout the 1620s and 1630s was often anxious, and
frequently angry. In 1622, soon after the respected
Powhatan werowance Nemattanow had been murdered, the Indians
killed nearly half the colony in a surprise attack. Then,
the company's charter was declared void, and the validity
of the colonists' titles to their land was threatened; not
until 1639 did Charles I decide to confirm them. In the
meantime, he gave part of Virginia's territory to Lord
Baltimore, a Roman Catholic, while various would-be monopolists lobbied to usurp control of the tobacco trade. Vir-

ginia's population grew rapidly and dispersed over a broad area. In 1634 eight shires were established, each with a county court, yet some colonists worried that this was evidence that Archbishop Laud intended to treat the Virginians as Englishmen had treated the Irish. In this tense atmosphere, Governor John Harvey, a former ship's captain, alienated the colonists whose support he needed, and showed himself unequal to the delicate task of being a governor. In 1635, virtually the entire colony supported the prominent councillors who engineered the Thrusting Out of Governor John Harvey. This coup d'etat, and the political situation revealed in its aftermath, also led to significant changes in Virginia's political institutions--changes defined in part by the increasingly important divisions to be found in the socio-economic order in Virginia.

The tobacco economy and society

During the colony's earliest years, both merchant and gentry investors generally agreed about the overall policies of the Virginia Company. Their lofty hope of planting a nation and converting the Indians coexisted nicely with hope for a profitable trade in silk, flax, grain, glass, or minerals. By about 1610, however, investors began to recognize the fact that their chance for profit was slim. In a massive study of English investments, Theodore K. Rabb determined that the end of 1609 marked an important change in the affairs of the Virginia Company of London: merchants, who

"never regard virtue without sure, certain, and present
gains," as a contemporary put it, fell behind the gentry
in their willingness to invest in Virginia. Trading companies such as the East India, Levant, and Muscovy companies
attracted the merchant investors and rewarded them with
substantial and relatively reliable profits, while the
proportion of gentry investors in the Virginia Company--
for whom the support of a great national enterprise offered
many intangible rewards--increased. In 1614, for example,
when Ralph Hamor sought to encourage investors "to persist
with alacrities and cheerfulness," he though that "the
worthier sort, I meane those Nobles and others of that
honourable counsell interested therein, neede no spurr,
theire owne innate vertue drives them a pace. The Merchant
onely wants some feeling and present return of those commodities which he is perswaded the country affordeth." In
time, with the election of Sir Edwin Sandys to the office
of treasurer in 1618, the gentry took over direction of the
Virginia Company from the merchants led by Sir Thomas Smith,
and ran it into bankruptcy by steadfast pursuit of the
program upon which all had agreed from the start. With the
development of the tobacco economy, the colony showed prospects of startling profits for individual investors, but the
company refused to give up its vision of a diversified
economy and continued to send colonists and resources to

Virginia to produce silk, flax, glass, iron, and other commodities that simply could not profitably be shipped to market in Europe.[36]

Company leaders, and colonists, presumed a fundamental relationship between social structure and political authority, and in doing so drew upon a medieval heritage: society was a hierarchy in which the socially superior were ipso facto political leaders. Whether shown in their choice of a baron as absolute governor, or in the knighting of governor-elect Yeardley, their expectation was that Virginia needed "good and sufficient men, as well of birth and quallyty to command," that Virginia needed representatives of the upper groups acknowledged to be the rightful rulers of English society. But in addition to reproducing in Virginia the complex social economy of England, the company also wanted to supplement that economy with tradesmen and industries that England lacked (silk dressers, Italian glassmakers, Dutch millwrights, Polish pitch-boilers, and French vine dressers and saltmakers) so that Virginia's products would benefit the mother country. Moreover, large numbers of the so-called laborers who came to Virginia during the first decade scarcely were laborers at all. Many were gentlemen's retinues and retainers, "that never did know what a dayes work was." Throughout the first quarter of the seventeenth century, Virginia remained an exotic curiosity for the English gentry.

Few well-born colonists saw themselves as permanent settlers. Many agreed with Robert Evelin, who crossed "the sea, a long and dangerous voyage with other men, to make me to be able to pay my debts, and to restore my decayed estate again." For most, Virginia was a temporary outpost, unless death intervened.[37]

Like the gentry investors, the colony's first generation of transient, well-born leaders were attracted as much by the prospect of glory as by the prospect of profit. Whether by sword or pen or both, men such as Smith, De La Warr, Pory, Gates, Sandys, Percy, and Thorpe lived by a Renaissance ideal ably summarized by Sir Humphrey Gilbert: "He is not worthy to live at all, that for feare, or danger of death, shunneth his countries service, and his own honour: seeing death is inevitable, and the fame of vertue immortall." Scarcely was fame or immortality to be won by settling in Virginia and growing tobacco.[38]

Elizabethan glory-seekers were not as plentiful in Virginia after the early 1620s. Their successors were men like William Claiborne and Francis West: men who owned trading vessels, amassed large tracts of land, and upheld the western terminus of the staple trade in fur and, especially, tobacco. From the ranks of these men emerged the indigenous colonial elite that came to dominate politics and society.

"All our riches for the present do consist in tobacco," Secretary John Pory wrote in 1619, "wherein one man by his own labor hath in one year raised himself to the value of

two hundred pounds sterling, and another by the means of
six servants hath cleared at one crop a thousand pounds
English." Pory admitted that these might be "rare examples,
yet possible to be done by others"--and others flocked to
Virginia to exploit the great tobacco boom of 1620-1630.
With few exceptions, Virginians during the boom were hard-
drinking men eager to turn a fast profit. Living in crude
dwellings; growing tobacco to the virtual exclusion of
other crops; relying on Indian trade or war for their supply
of corn; grasping land, servants, and cattle; they thought
of Virginia "not as a place of Habitacion but onely of a
short sojourninge."[39]

Irene Hecht's careful reconstruction of Virginia's
tobacco economy demonstrates the accuracy of contemporary
reports. Tobacco could be grown in Virginia with a very
low capital investment and sold in England at a very high
profit--Hecht's estimates of profit (based on the contemporary evidence, which is of varying reliability) range between 22 and 1000 percent. The social and political
implications of this situation are significant.

So long as tobacco offered exceptionally high profits,
Englishmen might hope to live briefly in Virginia, exploit
land, servants, and the market for all that could be had,
and carry wealth back to enjoy life a notch higher in English
society. So long as this ethos prevailed, Virginia remained
an outpost, peopled by vagrant profiteers.

As tobacco prices declined throughout the 1620s and

1630s, the _rate_ of profit available to entrepreneurs
eroded. Had tobacco prices fallen until production and
transportation costs exceeded market price, the planters
would have given up the business. The general increases
in immigrants, in acreage cultivated, and in tobacco exported,
demonstrate tobacco's continuing profitability, but the
erosion in the _rate_ of profit transformed Virginia. As
extraordinary levels of profit were reduced, new vagrant
profiteers were unable to enter the tobacco economy in the
way that men had in the 1620s, although established entrepreneurs continued to prosper. This had an important social
dimension, as the proportion of self-financed immigrants
to Virginia fell precipitously from more than 90 percent
of the 1624 immigrants to less that 10 percent after 1637.
"Broadly speaking," Hecht concluded, "there were two classes
of settlers coming to Virginia after 1624, those who could
pay their own way and those who could not," and by about
1635 only a small minority of Virginia's newcomers were
self-sufficient.[40]

Society and political institutions

By the mid-1630s Virginia had developed a two-class
society: the wealthy, powerful masters, and the poor, weak
servants and lesser planters. At the very top of the first
group were the commercial-minded planters who, by about
1635, had established their preeminence in a relatively

stable indigenous social order. Although the colony was
far removed from the gracious gentility of eighteenth-century
Westover or Gunston Hall, by the mid-1630s the change in
Virginia was palpable. Tobacco no longer grew in the streets
of Jamestown as it had in Argall's day, men now raised
cattle and corn as well. A six-mile palisade across the
Peninsula from the James to the York kept wolves from the
cattle, fences required by law kept swine out of the corn,
and brick houses began to appear among the cottages. Despite
a continuing imbalance between male and female colonists,
women were not so small a minority as they had been during
the boom (indeed, since women seem to have enjoyed a lower
rate of mortality in Virginia, the continuing sexual imbalance among new immigrants probably was greater than the
imbalance among the resident population).

Settled domesticity was in evidence, at any rate, on
the plantations of the elite. At Littleton, the home of
councillor George Menefie, on the James River a few miles
below the capital, grew rosemary, thyme, and marjoram, an
orchard of peach, apple, pear, and cherry trees, and a garden graced with "the fruits of Holland, and the roses of
Provence." At nearby Denbigh, councillor Samuel Mathews
had

> a fine house, and all things answerable to it,
> he sowes yeerly store of hempe and flax, and
> causes it to be spun; he keeps weavers and

hath a tan-house, causes leather to be dressed,
hath eight shoe-makers employed in their trade,
hath forty Negroe servants, brings them up to
trades in his house: He yeerly sowes abundance
of wheat, barley, &c. The wheat he selleth at
four shillings the bushell; kills store of
beeves, and sells them to victual the ships
when they come thither: hath abundance of kine,
a brave dairy, swine great store, and poultry;
he married the Daughter of Sir Tho. Hinton,
and in a word, keeps a good house, lives brave-
ly, and . . . is worthy of much honour.

Councillor William Claiborne's plan to reconstruct on a Chesapeake island the pleasures of his native Kent was disrupted when Lord Baltimore successfully claimed the island for Maryland. But when he founded Romancoke, in New Kent County, even Claiborne seems to have mellowed, giving up his swaggering military and trading exploits for a more sedate life as a planter and merchant. Councillor William Peirce, owner of plantations in Warwick and James City counties, kept a townhouse where in 1629 his wife said "shee hath a garden in Jamestown containing 3 or 4 acres where in one year she gathered near 100 bushells of excellent figs." Menefie, Mathews, Claiborne, and Peirce were typical of the second-generation Virginia elite whose lives centered on both agriculture and trade, men whose emulation of landed ease marked the end of the tobacco boom, men who dominated Virginia's society and politics and who controlled the ships (either as owners, part-owners, or factors) that carried Virginia's commerce. In both political and economic terms, it was their control of shipping that distinguished Virginia's second-generation elite from the rest of the colonists, and control of the tobacco economy that figured most prominently in Virginia politics. "Two things are necessarie for a merchant," a seventeenth-century maxim advised, "Money in the purse, and credit on the burse," and both were more secure when order prevailed, and most secure when the helm of the ship of state was manned by merchant-planters.[41]

George Donne, second son of the poet John Donne and a financially distressed would-be courtier, accurately perceived the emergence of a distinct society in Virginia by the later 1630s. Donne recognized that indigenous colonial leaders, especially on the Council, had emerged and that no governor could be successful who failed to contend with them. Donne was not a disinterested observer--he had come to the colony in 1637 when John Harvey returned as governor and then returned to England in 1638 to defend Harvey's interests at court--but his analysis of Virginia's political landscape was acute. The company outpost had become a society, and that society's natural leaders dominated the Council and frequently the governor.

An opponent such as Donne might prescribe a "sharpe and present cure to so increasinge an Evill, growne upp to maturity and ripeness in Faction," but the very presence of factions was evidence of the increasing political complexity of the society of commercial and lesser planters. Late in the 1630s an impoverished younger son like Donne might still set out for Virginia, hoping that an appointment as muster-master-general and a good tobacco crop would enable him to make money quickly and return home. But for many colonists the permanent trips home were pushed farther and farther into the future. For the elite there was time to be spent enjoying Samuel Mathews's "fine house, and all things answerable to it," or George Menefie's provence roses, or Mrs. Peirce's figs. Men who had been ready to exploit the tobacco boom only to return to England, had begun, by the 1640s, to make over Virginia in England's image. Virginians remained intensely commercial, but the colony was becoming a society. Most importantly, the colony had become their colony.[42]

Charles I had no choice but to send Governor Harvey back to Virginia in 1637 after he had been thrust from office two years earlier, but while Harvey tried to ruin his opponents and confiscate their estates, they successfully lobbied in London for his removal. Sir Francis Wyatt, serving again as governor from 1639 to 1641, calmed the colony and began a number of needed reforms. Tobacco prices were not improved, and the fear of a tobacco monopoly was still to be found. A small group of prominent merchant-planters, led by councillors Samuel Mathews, Sr., and William Claiborne, were secretly vying for control of the tobacco trade, control of Virginia, and control of Maryland as well.

From 1619 through the 1630s, the councillors and burgesses had met together with the governor in the General Assembly, and, as long as common interests overshadowed the separate interests that might tend to divide them, the unicameral assembly continued. The events of the 1630s, however, suggest that distinct interest groups, which were emerging within Virginia's increasingly stratified socio-economic system, could no longer be managed within that institutional framework. Soon after Sir William Berkeley became governor in 1642, the political and judicial reforms begun by Wyatt were brought to perfection.

Aware that the councillors who had thrust Harvey from office posed a potential threat to him, Berkeley saw that their economic and political goals differed from those of the smaller planters: Mathews, Claiborne, and their prominent allies in Virginia and London were seeking to monopolize the tobacco trade, while most of the other Virginians opposed monopolies and wanted to keep the tobacco trade open, especially to the Dutch. With Berkeley's apparent encouragement, the burgesses organized themselves as the lower house of a bicameral assembly in March 1643. Thomas Stegg, an associate of Mathews and Claiborne, appears to have resigned his Council seat and won election to the new

House of Burgesses in order to secure the Speaker's chair for his faction.

After 1643, with rare exceptions, the General Assembly met in two chambers. Legislation might originate in either house, but initiative generally fell to the governor and Council, whose approval was necessary before anything became law. By mid-century Virginia's constitution approximated the traditional mixed government of England, and in 1648 Virginia and Massachusetts Bay (where bicameral procedure began in 1644) were cited as precedents for the "Politique and Civill Government" of the proposed colony of New Albion:

> Virginia and New England is our president; First, the Lord head Governour, a Deputy Governour, Secretary of Estate, or Seal keeper, and twelve of the Councell of State or upper House . . . Next, out of Counties and Towns, at a free election and day prefixed, thirty Burgesses, or Commons. Once yearly . . . these meet, as a Parliament or Grand Assembly, and make Laws, or repeal, alter, explain, and set taxes and rates for common defence, and without full consent of Lord [i.e., governor], upper and lower House nothing is done.[43]

Although with Governor Berkeley's leadership Virginia remained formally loyal to the crown for as long as possible during the Civil Wars and Interregnum, in 1652 parliamentary commissioners William Claiborne and Richard Bennett negotiated a peaceful surrender. Sir William Berkeley retired to Green Spring, his plantation west of Jamestown, and between 1652 and 1660 the colony acknowledged "the Commonwealth of England as it is now Established, without Kinge or howse of Lords." The governors (Richard Bennett, Edward Digges, and Samuel Mathews, Jr.--merchant-councillors all) and councillors were appointed by the burgesses and derived their authority from the lower house. At first reluctantly, and then with increasing skill and self-confidence, the burgesses put their house in order, established committees to manage business, and fended off inappropriate claims of gubernatorial or counciliar autonomy. Crown and parliamentary lassitude in Virginia affairs since the mid-1640s had given the Virginia House of Burgesses confidence in its power of self-government, although the House always was reluctant to assert the radical populist basis of its authority. The burgesses' most assertive moment came in 1658, when, in a conflict with Governor Mathews and Secretary Claiborne and the Council, the House of Burgesses announced that the power was "resident only in the burgesses, representatives of the people, as is manifest by the records of the Assembly." When the burgesses met them head on, the governor and Council backed down.[44]

But the burgesses, too, were eager to back down from this dizzying height. After a tense period of uncertainty, Sir William Berkeley agreed to serve as interim governor after Samuel Mathews, Jr., died in January 1660. In May, Charles II had resumed the throne in England, and by October royal authority was quickly restored in Virginia. The colonists, their burgesses, and their governor, all relieved to have sovereignty and the crown resting again on "him, who by all Englishmen is confessed to be in a naturall politique capacity of being a Supreame power," quickly abandoned their ad hoc populist claims. But the habits of procedural sophistication that Virginians had learned in the previous three decades, and through which those claims had been exercised, never were unlearned.[45]

THE FOUNDING OF THE GENERAL ASSEMBLY:
The Governor, the Council of State,
and the Assembly of 1619

Between 1618 and 1643 the political institutions of the English outpost on the James River were transformed a third time as the settlement grew into a society. Two experiments had failed to foster a stable and profitable colony in Virginia. Government by president and council had allowed faction to tear apart the first outpost, leaving the starving survivors ready to abandon the attempt. The absolute governorship of De La Warr and his deputies had saved the colony and brought order, but had failed to make the enterprise profitable for company investors. In 1618, therefore, the Virginia Company of London chose a new governor to execute its new plan "to lay a foundation whereon A flourishing State might in process of time by the blessing of Almighty God be raised."[1]

George Yeardley, one of sixty subscribers to the company's Second Charter and a former soldier who had served in the Low Countries and accompanied Sir Thomas Gates to Virginia in 1610, was thirty years old when the company appointed him governor on 29 September 1618. His appointment confirmed by the quarterly court on 18 November, Yeardley was knighted at Newmarket on the 24th. By 8 December he had married Temperance Flowerdieu, of Norfolk, and on 10 January 1619 they sailed for Virginia on the George. After a "sore voyage," Yeardley and his wife arrived in Virginia on 19 April, carrying among their effects three documents that were to be the legal foundation for the flourishing state: Yeardley's gubernatorial commission, a commission to reestablish the Council and summon meetings of a General Assembly, and the instructions that came to be called the Great Charter.[2]

These documents and the new policies that they represented were the result of sometimes acrimonious debates within the Virginia Company of London between 1616 and 1618 that had led to a broad reorganization of the company's affairs. The machinery of the company itself had been improved, although in 1616 when Sir Edwin Sandys and his gentry followers demanded an audit of the company's books, the request had aroused ill feelings among the merchant leaders associated with Treasurer Sir Thomas Smith. In the long run, this demand for an audit marked the beginning of the company's strife-ridden decline toward its dissolution in 1624. Yet, the need to audit accounts and reform the administration was real: investors had subscribed variously in 1606, 1609, 1611, or 1616, some had paid only part of the amount subscribed, others none, and some had won their shares in the company's lotteries. Encouraged by the profit that could be seen in the production of tobacco, company leaders and investors hoped anew to realize profit in other commodities as well, and, as Craven observed, "men who had recently regarded Virginia as worthy only of scorn now found her worth quarreling about."[3]

In 1618 company members argued about who had been responsible for past mistakes, and two factions, one led by Robert Rich, second earl of Warwick, and his brother Nathaniel, and the other by Sandys, grew increasingly suspicious of Treasurer Smith's management. Nevertheless, Sandys did not succeed Smith as treasurer until 28 April 1619. Despite its other divisions, the company was united in its belief that the profit offered by tobacco could be realized on other commodities, too, and that with sound leadership, improved organization, and additional capital and labor, Virginia could at last become a model of the profitable, diversified colony envisaged by promoters such as Hakluyt.

"Towe supreame Counsells"

If the Virginia Company were to profit from the production of commodities raised on company-owned lands in Virginia, the colony's population had to be rapidly increased. During the first year of his administration, Sir Edwin Sandys was able to send 1,261 colonists to Virginia, half of whom settled on company lands and half on private plantations. Some four thousand new colonists went to Virginia during Sandys's administration. This successful effort to attract colonists rested on genuine reform and on a propaganda campaign in which printed tracts and pamphlets advised "that the Colony beginneth now to have the face and fashion of an orderly State, and such as is likely to grow and prosper."[4]

The so-called Great Charter, the instructions Yeardley carried to Virginia, was an important part of the reform of 1618. Having confirmed and expanded the policy of distributing land to individuals, the company sought to attract settlers with the promise that each could have a "share of Land due to him set out, to hold and enjoy to him and his Heires." The company proudly announced that "the rigour of Martiall Law" had been lifted and that in Virginia "the laudable forme of Justice and government used in this Realme [was] established and followed as neere as may be."[5]

This "laudable form of government by majestracy," as the Great Charter phrased it, was defined in the other two documents Governor Yeardley brought with him: his commission and the ordinance establishing "towe supreame Counsells in Virginia for the better government of the said Colony," the Council of State and the General Assembly. As had been the case with De La Warr, the important description of Yeardley's office was the term <u>governor</u>, for throughout the colonial period phrases such as "powers and Authorities incident to a Governor and Council in Virginia respectively" conveyed the real power of office. But of course Yeardley's appointment differed from De La Warr's in several important ways.[6]

Appointed for life, De La Warr had been allowed "free will and pleasure" to choose and displace his councillors and other officers (except for a handful of company-made appointments), license to leave the colony, and authority to appoint deputies in his absence. Yeardley and his successors, by contrast, had no decisive hand in conciliar appointments, were bound to govern in partnership with the Council, and had no authority to dismiss councillors with whom they might disagree. Gubernatorial absence was unusual in Virginia until after Bacon's Rebellion (only between 1710 and 1768 were absentee governors allowed to treat the office as a sinecure), and not until Culpeper's appointment in 1677 was another Virginia governor commissioned for life or given authority to suspend councillors from office.[7]

Rather than continuing the advisory council of De La Warr's administration, the reform of 1618 reestablished a Council of State as a powerful part of the colonial constitution. Between 1618 and 1660 commissions were addressed to both the governor and council. The governor was always named in the document itself, but practice varied with the councillors: prior to 1636 each member of the council was named in the address and frequently elsewhere in the commission; in 1637 and 1639 Charles I named only the governor and entered the councillors' names in the accompanying instructions; in 1641 and 1650 the practice of listing councillors by name was resumed. But whether the councillors were named in the commission itself is immaterial, because their authority always was conveyed in the commission, and it was expressed both in specific and in general terms.

The general statement that the councillors were to exercise the authority incident to a council, perhaps was as vague to the seventeenth-century colonist as it seems today. The modern distinction between council, a noun describing a group of persons, and counsel, a noun meaning advice or a verb meaning to advise, was only beginning to emerge in early seventeenth-century English political usage, although the distinction can be seen in the Latin roots concilium and consilium. More importantly, regardless of spelling, the word carried no specific definition of authority: a council might have deliberative power or it might have only an advisory function. Council of State was equally ambiguous

This fundamental ambiguity is seen even in the Virginia Company of London's most specific descriptions of the colony's council: Council decisions were to be taken by majority vote, with the governor casting the deciding vote in the event of a tie. "For the time being," the company said in 1618, the governor could alone summon the councillors to meet in emergency sessions, and he could sign warrants for the execution of council orders. But even his "absolute power and authority . . . to direct, determine and punish . . . emergent buisness, neglect or contempt

of authority—in short, his power to act decisively in the face of crisis—
was hedged with restrictions. Notably, a governor could not act
against a councillor except by vote of a majority of the councillors
at a quarter court.[8]

The line between gubernatorial and counciliar authority never was
clearly marked. During emergencies a governor was expected to exercise
leadership equal to the occasion, lest the colony again witness the
vicissitudes of its earliest years, but how much authority did that
require? and who was to judge if it were rightly used? and by what gauge?
Such queries are, of course, only the local versions of the bedeviling
seventeenth-century questions about authority in general: where was it?
who had it? how could one know? The Virginia Company leaders had no
prescient answer to these questions. They wanted a governor strong
enough to be effective, but they did not want to reproduce De La Warr's
office and entrust it to a parvenu like Yeardley. While the General
Assembly was in session the governor enjoyed a power of veto, but during
the ordinary meetings of the council his constitutional position was
primus inter pares, first among equals. And the pattern survived the
company, for even after Governor John Harvey had been thrust from office
in 1635 by the members of the council, Charles I sent him back to Virginia
with no clearer and no more forceful definition of his authority than
he had had. For the company and for the crown, the office of governor
and the office of councillor were defined by the terms; neither company
nor crown was willing to attempt a more precise definition.[9]

If the company was unwilling to attempt a more precise constitutional
definition of the offices of governor and councillor, at least its thinking

was now distinctly political thinking, and its solution to the problem of governing Virginia was an appropriately political solution. "In a world where the ancient landmarks were fading, where the will of God was becoming ambiguous to man's reading," Perry Miller observed, "the one remaining certainty, the one institution which could plead at least the excuse of utility, was the organized rights of Englishmen, exercised and protected in an elective assembly." The bedeviling problem of authority might not be resolved, but at least some means might be contrived to soften its force, to prevent disaster, and to encourage accomodation and order. All the better for the company if the mechanism of an elective assembly could be displayed as further inducement for Englishmen (between 27 and 40 percent of whom voted in parliamentary elections) to settle in Virginia.[10]

Attractive as the General Assembly may have been to adventurers and would-be adventurers, however, its chief utility was to the company. Periodic meetings attended by elected representatives as well as the governor and councillors better enabled the company's Virginia leaders to adapt their instructions to the colonial situation and to give their measures the added force of having been "decided, determined and ordered by the greater part of the voices then present." The assembly, summoned "yeerly, of course, and no oftner but for very extreordynarie and important occasions," was a sure safeguard against either the potential abuse of authority by a governor such as Yeardley, who lacked De La Warr's social claim to rule, or by the members of the Council. During meetings of the General Assembly it was also prudent, as a safeguard against abuse by the

councillors or elected members, to reserve "alwaies to the Governor a
negative voice" that he did not enjoy in council meetings. The Virginia
experience that enlightened James Madison's contributions to the Federalist
Papers began here. Real political institutions were replacing the military
state. According to an anonymous contempory who formulated another plan
of government for Virginia, the grand object of a prosperous settlement
was to be accomplished by adopting "Aristotle's rule . . . that, that
right which works most to the attaineing of politick End must be preferred."
"Layeing aside force and our coactive power," he continued, the company
might "by our justice and bountie marrye and combinde those of our
provinces to us and our soveraigntye in naturall love and obedience."[11]

The secret, then, to successful colonial government was to delegate
sufficient authority within a well-ordered system of government, to count
on the inherent nature of a governor to supply the energy, and to provide
that "theire jealousys one of each other will by maintaineing that
equalitye [i.e., balance] keepe anie one either from usurpinge further
authoritie . . . then our forme doth give him." Was it not "better to
authorize one sett forme of government" by governor, Council, and General
Assembly "and soe leave the lawes to bee ordainedd accordinge to that forme,"
than to have the company "give lawes and government . . . to the planters in
Virginia as if they were tenantes or servantes"? The Virginia Company's
reform program, as Craven has emphasized, worked to strengthen the company's
position and its officers' authority in the colony by establishing the
political machinery—part of which consisted of elected representatives—
through which a better understanding of company policy and a better spirit
of cooperation could be promoted among the colonists.[12]

In a significant way, both the observations of the anonymous contemporary and the reforms of the company approached the problem of order and authority from a fresh angle: each anticipated the emergence of a political community. The observer recommended a "sett forme of government" within which all the traditional wisdom of political science would be appropriate. After citing Aristotle by name, in a note he couched his advice in the terminology of English Machiavellian treatises: "Reade the treatice uppon the word Policie." Similarly, having decided to imitate the government of England "as neere as may bee," the Virginia Company of London was consciously establishing circumstances within which the arts of political management had space to function. The governors' and councillors' eventual transition from commanders to politicians was begun. The addition of a representative dimension to the government of Virginia opened the way toward political community. From the community, in time, came a stable, cis-Atlantic polity that first augmented and eventually supplanted rule from without.[13]

The General Assembly of 1619

On 19 April 1619 Governor Sir George Yeardley arrived in Virginia, and late in June he "sente his summons all over the Country" and "caused Burgesses to be chosen in all places." Twenty-two men were elected from eleven plantations to meet with Yeardley and the Council of State in a General Assembly. Unfortunately, especially in light of recent studies that suggest that the English franchise extended to as many as four out of ten adult males in this period, no evidence about the electoral procedure survives.[14]

H.R. McIlwaine thought that the title <u>burgess</u> was used in the sense of "an inhabitant of a borough" (in which sense it was used as early as 1225 in England). McIlwaine failed to recognise that the Virginia Company had used the term <u>borough</u> in its instructions to Yeardley, and that the post-parliamentary (ca. 1472) meaning of <u>burgess</u>, as a borough's representative in Parliament, was therefore entirely appropriate. In contempory English political theory, the third estate was represented by the two lowest of the six orders in Parliament: the House of Commons comprised knights of the shires (the fifth order) and citizens and burgesses (the sixth). Virginia had no shires in 1619, but it aspired to cities and boroughs and the word <u>burgess</u> was used to name the representatives "elected out of each Incorporation."[15]

The term has more than semantic interest, for the post-parliamentary definition implies the representational nexus without which a General Assembly had no value either to the company and its officers or to the colonists. In Virginia, as in England or on the Continent, a representative was useful to the central administration only insofar as his assent bound the populace for whom he spoke to abide by the measures to which he agreed. In turn, of course, a central administration, too, might be bound.[16]

The local interest is less important for the understanding of the General Assembly of 1619 than for the subsequent development of political institutions and a genuine political community in seventeenth-century Virginia. From the local point of view in an operating representative system, a representative was an attorney empowered to speak for his locality. His summons to Parliament afforded an opportunity to lay local grievances before a central assembly. But the effective operation of this aspect of representation requires a sense of corporate interest or identity, which in turn is a dimension of political community. If the argument is followed a bit further, one finds the circumstances of an integrated, national political community in which the representative's role as attorney for a narrow, local constituency is diminished. Eighteenth-century England was such a community, and the familiar Burkean assertion that representatives in Parliament consult "not local purposes, not local prejudices . . ., but the general good, resulting from the general reason of the whole," was an expression of a more generalized or transcendant sense of political community. The aspiration toward Burkean representation seems to correspond with parliamentary representation in a stable, relatively homogeneous social order and political culture. Virginia in 1619 had few claims to political or social cohesiveness, yet the case was far different twenty years later. Representation in 1619 supplied the framework within which residents of the colony eventually would identify and assert their corporate interest. Conversely, the subsequent emergence of an assertive, well-ordered representative assembly is a visible gauge of the colony's transition from outpost to society.[17]

The members of the General Assembly gathered in Jamestown on Friday morning, 30 July 1619. Governor Yeardley took his seat in "the Quire of the churche," and "nexte him on both hands" sat councillors Nathaniel Powell, Samuel Macock, and John Rolfe. John Pory, "then appointed Speaker, . . . sate right before him." Although the burgesses are listed early in Pory's report of the proceedings of the first assembly, until certain preliminary ceremonies had been completed they did not become members of the assembly; simple failure to appreciate the straightforward chronology of Pory's narrative has led many historians into misconceptions.

Three things happened before the burgesses individually took the oath of supremacy and were admitted into the assembly. First, Secretary Pory, a councillor, was appointed Speaker. Second, John Twine and Thomas Pierse (about whom scarcely anything else is known) took their places respectively as "clerke of the General assembly" and "sargeant." Finally, the Reverend Richard Buck, minister at Jamestown since May 1610, led the assembled colonists in prayer, asking "God to guide and sanctifie all our proceedings, to his owne glory, and the good of this plantation." When Mr. Buck finished the prayer, the elected representatives left the choir "to retyre themselves into the body of the Churche," where they awaited formal admission to the assembly.

John Pory's appointment as Speaker is widely misunderstood. Regardless of the later history of colonial assemblies, the burgesses had nothing whatever to do with Pory's position—his appointment had been arranged before they were formally admitted to membership in the assembly. Moreover, Speaker Pory executed only some of the presidential functions of a Speaker of the House of Commons, and nothing of the ancient role of "speaker-forth," or spokesman for the Commons. John Pory was Speaker of the assembly because he was secretary of the colony and, as secretary, in the best position to arrange the working papers of the meeting, to oversee the recording of its deliberations, and to conclude the paperwork generated by its actions. In this respect, the explicit definition of the secretary's responsibilities during meetings of the assembly of the Bermuda colony during the 1620's is instructive:

> The Secretary shall also in all generall Assemblies, hold the place of Speaker: and have care that all things

proceed and passe in due order; and shall keepe a

Register Booke of all the Acts there passed.

The membership and leadership of the Bermuda Company being drawn almost entirely from the Virginia Company, the Bermuda instruction may have been based on a Virginia model. In any case, the responsibilities it described were those that Pory actually had at Virginia's first assembly (The Bermuda Company also provided that "the Governor shall act as President, to moderate the Assembly," in the same way that Governor Yeardley presided over the Virginia assembly.) Pory's duties—reading documents aloud, organizing Yeardley's instructions (the Great Charter) into four books, writing and reading the assembly's orders, reading aloud the laws a last time before final passage, and making copies of documents for each locality—were more secretarial than presidential.[20]

After the officers had been named and the prayer ended, the elected burgesses passed "the barre"—marked by the rail that separated the choir from the narthex—and retired into the narthex so that they "might proceed with awfull and due respecte towardes his Lieutenant, our most gratious and dread Soveraigne." From their places in the narthex "they were called in order by name, and so every man . . . tooke the oathe of Supremacy, and then passing the bar into the choir entred the Assembly." None hesitated to take the oath, and all were "fully admitted" except those to whom Pory and Yeardley took exception.[21]

Because the decisions on the admission of members involved an important aspect of English parliamentary privilege, an assembly's claim to determine its own membership, the assembly's actions are frequently cited as an early precedent. However, the decisions on the two cases that arose had a more immediately significant dimension that is often overlooked. The assembly's actions corresponded exactly with Yeardley's instructions from the company: by action of the assembly one colonist was induced to comply with company policy, and another colonist's refusal to comply was made to affront not only the company and its governor but the common interest of all the colonists as well.

Twenty burgesses from ten vicinities had been admitted to the assembly and only the two representatives "for Captaine Wardes plantation" remained in the narthex. Pory challenged the right of Captain John Ward to participate in the assembly on either of two grounds: either Ward was ineligible because he had situated his private plantation on company-owned land without a commission from the company, or he had settled on a tract owned by John Martin, in which case, with burgesses for Martin's Brandon already admitted, "there could be but two Burgesses for all." Captain Ward was ordered to leave (the other burgess-elect, Lieutenant Thomas Gibbes, probably accompanied him), the assembly considered the matter, and "after much debate" offered to admit Ward and Gibbes if Ward agreed to seek a commission from the Virginia Company for his plantation. Ward agreed, "the whole Assembly" voted to admit them, they took the oath, and they entered the assembly in the choir. [22]

Yeardley was not as familiar with procedure as Pory, for all the burgesses had been admitted when "the Governour himselfe" challenged the credentials of Thomas Davis and Robert Stacy, who had been seated for John Martin's plantation, Martin's Brandon. He had come prepared to make the challenge, however, for he had brought with him a copy of Martin's patent from the Virginia Company, a generous grant of five thousand acres free from any obligation to the colony or its government "save only to defend it against its foreign and domestical enemies."[23]

Yeardley knew that Martin had friends and relatives in high places. His father Sir Richard had served as warden and master of the mint, alderman and thrice Lord Mayor of London; his sister Dorcas had married Sir Julius Caesar, a member of the Privy Council. Martin himself was an ancient planter who had served on the Virginia Council of State from 1607 to 1610 and had returned to the colony in 1616 with his extraordinary patent and immediately embroiled himself in controversy with other planters and with many members of the company. Nevertheless, Yeardley's instructions set forth the company's desire to bring all private plantations (including Martin's, which was expressly named) "into one body corporate . . . under equal and like laws and orders with the rest of the colony."[24]

Governor Yeardley used the General Assembly to bolster his authority in an attempt to win Martin's voluntary compliance with the colony's government as required by his instructions. The assembly's first order "touching a clause in Captain Martin's Patent" offered Martin a clear choice: if he refused to "give over that parte of his Patente," the assembly was ready to order the Martin's Brandon burgesses "utterly to be excluded, as being spies, rather than loyal Burgesses." The debate expanded into a general consideration of Martin's potentially disruptive presence in the colony. A complaint was registered against Martin for allowing the crew of his shallop to force Indians to sell them corn. One Thomas Davis (apparently one of the Martin's Brandon burgesses whose admission was in doubt) testified against Martin under oath before the assembly, and Yeardley evidently informed the assembly that Chief Opechancanough himself had complained about Martin. An order was drafted

against Martin requiring him to secure the governor's
permission for trade with the Indians and to deposit a
bond for his crew's good conduct. Thus far Yeardley had
been able to secure popular endorsement of his authority
through the assembly's actions and, apparently, the assembly had drawn one of Martin's burgesses into testifying
against him. Finally, "a letter or warrant was drawen in
the name of the whole assembly to summon Captaine Martin
to appeare before them." Three days later Martin "made his
personall appearance at the barre," heard Pory read the
orders against him, and "pleaded lardgely for himself."
Martin's appearance was itself a victory for Yeardley,
and although Martin refused to surrender any part of his
patent, he agreed "(his Patent notwithstanding)" to post
bond for his men's good behavior. The Martin's Brandon
burgesses were denied seats in the assembly and the question
of Martin's patent was left to the Virginia Company, but
through the assembly Yeardley had gained a greater measure
of compliance to his instructions than might otherwise
have been the case.[25]

"These obstacles removed," Pory wrote, the assembly was
ready to turn to the business at hand. Pory briefly recalled
the reasons for their meeting, much as the lord chancellor
might read the crown's speech before the king, lords, and
commons at the opening of Parliament. "Which done, he read
unto them the commission for establishing the Counsell of

estate and the general Assembly." Then, "having thus
prepared them" with his own admonition and with the commission "wherein their duties were described to the life,"
Pory read for the first time the Great Charter, which he
had divided into four sections, or "books." He read the
first two books again that morning (30 July) "for expeditions sake" before each was referred to a committee of
eight burgesses.[26]

The assembly's use of committees is important, but
unfortunately few pre-Restoration records survive to reveal this aspect of internal procedure. Pory's record
of the General Assembly of 1619, more detailed than any other
in this respect, suggests that Virginians followed contemporary English usages. We do not know how the committees were
appointed, just as we do not know how Pory was appointed;
we do know that two groups of eight men each--all burgesses
--were named as "Committies." Pory's use of the term
committee here reflected the older Elizabethan meaning of
an individual to whom a charge, trust, function, or
particular item of business was delegated or committed.
Modern committee procedure was a sixteenth-century development, and the modern, corporate sense of the word appears
occasionally in Pory's report, too.

At first, committees of the House of Commons had been
appointed to draft bills that accorded with the sense of the

House, but by the beginning of the seventeenth century the practice of sending a bill to committee after its second reading had become regular. The two 1619 Virginia committees were composed only of burgesses, but they seem to have had a basically passive role: considering and approving documents submitted to their attention, but not drafting proposals themselves. The drafting of orders, petitions, and laws remained in the hands of "the Governour and those that were not of the Committes." These "Non Comitties"--whose deliberations continued in the absence of the sixteen committee members--included the four councillors and four burgesses (Thomas Gibbes, Edward Gourgainy, John Polentine, and Ensigne Washer, each of whom, being listed second in Pory's report, probably was the less prominent burgess from his plantation).[27]

The two committees met outside the church in the afternoon, and, after three hours, returned "their opinions concerning the two former bookes." The next morning, Saturday, 31 July, the whole assembly reviewed the committees' opinions and agreed to six petitions to the Virginia Company. Neither committee had drafted formal petitions, however; the requests reached the company in Pory's report of the assembly proceedings. Five of the six petitions either asked that company policy be clarified or suggested specific ways that it might better be implemented. The last asked that "the savage name of Kiccowtan" be replaced (it

became Elizabeth City, in honor of the daughter of James I).
The two committees then reported that "they had observed in
the two latter bookes . . . nothing therin subject to exception."
Throughout the rest of the assembly session, the
two committees continued to offer passive approbation to
documents drafted by the governor, councillors, and "Non
Committies." Late Saturday afternoon they were given the
text of laws derived from Yeardley's instructions "to be returned
by them into the assembly on Munday morning." On
Monday, 2 August, the assembly heard the committee reports
and adopted a dozen such laws. [28]

In the assembly's handling of the "thirde sort of lawes
(suche as might proceed out of every mans private conceipte)"
the same passivity is seen in the committees. After being
read early on Tuesday morning, 3 August, these laws were
divided into two groups and referred to "the same Committies
which were from the beginning." Committee members, however,
seem not to have hurried from the room to confer, for the
assembly next dealt with a petition from William Powell and
heard the second reading of the laws drawn for Yeardley's
instructions. Inasmuch as committee member Powell was present
to offer his petition, and as the laws from Yeardley's
instructions were "one by one thoroughly examined, and then
passed once again [by] the generall consente of the whole
Assembly," it seems likely that the committees did not meet
until after the morning session had ended. In any case,

that afternoon they reported on the private laws, "the
discussing wherof spente the residue of that daye." Clearly,
the burgesses had little hand in drafting those laws, and
the only thorough discussion occurred while the governor,
councillors, and burgesses met together on Tuesday afternoon and Wednesday morning.[29]

By Wednesday, 4 August, several members of the assembly,
including Governor Yeardley, had fallen victim to the "extream
heat" of a tidewater summer; one burgess had died on Sunday.
Yeardley resolved to end the meeting. Secretary Pory read
aloud the legislation passed earlier "to give the same yet
one reviewe more," and, no changes being made, went on to read
the private laws, which were "thoroughly discussed" once more
and passed by the whole assembly. The stifling heat and its
"alteration of the healthes of diverse of the general Assembly" may have contributed to the prompt rising of the assembly,
but the function of the burgesses and their committees--the
approval of documents and policies drafted by others--scarcely
could have been diminished by the weather.[30]

Like the Council of State, of which it was basically an
expanded meeting, the General Assembly of 1619 acted as a
court of justice and drew no line to distinguish lawmaking
from the administration of justice. Four items of business
that today would be characterized as judicial were dispatched
by the governor, councillors, and burgesses meeting at Jamestown in 1619. From them a common pattern emerges, illuminated

by English parliamentary practice. Three of the four cases were brought to the assembly's attention by petitioners: burgess William Powell petitioned for justice against one of his servants; councillor John Rolfe petitioned for redress against aspersions cast upon him by John Martin; and the inhabitants of Pasbehegh presented "a petition to the general assembly to give them absolute dischardge from certain bonds." The fourth case involved charges made against Captain Henry Spelman by Robert Poole in "a relation upon oath."[31]

The first three petitions demonstrate the futility of attempting to distinguish the assembly's legislative and judicial functions according to a modern constitutional definition. Just as legislation in Parliament had derived from petitions for redress of grievances, so public demand in Virginia inspired some lawmaking. Petitions could initiate the dispensation of justice by general law, by judicial determination and order, or by private bill. Powell's and Rolfe's petitions, which would as easily have come to the General Court as to the General Assembly, probably came to the assembly simply because it happened to be in session at the moment. In the first case, the assembly heard testimony given under oath, found Powell's servant Thomas Garnett guilty of immorality and slander, and, with "the Governour himselfe giving the sentence" as he did in the General Court, ordered that Garnett "should stande fower dayes with his eares nayled to the Pillory . . . and every of those fower dayes should be publiguely whipped." Rolfe's petition was more difficult. John Martin was no servant indeed, and he could scarcely be judged by the assembly while his patent exempted him from the colony's jurisdiction and while his brother-in-law sat on the Privy Council. Rolfe's petition against Martin (along with the determination of what Garnett owed Powell for the neglect of his work) was referred to the Council, or General Court.[32]

The petition from Pasbehegh, a suburb of Jamestown, was a different matter. Introduced on Wednesday, 4 August, either by the locality's burgesses (as Pory's report seems to suggest) or by the inhabitants themselves from the bar, the petition requested discharge from a contract with Samuel Argall, De La Warr's last deputy governor, for clearing land at a cost of six hundred fifty pounds sterling. No testimony was heard, for the facts were not in dispute. Two problems faced the assembly: the land in question was granted to Governor Yeardley in the Great Charter that the assembly had affirmed on Saturday, and the assembly members were doubtful "whether they have any power and authority to dischardge the said bonds." Details about the contract are unclear, but from the distance of three centuries it appears that the inhabitants of Pasbehegh wanted the equivalent of a private bill to nullify a contract and its financial obligation, and that the assembly, doubting that its authority extended to the passage of such a bill, merely endorsed the petition and sent it on to the Virginia Company.[33]

The trial of Captain Henry Spelman was notable for the assembly's reluctance to convict in a treason case or to base a severe sentence upon only one man's testimony. Robert Poole, an interpreter, accused Spelman, another interpreter, of threatening the peace by disparaging the governor in a meeting with Opechancanough. Apparently Poole's written "relation upon oath" was read to Spelman as he stood at the bar to answer its charges. Spelman denied "the greattest parte" of the accusations, but "acknowledged some for true." Among the latter was "onely one matter of importance, and that was, that he had informed Opochancano, that within a yeare there would come a governour greatter then this nowe is in place." Spelman's remarks to the Powhatan chief might bear a favorable construction--as a firm warning that the English were not going to weaken--but the assembly concluded that his comments weakened Yeardley's reputation and "alienated the mind" of Opechancanough.[34]

The case was a sensitive one, and trustworthy evidence was always difficult to obtain in cases that involved Indians and Europeans, which frequently arose in frontier trading areas where the line between war and peace or the distinction between friendly and unfriendly parties on either side often was obscure. Moreover, Virginians were uncertain about whether a policy of friendship or of hostility was the better course, and Indian affairs evoked strong emotions for they affected the immediate security of every person in the colony. Pory himself seems to have thought that Spelman deserved harsher punishment than he received, yet by January 1620 his opinion of Spelman's accuser had fallen, and in retrospect perhaps Pory recognized the soundness of the assembly's moderate course. However that may have been, despite his apparent bias Pory reported that the assembly carefully and judiciously handled a serious, emotionally charged case. [35]

Unwilling to act on "Pooles testimony onely," the assembly convicted and punished Spelman only as a result of "his confession above written," rather than "out of any other proofe." Yeardley favored censure and lenient punishment rather than execution for treason, and after they had debated the case the "whole court" of the assembly agreed "by voices." Although these cases established the assembly's judicial function in Virginia--a role not lost until the 1680s--that judicial role was but one face of a narrow competence limited in 1619 by: the company's instructions, the laws of England, the ability of the governor and councillors to guide the burgesses, and mundane things like the fact that the burgesses' committees had little time to initiate anything. [36]

One of the General Assembly's final acts on 4 August

1619, however, was to ask that the company "make good their promise sett downe at the Conclusion of their Commission for establishing the Counsel of Estate and the General Assembly, namely that they will give us power to allowe or disallowe of their orders of Courte." Among all the records that survive from the assembly of 1619, this is the one indication that more assertive aspirations might mark the future of representative assemblies in colonial Virginia. When Yeardley prorogued the assembly on Wednesday, 4 August, both he and the Virginia Company might look back on the event with satisfaction about its accomplishments and about the reforms that had brought it into being. The representative assembly brought popular support to company policy and government authority.[37]

It also permanently altered the nature of government in colonial Virginia by supplying the mechanism with which the colonists could define their interests and discover politics. The seventeenth-century question of the location of political authority might continue to bother Englishmen on both sides of the Atlantic, but in their polite request that the company make good its promise, colonial Virginians quietly announced that they had some inkling of whose answer they trusted.

3

THE FOUNDING OF THE HOUSE OF BURGESSES:

The Dissolution of the Virginia Company,

Uncertainty and Coup d'Etat,

and Reform, 1624 - 1643

Between 1618, when the Virginia Company of London established colonial government by governor, Council, and General Assembly as a part of its last hopeful attempt at a profitable colony, and 1624, the company declined toward bankruptcy. Fortunes began to be made in tobacco, but they were private fortunes. None in the company challenged its unrealistic adherence to diversified commodity production; members of the faction-ridden Virginia Company attacked not policies but each other. The merchants associated with former treasurer Sir Thomas Smith, whom Sir Edwin Sandys had succeeded in 1619 in the gentry takeover of company leadership, prevented Sandys's reelection in 1620, but the election of Henry Wriothesley, third earl of Southampton, as treasurer brought no change in policies or subordinate leadership. On 24 October 1623 the Privy Council established a commission headed by Sir John Harvey, which investigated conditions in Virginia the following spring. On 9 May 1623 another commission, headed by Sir William Jones, had also been given formal authority to investigate the company. The latter commission acted as receiver for the company during the year prior to its dissolution on 24 May 1624.

It is fitting that James I had challenged the failing company with a writ of *quo warranto*, which asked by what warrant the company presumed to exist, for the dissolution of the Virginia Company brought colonists fifteen years of especial uncertainty in an age of uncertainty. Two years earlier, on 22 March 1622, the colony had been nearly exterminated in a surprise Indian attack coordinated by Opechancanough that began a decade of intermittent conflict between the colonists and their Indian neighbors. Tobacco prices, falling sharply after 1624 and cutting into the boom-time margins of extraordinary profit, contributed to a sense of malaise. From the small planters, who had not yet had full benefit of the boom, came complaints that merchants were engrossing food and commodities and selling them at unfairly high prices. (Some of the complaints were registered against larger planters, whose fortunes had come in the boom.) Everyone in Virginia was uneasy about the legal status of land titles, and then in the mid-1630s the crown allowed Lord Baltimore, a catholic, to establish Maryland on territory that Virginia long had claimed as its own. Maryland threatened Virginia's prospect for continued expansion and trade into the upper Chesapeake and along its northern tributaries, and the colonists' frustration and anger erupted in 1635, when virtually every politically significant colonist joined in a peaceful <u>coup</u> that threw Governor Sir John Harvey out of office and sent him packing to England.[1]

Dissolution and Uncertainty

Between 1624 and 1639, the colonists' two concerns, about which repeated complaints were made, were the uncertainty of their land titles and the uncertainty of the continuation of their form of government.[2] The <u>quo warranto</u> proceedings against the Virginia Company of London had ended in a king's bench judgment that the company's charter had been defective from the beginning. In turn, this undercut the legal validity of the corporate actions upon which the entire life of the colony depended.

As royal authorities assumed direction of the company's affairs, all parties seemingly agreed that the Virginia planters eventually would have clear title to their lands. Professing to "marvell that any should be so farr mistaken," in October 1623 the Privy Council promised that "no man shall receive any prejudice but shall have his Estate fully and wholly conserved." The royal commission headed by John Harvey gave similar assurances the following spring, and on 13 May 1625 newly crowned Charles I assuaged the planters' doubts by pro-

claiming his intention to "settle and assure the
particular rights and interests of every Planter and
Adventurer." The colonists, however, remained skeptical.
Governor Sir Francis Wyatt, who had been appointed by
the company in 1621 and confirmed by the crown on 26
August 1624, stopped issuing land patents on 20 January
1625 until the legal doubts could be resolved. Wyatt's
action probably was prudent, but surely it did not allay
anxiety; others reported that the suspicion and anger
"which hath bin bred by the late Quo Warranto" would
subside only when land titles had been clearly confirmed.[3]

Virginians had good reason to doubt royal assurances
about their land titles: having recently witnessed the
undoing of a charter bearing the king's great seal, of
what permanence were the private deeds that derived from
it? Indeed, the crown's assurances themselves came with
unsettling reservations. Royal proclamations announced
the king's intention to alter Virginia's system of
government. None could be sure what was intended, but
clauses such as "otherwise then should be of necessity
for the good of the publique," or "untill some other
constant and setled sourse be resolved upon," only
reminded Virginians that they had not heard the last word--
and that it would be someone else's final word. Court
intrigue might be devastating. Virginia colonists

feared for their future, and "for the security of their persons."[4]

An ominous possibility was that their future would be subject not just to conventional selfish court politics, but that they might fall subject to men whose conscious design was to rule Virginia as another Ireland and to treat "the planters in Virginia as if they were their tenantes or servantes." The presence of Lords Chicester, Carew, and Grandison on the Mandeville Commission, which had been established on 15 July 1624 "for settling a Government in Virginia," suggested that Irish policies might be adapted to Virginia under royal rule. As lords deputy of Ireland from 1604 to 1615 and 1616 to 1622, respectively, Chicester and Grandison had displaced the native inhabitants of Ulster: they had been declared tenants at will, their land titles denied, and their estates distributed to new (often absentee and usually English or Scot) owners.[5]

Sugh a design never was executed. The Mandeville Commission fell into inactivity after the death of James I, and the disposition of Virginia affairs remained unsettled until about 1640. The important fact is that land titles and tobacco monopoly projects became inextricably tied to the development of Virginia's royal government during those years of indecision. Fearing

that the Mandeville Commission intended "to exercis the
same Tiranny uppon our persons, which already . . . they
execute uppon our fortunes," the General Assembly of
1625 unanimously dispatched Sir George Yeardley to England
with its petition to the king, "the importance of the
cause requireing no lesse than" the man Charles I had
named to succeed Wyatt as governor in 1626. As agent for
the assembly, Yeardley requested a charter with eleven
guarantees, including the immediate shipment of needed
supplies and soldiers for defense against Indians, security
against the intrigues of factious persons and tobacco
monopolists, and confirmation of the colonists' land
titles and "their liberty of General Assemblyes."[6]

Yeardley admitted the planters' willingness to accept,
for the time being, Charles I's "royall assurance" about
the matters at issue, but he left no room for doubt that
Virginians wanted a permanent charter: they wanted "a
new Patent to confirme all their dividend of land, with
all such priviledges as formerly they enjoyed, and with
more ample as their Lordships shall think meete, and for
their full assurance therof to have it confirmed by act
of Parliament else they think it may be revoked as the
former."[7]

Virginia never got such a charter. Charles I issued
a royal proclamation on 13 May 1625, apparently in direct

response to the assembly's petition, but the proclamation was a disappointment. Reservations were too noticeable. The king assured planters that land titles were secure, unless necessity forced his hand. He promised "one uniform course of Government, in, and through all Our whole Monarchy" and that the Virginia Company would not be revived, but held it to be impolitic "further to communicate the ordering of State-affairs." He announced his intention to continue the Mandeville Commission, but at the same time suggested two councils, one in England and one in Virginia. Finally, he affirmed his resolution to control the tobacco market, promising that his agents would buy tobacco at reasonable prices, "but the maner thereof, Wee will determine hereafter at better leisure." Charles I's unsettling missive, entitled a <u>Proclamation for setling the Plantation of Virginia</u>, failed to answer the Virginians' questions and fell short of their hopes—it was vague where they had sought certainty, it was inflexible where they had sought change.[8]

On the other hand, the crown's indecisive course after the dissolution of the Virginia Company allowed Governors Wyatt and Yeardley and their successors to permit the continued operation of pre-dissolution institutions, and in the long run the colonists gained full sanction for them. Between 1624 and the early 1640s,

Virginians affirmed their claim to full political rights and avoided subjection to Irish colonial policies. Taking advantage of the crown's vacillating treatment of the tobacco trade, they secured first ad hoc and then formal recognition of their General Assembly.

In 1624, with the company's divisions and mismanagement apparent, James I set the course of royal tobacco policy for the next dozen years; his policy was predicated on a monopoly for the importation of tobacco into England. James I never got his monopoly, but in the attempt Virginia got its General Assembly recognized and confirmed. In September 1624 James I prohibited the growth of domestic tobacco or the importation of foreign tobacco, and in November he ordered that all colonial tobacco (from Virginia and Bermuda) be imported at London, where a group of six merchants was commissioned to oversee the trade. For the Virginia colonists, however, the important development had come in the king's 2 July 1624 letter instructing Solicitor General Sir Robert Heath to contract with the planters and adventurers of Virginia and Bermuda "for all their tobacco to be delivered for the king's use."[9]

During the next decade, each time the crown resolved on a plan to manage the tobacco trade, the Virginians were asked to agree to a contract. Because the king sought the colonists' agreement and because the agreement

of an assembly of representatives would bind those who
had elected them, the king found it in his interest to
countenance, indeed to require, successive meetings of
the General Assembly. At the same time, through the
assembly the colony came to see itself as a community.
It discovered and defined its common interest in contra-
distinction to the interests of the crown and the tobacco
monopolists.

The first General Assembly after the dissolution of
the Virginia Company met in 1625, before the crown had
initiated its new tobacco policy and before word of James
I's death on 27 March 1625 had reached Virginia. During
this especially unsettled time, the governor and Council
took an important decision. In April they issued writs
for elections to the commanders of plantations, and in
May they convened a General Assembly to consider things
"which nerely concern the generall Estate of the Colony."
The continuation of General Assemblies was far from
assured, and Governor Wyatt had no specific royal authorization to summon one. He did have authority, by
virtue of his 1624 commission and the crown's indecision
that it represented, to govern "as fully and amplye as
anie Governour and Councell resident there at anie
tyme within the space of five yeares now last past."[10]

Possibly the presumption of royal antipathy toward

General Assemblies is the historian's inheritance from
the whiggish interpretation of the Stuart period of English
history. During the 1620s and 1630s, Charles I's attitude
toward Virginia's General Assembly seems to have been less
antagonistic than unconcerned--indeed to suggest that he
had "an attitude" at all seems presumptuous. Nevertheless,
Wyatt and the Council seem to have taken great care to
summon the assembly of 1625 in language that was inoffensive.
They avoided the words General Assembly in their summons
for elections, and the assembly itself followed suit in its
petition to the king from "the Governour Counsell and
Collony of Virginia assembled together," and its petition
to the House of Commons from "the Governor Councell and
Colony of Virginia." Yet repeatedly in Wyatt's copies of
the assembly's papers, the 1625 meeting was called a
General Assembly.[11]

    Why, apparently, were they so careful in their choice
of terminology? Probably because they were uncertain
about the continuation of their forms of government and
certainly because at least one colonist, Captain John
Martin, favored giving Edward Ditchfield and several
other merchants a monopoly for tobacco. Martin's extraordinary patent for Martin's Brandon had been altered
following the assembly of 1619, and he had been returned
to the Council, in which capacity he was present at the

assembly of 1625. The record tells that when a resolution against the Ditchfield tobacco contract was offered, most of the members of the assembly (presumably everyone but Martin) agreed that the contract would be "hurtfull and prejudicial both to his Majestie, the adventurer and planter and to the Colonies themselves, for the benefitt and advancement whereof his Majesties most graciously hath granted them the sole importacion." But, the record continues, when this was "putt to the Question in the generall Assembly, Capt[ain] John Martin refused to give his answer for No." Not only did Martin want to say Yes to the contract, he thought "that the Governor and Counsell had no power to calle a generall Assembly, neyther could they justify the doinge thereof, And that he for his parte would have noe hand in it." "Yf they called the kings wisdom in question" by rejecting the tobacco contract, Martin warned, "for anything he knew, the Kinge might proclayme them Traytors." Martin's vocal presence caused the colonists to avoid contention over their institutions, for their immediate object was to prevent the colony's "inevitable destruction" at the hands of Ditchfield and the tobacco monopolists.[12]

The death of James I disrupted Ditchfield's attempt to gain a monopoly, but soon after Charles I was crowned,

Sir Edwin Sandys sought a monopoly of tobacco importation and the reincorporation of the Virginia Company. Sandys's plan failed, too, and the tobacco trade remained open. Then, pressed by financial need, on 31 January 1627 Charles I again turned to the idea of a tobacco monopoly. He commissioned six merchants to enforce the restrictions against domestic tobacco production, to import and sell small amounts of Spanish tobacco, and to negotiate a contract for the importation of colonial tobacco as a crown monopoly. Commissioners Edward Ditchfield, Reuben Bourne, George Bromley, Sir John Wolstenholme, Abraham Jacob, and Henry Garwaie promptly set out to obtain a contract with the Virginia and Bermuda planters.[13]

As it happened, a group of prominent Virginia merchants and planters then in England (many of whom would come to be associated with the Mathews-Claiborne faction during the 1630s and 1640s) met with Wolstenholme on 7 April. They heard the monopolists' terms and declared them insufficient "to maintayne soe many people, as were in both those plantations." Four months later, in August, Charles I proclaimed that colonial tobacco be imported only under a special license, and that it be sold by importers only to his commissioners at prices agreed upon between them and "the Owners or Factors."[14]

In November 1627--in an action widely and properly

recognized as royal acceptance of the continued existence of Virginia's assembly--Charles I proposed his monopoly to the Virginians and directed that an assembly be summoned to conclude the bargain on behalf of his subjects in the colony. Repeatedly thereafter, Virginians elected burgesses to meet with their governors and councillors to consider the king's successive proposals for tobacco contracts. The assembly of 1628 announced that the very word <u>contract</u> became "a terror and discouragment to the whole Colony." That same assembly offered to accept the absurdly high price of 3s6d per pound in Virginia or 4s per pound in England, and ordered Edward Bennett and Michael Marshart to join former governor Sir Francis Wyatt in England to "either refuse the propositions of this Contract, or . . . establish a sure and certaine meanes of our subsistance."[15]

For several years the pattern held: the king proposing contracts, the assembly rejecting or politely ignoring his offers and thanking him for "his Princely care for us his people." The process had far greater significance than either the subject or the result. Tobacco kept the General Assembly of Virginia alive after the dissolution of the company. By autumn 1628, Charles I and his Privy Council had quietly, but fully, accepted the General Assembly as a permanent feature of Virginia's colonial government. Couched in the frustratingly vague terms that had become all too familiar to the colonists, the king's letter of 12 September 1628 again promised confirmation of the colonists' land titles and other privileges. This time, however, the accompanying instructions--a private communication-- were more specific. In them the Privy Council expressly directed that two items of imperial concern be referred to the General Assembly of Virginia. "His majesties will and pleasure" was that measures be taken to preserve neat cattle and that the problem "be declared to a Grand Assemblee." Another necessity was navigational beacons, which the Privy Council wanted erected and maintained "at the charge of the Countrie as shall be determined in a Grand Assembly."[16]

Thus, in addition to acknowledging the General Assembly of Virginia as the colonists' representative in negotiations with his tobacco agents, Charles I found it convenient to entrust a colonial legislature with responsibility for local ordinances and finance. Some of the legislation passed in 1629, 1630, and 1632 attended to the Privy Council's concerns for cattle and beacons, but of course the Virginians passed other legislation, too, and made their own provisions for revenue through self-imposed taxation. Of course, it remains true--as has been widely recognized--that the General Assembly was not specifically named in a royal governor's <u>commission</u> until 1639, and that continued court intrigue and indecision kept land titles insecure until that same year. Nevertheless, the record plainly shows that the king and his ministers treated Virginia's unicameral assembly as a legitimate body after 1628, and that Virginians had come to cherish their General Assembly as a means to define and protect the interests of their maturing community.[17]

Regrettably, no other journal as complete as John Pory's survives from the period before 1680, but enough information is extant to show that in its general internal organization the assembly followed until 1642 the pattern established in 1619. Governor, councillors, and burgesses met together in a single chamber. Deliberations began when the governor and councillors swore the necessary oaths and administered them "afterwards to all the burgesses." Each morning the members of the assembly attended "devine service, in the roome where they sitt, at the third beatings of the drum, an hower after sun rise." Members were fined 2s6d for unexcused absences. Subjects for legislation or deliberation might come to the assembly's attention from the king's instructions, through the governor's or Council's initiative, from a burgess, or as the result of a petition.[18]

The assembly debated "many matters"; some were formulated as propositions, "put to the question," and decided by vote of "the major part" or the "opinion of the most voices." As in 1619, some matters were referred to committees, but because the surviving records (mostly statutes, orders, and the like) tend to report the results but not the process, it is impossible to determine how frequently the assembly relied on committees or whether, as may be likely, committees were composed solely of burgesses as in 1619. From 1619 to the early 1630s, in general it seems that meetings of the General Assembly had come to be seen as beneficial events in the year-to-year life of the colony.[19]

Uncertainty about land titles and pressure to contract for a tobacco monopoly continued, but by 1630 Virginians had witnessed the passage of several years without disaster. For some of the most prominent planters the late 20s and early 30s brought prospects of a lucrative trade connection Virginia and London. Some flirted with the prospect (anathema to their neighbors) of participating on the monopolist's side of a tobacco contract, and some of the same men were drawn into the fur trade of the northern Chesapeake Bay. The declining margin of profit in the tobacco trade discouraged newcomers and encouraged large-scale operations and some diversification. But even as the General Assembly was becoming the vehicle to define and secure the community's interest in the face of external challenges, social cleavage and economic disparity were emerging in Virginia.[20]

Faction and Coup d'Etat

The central event of the 1630s in Virginia was the Thrusting Out of Governor John Harvey in 1635. To understand that event and its context is to understand much about politics and institutions in the emerging society of colonial Virginia. First, the fundamental constitutional question involved in the coup d'etat has been widely misunderstood. The Thrusting Out was neither a rebellion against royal authority nor an impeachment. Rather, the struggle between Harvey and his councillors occurred because they disagreed with one another and there was no provision for such disagreement: the line between gubernatorial authority and conciliar authority had remained unclear. Harvey insisted that he was the king's lieutenant capable of acting without regard to the Council, and the councillors insisted that the governor was primus inter pares. The latter position seems a more nearly accurate reflection of the terms of Harvey's and his predecessors' commissions, and, especially in light of that consideration, a more capable governor might have prevented the issue from being pushed to extremes. Harvey was unequal to that task.[21]

Every existing source of conflict between a governor and the colonists seems to have flared up during Harvey's first years in Virginia, and in 1632 the crown added a new one. Charles I gave Virginia's northern Chesapeake Bay area to Lord Baltimore and directed Harvey to assist the Virginians' hated rival. When Harvey, whom a close friend had described as "a proper man, though perhaps somewhat choleric and impatient," zealously assisted the Marylanders, he quickly lost all hope of support from the prominent Virginians who comprised the Council. Throughout the 1630s, the political strife arising from a number of conflicting interests caused several factional groups to appear. The most important group was that cluster of wealthy Virginia planters and merchants associated with Samuel Mathews, Sr., "the head & cheefe support," and William Claiborne.[22]

During the 1620s the economic interest of the planters who came to form the Mathews-Claiborne faction--to dominate the tobacco economy by controlling the export trade--would have placed them at odds with everyone else in the colony (had they settled on such a policy, or found opportunity to advance it). But other dangers were more immediate during the 1630s, and the readiness of the merchant-councillors to monopolize the tobacco trade was momentarily overlooked, as the entire colony's political community, in its first concerted political action, expelled a governor whose conduct offended all but a small number of colonists.

The Mathews-Claiborne faction was "nourished from England" with "many letters and secrett intelligences," Governor Harvey wrote in 1635. They had "many meetings and consultations," he concluded, and "I doubt not but to find notable combinations." Just how notable the transatlantic combination of his opponents really was, Harvey had no inkling. In the deposition of Governor Harvey, Mathews and his circle worked closely with Sir John Zouch, Sir John Wolstenholme, and William Button, all of whom had interests in the possible revival of the Virginia Company as a trading corporation. The opposition to Harvey, however, for all its importance in the subsequent political life of Virginia, was incidental to the common ground of the merchant-councillors' interest: the Mathews-Claiborne faction upheld the western terminus of a transatlantic trading connection. At the eastern terminus stood a circle of the leading new merchants of London, in the center of which stood Maurice Thompson, "the non-company, interloping merchant par excellence," a leading proponent of the anti-Dutch mercantilism embodied in the Navigation Act of 1651, and a robust puritan who "was once a poor fellow in Virginia, but got a great estate." The names of the members of the Mathews-Claiborne faction appear and reappear not only in the history of the Thrusting Out of Governor Harvey, but throughout every aspect of Virginia history between 1630 and 1660.[23]

The faction's roster would include Mathews, Claiborne, John West, and John Utie, who were members of the Council

of State when it agreed to a contract that gave Maurice
Thompson, Thomas Stone, and William Tucker (another
Virginia merchant-planter and Thompson's brother-in-law)
a short-lived monopoly of the tobacco trade under which
they imported 256,700 of the 405,000 pounds of tobacco
shipped from Virginia to England in 1633. Thompson and
Claiborne and others formed the company that sponsored
Claiborne's colony on Kent Island in the northern Chesapeake, which fell within the boundaries of Maryland and
caused decades of conflict, and in 1639 Mathews, Claiborne,
Thompson, and others joined to petition the Privy Council
for a grant of all the land between the Potomac and Rappa-
hannock rivers.[24]

Three other members of the faction were Thomas Stegg,
Richard Bennett, and George Menefie. Stegg was the Virginia
factor, or agent, for Thompson and Mathew Craddock, as well
as a partner to Claiborne, Thompson, Jeremy Blackman and
others in the purchase of Berkeley Hundred in 1636. Later,
armed with a commission from the earl of Warwick, Stegg
preyed on royalist shipping in the name of Parliament. He
joined the Council after 1639, but vacated his seat in 1642
(for important tactical reasons that soon will be evident).
Bennett, who was younger than the others, stepped into his
family's business interests, which included Virginia tobacco
and Newfoundland fish. Menefie seems to have been independent of Mathews and Claiborne until after the Thrusting Out.
Initially his interests and connections paralleled theirs.

In the 1620s Menefie contracted with the Jamestown planters to sell their tobacco for a 12 percent commission. He was Virginia factor for John Ferrar, John Bland, Abraham Jennings, and Company, and he traded with Samuel Vassall and Peter Andrews, both members of the circle of interloping London merchants. In addition, Menefie, through his first wife, was related to interloping merchants Tobias and William Felgate; the latter was Maurice Thompson's brother-in-law.[25]

At the eastern terminus of this trading system, eight of the forty merchants who imported ten thousand or more pounds of American tobacco in 1633, 1634, or 1640 (years for which data are available) were closely linked to the Mathews-Claiborne faction. Twenty of the forty merchants associated with Maurice Thompson had business ties to members of the faction. These forty merchants represented "only the cream --perhaps the top 10 percent--of the total colonial trading group." They tended toward a puritan religious outlook, and most took the parliamentary side in the Civil War. But their program was not principally a religious or political one: their program was embodied in the Navigation Act of 1651 --of which Maurice Thompson was principal draftsman--which replaced England's company-based monopolies of the commodity trades with a vision of a comprehensive national monopoly in which overseas trade was carried in English bottoms to and from English ports. They favored low duties on imports from English plantations, freedom of re-export, and the

exclusion of foreign tobacco (especially Spanish) and
merchants (especially Dutch) from the colonial trade. They
were hostile toward Maryland, Spain, and Holland. Few
Virginians consciously supported this program, but the few
were powerful throughout the 1630s, 40s, and 50s. With their
ships and their partnerships, they formed a notable combination indeed.[26]

Possibly, if circumstances had been different, Sir John
Harvey might have been modestly successful as a governor.
He had had some experience in the colony during the 1620s
(when he and Mathews were fellow members of the investigating
commission that bears Harvey's name) and he knew enough
about the colonists' anxieties to request of the Privy
Council, upon the occasion of his appointment as governor
in 1629, that the king "extend his favour to the planters,
for a new confirmation of their lands and goods by charter."
The answer was succinct: the Privy Council would settle these
matters "by calling in the former books and charters at a
convenient tyme." Having received the same answer that
Virginians had become accustomed to hear from the crown's
authorities, Harvey decided that he could not issue land
patents even though his immediate predecessors had been
doing so since 1626. Perhaps his decision found favor among
members of the Privy Council (though it is difficult to
believe that they paid it any attention), but it was unpopular in Virginia.[27]

A former ship's captain, Harvey was not the man to win

a colony's willing compliance with unpopular crown policies.
His inflexible, sometimes intemperate, habit of treating
councillors and colonists alike as though they were fractious
sailors made things worse. Even when he kept his temper,
his actions seem as though they were part of a self-
destructive plan to alienate the very men whose support he
needed. Upon his arrival in spring 1630, he prosecuted
former acting governor Dr. John Pott for his interference
with William Capps's assignment to give Charles I an account
of the state of the colony. Pott was released because he
was the colony's only doctor; it is difficult to see any
advantage in Harvey's decision to prosecute the case, and
the trial only bred ill will among the colonists and councillors. In England, meanwhile, the Mandeville Commission that
had engineered Harvey's appointment was dissolved in 1631
and replaced by a new commission headed by the earl of Dorset.
The Dorset Commission included many former members of the
Virginia Company of London and some notable friends of
Mathews and Claiborne, including Wolstenholme, former governor Wyatt, Nicholas Ferrar, George Sandys, and Sir John
Zouch. Not surprisingly, the commission recommended that
the Virginia Company be given a new charter.[28]

Word of the formation of the Dorset Commission reached
Mathews in letters from Dorset, Wyatt, Ferrar, and others
before it reached Harvey. In December 1631 the eleven members of the Council of State, certain that they had out-

flanked the unsuspecting governor, signed a formal document
of accord in which they agreed to treat Harvey with "all the
service, honor and Due Respect which belonge unto him as his
Majesties Substitute," in exchange for Harvey's promise to
"follow such instructions only as are contayned in his Majesties Commission and Instructions which wee have Received."[29]

When the attempt to revive the Virginia Company
foundered, however, Wolstenholme, Thompson, William Tucker,
and Abraham Dawes arranged the monopoly to which the Virginia
councillors agreed despite Harvey's resolute opposition.
Harvey poised himself as an obstacle to the restoration of
the Virginia Company and the tobacco contract. He excoriated
the monopolists for offering a penny a pound for Virginia
tobacco "when our intruding neighbours, the Dutch, doe allow
us eighteene pence per pound." Because the restoration of
the Virginia Company offered the prospect that land titles
might be confirmed, however, Harvey won no favor among the
colonists at large. Even had Harvey seen the opportunity
to curry favor among the lesser, non-mercantile planters,
however, the arrival of Lord Baltimore's settlers aboard
the Ark and the Dove in 1634 dashed any hope of doing so.[30]

Virginians strongly opposed the establishment of
Maryland, a colony carved from the limits of their own--
limits that they had hoped a charter might secure--and
settled by many Roman Catholics. William Claiborne came

into immediate armed conflict with the Maryland colonists over his trading post on Kent Island, and according to Harvey, Virginians "would rather knock their cattell on the heads then sell them to Maryland." Nevertheless, Harvey did all he could to fulfill his order to assist Baltimore and his settlers. Relying increasingly on the claim that he was the king's lieutenant, Harvey progressively affronted each of the prominent Virginians whose support he needed to survive.[31]

No more poignant chronicle of his political failure can be found than that in his own 1635 report to the Privy Council. Listing his opponents by name, Harvey reported the reasons for their animosity: Wolstenholme "had kept the countrey in expectation of a change of Governor and the renewing of a corporation." Mathews had "particular quarrels" because Harvey had "endeavoured to obey his Majesties command in assisting Captaine Yonge," a Maryland trader, by forcing one of Mathews's men to repair Yonge's ship without compensation or Mathews's permission. Councillor John Utie bore a grudge because Harvey had "called often upon him to give an account of a great stock of Cattell which belong to his Majestie since the dissolution of the Company." Claiborne opposed him because he had "endeavoured to discover his practice with the Indians against the Lord Baltemore's plantation in Maryland." Councillor William Peirce was "discontented" because Harvey had "comitted one Walker (the

Master of a shipp wherein he is a partner) for his saucy behaviour before mee and the Councell of Virginia." Former acting governor Pott retained "an old grudge" over his trial. And, his brother, Francis Pott, had been displaced from the captaincy of the fort at Point Comfort, "whereof he still retaynes the memory." In this document Harvey did not mention that he had thrown Councillor Sir Thomas Hinton into prison for insulting him, or that he had knocked out some of Councillor Richard Stephen's teeth with a cudgel--nevertheless, Harvey's catalog of enemies was a virtual Who's Who of the colonists whose support he needed.[32]

By 1635, he having alienated most of his councillors, Harvey alienated the colonists at large when they learned that he had refused to transmit to England a resolution, signed by all the burgesses at the assembly of 1628, that emphatically rejected the king's proposal for a tobacco contract. Harvey held the original, which bore the burgesses' signatures, because he feared the crown's displeasure; he sent a copy to Sir Francis Windebanke, secretary of state and a known opponent of the movement to revive the Virginia Company. Taking Harvey's actions to be hostile to their interests, the colonists and councillors met in a series of "secret and unlawfull meetings," as Harvey put it. On the evening of 27 April 1635 a messenger brought Harvey word of a meeting in York County, immediately north of Jamestown, that day at which Francis Pott, Sheriff William

English, and former burgess Nicholas Martiau had circulated a petition criticizing Harvey for his refusal to forward the assembly's resolution and asking "the councell for some speedy redress of these evills which would otherwise ruin the Colony."[33]

Events now moved quickly. Harvey had Pott, English, and Martiau arrested and, without concurrence of the Council, appointed "a new sheriff at James Citty," who, Harvey's opponents claimed, was "a defamed fellow to whom he committed the Keeping of the Prisoners in Irons." The next day he demanded that the Council agree to punish the three "chiefe actors" under martial law. The councillors "desired that they might have a legall tryall."[34]

Uncertain of how many councillors were united against him, but certain that some had had a part in the secret meetings and the petition, Harvey demanded that each councillor, without consultation, write his answer to the question, "What do you think they deserve that have gone about to persuade the people from their obedience to his Majesties substitute?"[35]

"I begin with you Mr. Menefie," Harvey said.

"I am but a young lawyer," George Menefie responded, "and dare not upon the suddain deliver my opinion."

"That should be his answer under his hand," Harvey curtly replied. Nicholas Ferrar attempted to complain, but Harvey cut him off.

"I conceive this a strange kind of proceeding," Mathews interrupted. Harvey commanded him to be silent in the king's name, but Mathews continued: "There was no Presedent for such a command, But it was by a Tyrant, meaning that passage of Richard the third against the Lord Hastings."

The meeting quickly degenerated into "many bitter languages" without result, but the crisis had come. Mathews saw the dangerous parallel to that passage in Shakespeare's Richard the Third: Harvey was Richard, duke of Gloucester, saying, "I pray you all, tell me what they deserve/ That do conspire my death with devilish plots . . .?" Menefie, if he were not careful, was Hastings. If, opting for martial law and following the script, he answered "death," then Mathews feared that Harvey would follow Gloucester: "Thou art a traitor! Off with his head!"[36]

The next day Harvey gathered his councillors again and asked whether they knew why the colonists were aroused against him. Menefie, who still was independent of the Mathews-Claiborne faction and trying to discover a conciliatory course, replied that "the chiefest cause was the detayning of the Letters to his Majestie and the Lords." Harvey immediately concluded that Menefie had been privy to the supposed plot. "Rising in a great rage," Harvey struck him on the shoulder and shouted, "I arrest you of suspicion of Treason to his Majestie." John Utie replied, "And we the like to you sir," and Utie and Mathews held Harvey in his chair. At a signal from John Pott, forty armed men surrounded the house.[37]

The Council put Harvey under arrest, Secretary Richard Kemp took custody of his commission and instructions, which were publicly read--an act which testifies to the councillors' apparent belief that they acted legally--and the councillors took "time to consider of a safe course for the satisfying the Inhabitants Petition and the safety of the Governours Person."[38]

Having determined that, according to the king's commission appointing the governor and Council, the councillors were empowered to elect a successor in the event of the governor's absence or death, the Council chose John West to be governor "until his Majesties further pleasure," and summoned a General Assembly to meet on 7 May 1635. The assembly resolved that the colony's grievances "should be presented to the Right Honorable Lords Commissions for Plantations, and on 23 May Francis Pott and Thomas Harwood, a burgess at the assembly of 1635, took custody of Harvey and sailed for England. The Thrusting Out of Governor Harvey was over, and the Mathews-Claiborne faction held sway until Harvey's return to the colony in 1637.[39]

The coup had absolutely no effect on the powers given to the governor of Virginia. In his dealings with the Virginia councillors Harvey had stressed the vicegerency inherent in the term governor, as when he claimed in 1635 that although "by the Commission all things are to be ordered by the Governor and councell, only the Governor is of the

Quorum"--that is, only the governor had to be present for an order to be legal. But in fact Harvey knew, as he had written to Windebanke in 1634, "that my power heere is not great it being limited by my commission to the greater number of voyces at the Councell table." This was precisely the constitutional position to which the Council had secured Harvey's concurrence in the 1631 document of accord, and it was the standard against which the councillors criticised Harvey for usurping "the whole power, in all causes without any respect to the votes of the councell." Harvey, they complained, reviled them in open court and claimed them to be "assistants onely to advise with him, which if liked of should pass, otherwise the power lay in himselfe to dispose of all matters as his Majesties substitute."[40]

If Harvey's claim had been correct, then surely the crown would have attempted to clarify the ambiguity that had been inherent in the commissions since the end of the military regime: the uncertainty as to whether the governor was *primus inter pares* or *governor*. The crown's position was as clear as could be expected: despite Harvey's request for additional power, and Lord Baltimore's recommendation that he be given additional power, the governor's powers were unchanged in the commission Harvey carried back to Virginia in 1637. Charles I knew that he had to send Harvey

back to Virginia if only for a day, but he did so without
enthusiasm and without bestowing signs of favor. Harvey
requested that he be transported to the colony in a royal
vessel as "an honor to the King's governor" and a gesture
to "check the boldness of the offenders in the Colony."
He was given the <u>Black George</u>, an unseaworthy craft that
leaked so badly that Harvey had to turn back and sail to
Virginia as a passenger aboard regular shipping.[41]

    Although in the immediate aftermath of the <u>coup d'etat</u>
Virginians witnessed a period of intense and bitter strife,
Harvey's few supporters quickly faded from view and within
a few years personal antagonisms spawned in the events of
1635 scarcely were to be found. Formally acquitted of the
charges leveled against him, Harvey arrived in Virginia on
18 January 1637 and set out to crush his enemies and confiscate their estates. The circumstances suggest either that
Harvey remained unaware of the tenuous nature of the crown's
support, or that he was fully sensible of the crown's lack
of faith in him and that this awareness drove him to greater
rashness. Acting on Harvey's request and Lord Baltimore's
second, the Privy Council had agreed to order the arrest of
Mathews, Utie, Menefie, John West, and William Peirce.
Gleefully Harvey sent them to England, for he had begun to
confiscate their properties, and he had vowed not to leave
Mathews "worth a cow's taile."[42]

Mathews and the others were perhaps more dangerous to Harvey in England than they were in Virginia. They secured orders from the Privy Council requiring Harvey to restore their properties, which reluctantly he did. Finally, spreading gossip about his conduct throughout London, Harvey's enemies and their influential English allies succeeded, on 11 January 1639, in having Sir Francis Wyatt appointed governor.[43]

Wyatt had remained familiar with Virginia during the decade and a half after he had left in 1626. His ability was well known, as he had guided the colony through the post-massacre recovery and through the dissolution of the company, and he had always been allied with the friends of the old company. He had most recently served on the Dorset Commission in which capacity it seems likely that he had written key items into his new instructions. The scion of a prominent gentry family in Kent, Wyatt brought more social bearing to the office than _parvenu_ governors such as Yeardley and Harvey. On the constitutional question of gubernatorial vs. conciliar powers, Wyatt's commission gave him no more power than any other governor since De La Warr: he was _primus inter pares_ in point of law. But Wyatt did bear instructions that brought fifteen years of uncertainty to a close and transformed the political life of the colony. His instructions provided for the calling of annual meetings of the

General Assembly and for the confirmation of "lands to the present planters and possessors."[44]

Once the crown had affirmed the colonists' titles to land, the principal common interest that had united greater and lesser planters was gone. Once Harvey--who had unified the colonists by his assistance to Maryland, greed, temper, land policy, and support of royal tobacco contracts--was gone, the social and economic distance that separated the merchant-planters from the rest of the colonists became more apparent. And, having been tested in the Thrusting Out, the Mathews-Claiborne faction had emerged as a more formidable political element than it might otherwise have been. The coup d'etat had no immediate constitutional effect on Virginia, but it revealed the structure of Virginia's political community to interested observers, and within a few years this revelation had significant effect. Immediately upon his forced arrival at Plymouth in 1635, Harvey had written to inform the Privy Council of his misfortune and to complain that Virginia's unicameral assemblies "being composed of a Rude, Ignorant, and Ill-conditioned people were more likelye to effect mutinye than good lawes and orders, especially whilst the Councell gave them such examples." Harvey's close associate George Donne, however, put the situation in familiar political terms in 1638: Virginia's "Aristocracie Those of that Council," Donne observed, had learned "to eye Authority and to dispute power with their Governor."[45]

The crown's affirmation of Virginia land titles also altered the lesser planters' interests in politics. The revival of the Virginia Company sought by allies of the Mathews-Claiborne faction had been attractive to the lesser planters because it would have undone the quo warranto decision against the company's charter, thereby affirming both the charter and the titles derived from it. But with their land titles secure, the possible restitution of the company now was inimical to the lesser planters' interest. If, as the proponents of a revived company claimed, "the King had no right to confirm their grants," said the colonists, then "our land held by immediate grant from his Majesty must be void, and our possessions must give place to their [i.e., the company proponents'] claim, which is an invincible argument of ruin and desolation to the Colony." Freed from the necessity of accepting a company monopoly of the tobacco trade in exchange for secure title to their lands, after 1639 the lesser planters opposed any attempts at monopoly or at the exclusion of Dutch merchants from the colonial carrying trade. A shrewd governor might notice the lesser planters' interest, and find it useful.[46]

Precisely the opposite positions held for the Mathews-Claiborne faction after 1639. The restitution of the company posed no threat to them, for if the company were revived they would control it. A company-held monopoly and the exclusion of Dutch traders were their objects. For Mathews and Claiborne, and it seems for Sir Francis Wyatt and George Sandys, and for the entire network of merchants and planters associated with them, the monopolies to be prevented were only those that they did not control. Most Virginia colonists opposed all monopolists; the merchant-councillors opposed rival monopolists. Harvey's failure had highlighted the potential dangers that faced a governor in Virginia, "especially whilst the Councell gave [the burgesses] such examples," and the sudden resolution of fifteen years' agitation for confirmation of land titles and the General Assembly, exposed the divergent interests that might be represented in the assembly by the councillors, on the one hand, and the burgesses, on the other.[47]

The Reform of 1639-1643

Virginia in 1639 was a different sort of place than it had been twenty years earlier. Indians still posed a military threat, but it was much diminished. In 1622 Opechancanough's warriors had killed more than three hundred fifty colonists, including six members of the Council of State, "and burst the heart of all the rest," but in 1644 the old chief led his last attack, in which about five hundred colonists, mostly residents of the outlying settlements, were killed.

The social impact of the loss of 6 percent of the Chesapeake area's English population was far less severe than the earlier loss of half the colony's population in an attack that had threatened the whole enterprise.[48]

Virginians were more secure and their community and government--like the brick houses that they were beginning to erect--were more stable. During the 1630s--rather than the massacre, famine, or disease of the colonists' earliest days--they had confronted difficulties amenable to political resolution, and they had used statecraft to achieve their goals. Disputes over tobacco contracts and land titles, the continued meetings of the General Assembly, and the Thrusting Out of Governor Harvey--these were experiences through which the Virginians had learned the power of a politically engaged community, and sampled the multitude of objectives toward which political actions might be directed.

Save for the founding of Maryland, which was accomplished despite Virginia protests, the battles of the 1630s had been won, and in 1639 the colonists were able to address a new problem borne of the numerical increase and geographical dispersion of the colony's population. Alterations in Virginia's central and local administrative and judicial institutions were necessary. Planters at Henrico, or Lower Norfolk, or on the Eastern Shore could not troop to Jamestown to prove wills, settle small debts, collect or pay taxes, punish drunkards and fornicators, and arrange routine main-

Chapter 3, figure 1: Population growth in Virginia, 1610-1660

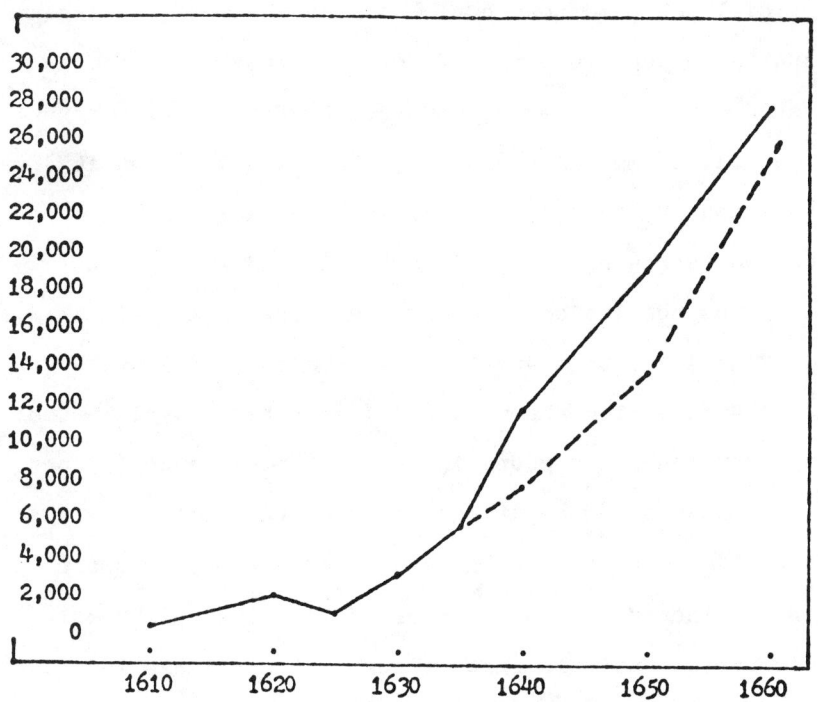

The solid line represents population figures from the United States Bureau of the Census, Historical Statistics of the United States: Colonial Times to 1970 (Washington, D.C., 1975), 1168. The broken line shows lower post-1634 estimates from Edmund S. Morgan, American Slavery--American Freedom: The Ordeal of Colonial Virginia (New York, 1975), 404.

tenance of such things as jails, ferries, and bridges.
And, officials at Jamestown could not have handled successfully such an extensive array of detailed local responsibilities even for the increased population of the settlements in the capital's immediate environs. Between 1624 and 1634 the population of James City, Charles City, and Warwick counties had increased from 847 to 2,208, and throughout the colony the population had increased rapidly as well: from 1,227 in 1624, to 4,909 in 1634, and to 10,442 by 1640. During the same period the market price of tobacco plummeted: from thirteen pence per pound in 1624, to five pence in the mid-1630s, to three pence at the close of the decade.[49]

Population increase and a tightening economy accompanied a tremendous increase in the number of lawsuits in the colony's courts--a statistic that is the best available index of the general administrative burdens put on the existing political system. The number of actions in the Accomack County Court, for example, increased five-fold between 1632 and 1638, from 40 to 249. More than 80 percent of these cases concerned debts. In 1639 the settlement of debts in court was suspended by proclamation, and in January 1640 the assembly passed a number of laws designed to relieve indebted planters and improve tobacco prices, which had fallen from the levels that once promised extraordinary profits to successful enterpreneurs. The burdensome caseload has paramount importance today because it set the stage for permanent change in the structure of Virginia government. From reforms begun for "the better ease of the Country and quicker dispatch of business," a bicameral assembly emerged that lasted without significant institutional change until the 1680s, and, in a general sense, to the present day.[50]

As early as 1624, the geographic dispersion of Virginia's increasing population had brought modest changes to the colony's political institutions when the assembly had established the first two monthly courts, at which plantation commanders decided suits up to the values of one hundred pounds of tobacco. Five more monthly courts had been created in 1632, and in 1634 the assembly had established eight shires--one supplanting each of the monthly courts and the eighth to serve Jamestown--whose commissioners were empowered to hear petty criminal cases and suits to the value of ten pounds sterling. These changes had relieved the governor and Council of some time-consuming business, made it easier and less costly for planters to conduct routine legal affairs, provided for the beginning of a uniform system of local administration throughout the colony, and fostered representative government and political stability by supplying fixed electoral districts. Yet these changes had taken no powers from the governor and Council or the assembly: county commissioners were required to deliver "a true copy of all your proceedings at every Quarter Court unto the Governor and Council," and members of the Council could sit as senior justices in the county courts and, in emergencies, "keep a court in the absence of those of the Quorum."[51]

Local bodies that extended central authority freed the governor, Council, and assembly from the press of minor details. Unwilling to waste much time on a suit "concerning damages done by hogs," for example, in March 1642 the governor and Council directed that it "be heard and determined by the commissioners of Lower Norfolk"; the county court, in turn, impanelled a jury that found for the defendant and made "final determination of the said suit." Similarly, the governor and Council referred to the county commissioners a case concerning an orphan's estate. The county commissioners had been unsure of their interpretation of the relevant statute and had asked "to have the act explained"; the Council dispatched a one-sentence answer. In both instances, as in scores of others, central authority and uniform interpretation of law was upheld without all the encumbrances of centralization. An avenue of appeal remained available--first to the Council and then to the General Assembly--but most legal business could be resolved without a trip to Jamestown.[52]

The reform of the judicial system begun under Sir

Francis Wyatt was possible, it seems likely, because Wyatt stood in close proximity to the merchant-councillors and because his second administration was something of a caretaking operation near the end of his career. The old veteran had been dispatched to the front to put things in order. Before his efforts had been completed, however, Wyatt's successor arrived. To Wyatt's successor fell both the task of completing the reform, and the opportunity to modify it if he would or could.

Governor Sir William Berkeley, thirty-four years old, a polished courtier and playwright with a master's degree from Merton College, Oxford, arrived in Virginia in February 1642. In the absence of extant documents telling of his intentions, they must be read from his actions, and the state of the evidence requires that the historian reconstruct plausible motives from the circumstances. "Subtle conjectures at the secret aims and inward cogitations of such as fall under their pen . . . is also none of the least virtues in a history," said Hobbes of Thucydides, so long as the historian does not "enter into men's hearts further than the acts themselves evidently guide him."[53]

Berkeley's actions upon his arrival in Virginia are revealing in three ways. First, we see that he intended to continue Wyatt's needed reforms. Although the assembly Wyatt had summoned on 12 January 1642 stood in adjournment until 18 April, Berkeley, a new governor, did not summon new elections. Instead, he chose to reconvene the

unicameral General Asembly on 1 April and again on
2 June. At the latter meeting the General Assembly
completed the reform legislation that had been discussed
in January. Berkeley had had time to give the legislation
careful review himself, and a contemporary statement
tells that he had reconvened the old assembly, rather
than call for new elections, in order to "prevent all
doubts" about the "acts already agreed upon" and to conclude
"the many and weighty business begun in the present
Grand Assembly."[54]

Second, in the expressed reason for reconvening the
old assembly in June rather than conducting new elections,
we see a concern for English parliamentary practice as
it applied to analogous situations. Virginia's own
constitutional development to date had been vague as to
whether the arrival of a new governor demanded new elections
(it later did) or whether the dissolution of an assembly
killed uncompleted legislation (it later did). The important
thing is not whether this or that English parliamentary
procedure happened to have been applied, but rather that
Berkeley and his fellow colonists readily assumed that
the model of English parliament was analogous to Virginia's
General Assembly.[55]

Third, Governor Berkeley summoned the 1 April meeting
of the old assembly for an important and revealing reason:

the assembly took prompt action against the efforts of
George Sandys (and unnamed others) to revive the Virginia
Company, news of which Berkeley probably had carried to the
colony. The April assembly met briefly, adopted a
Declaration against the Company, dispatched it to England,
and adjourned. The General Assembly of Virginia had
gone on record in opposition to an attempt at monopoly.
This had been done before, but in 1642 George Sandys
claimed to speak for the Virginia colonists when there
can be no doubt but that he spoke for the merchant-
councillors and their allies. Sir William Berkeley
cannot have failed to notice that this knot of planters,
merchants, and advocates of a revived Virginia Company was
the group that had successfully ousted Governor Harvey.
In short, by his actions between his arrival in February
and the meeting of the assembly in June, Berkeley demonstrated his willingness to study and complete the reform
legislation, his inclination to imitate English parliamentary models, and his readiness to stand aloof from the
Mathews-Claiborne faction and ally himself with the best
interests of the lesser planters.[56]

Few records survive, but clearly the assemblies of
1640, 1641, and 1642 worked harder and longer than usual
in their efforts to reform the colony's government. In
1641 the "well ordering and setling of many Weighty Affaires

Controverted and Concluded" by the assembly took so much "more tyme then was at first expected" that Wyatt had postponed the March quarter session of the Council for four weeks to allow "the Counsell and the Burgesses such as have causes depending to settle theire domesticall Affaires and returne again." Berkeley had the same experience. His month-long assembly in June 1642 exceeded "customary limits of time" but had produced laws so "few in number" that the members published an apologetic Remonstrance directing their constituents' attention to the judicial reforms that had been made, and to the other, unnamed "benefits redounding" to Virginia as a result of their "consultations."[57]

No manuscript copy of the legislation of June 1642 survives, but probably all the recent reforms were enacted again in March 1643, when the assembly rewrote the entire legal code. The results of the 1643 revisal--as the assembly called its periodical procedure of repealing all the laws and then reenacting them so that clean copies of the statutes, as they had been amended over the years, could be prepared and distributed by the clerks--do survive: among the seventy-three acts passed in the revisal of 1643, five acts of 1641 and eleven acts of 1642 can be identified. From them one learns that the assembly of June 1642 had protected officers of the law from suit for actions taken in performance of their duties; defined the county court's role in handling land grants and orphans' estates; specified meeting schedules for the quarter court and rules for serving writs and for arrests; affirmed the right to jury trial when requested by either party in a civil case; and staggered meeting days of the county courts "for the convenience of those having business in more than one court." In sum, the June 1642 assembly completed a reform of the colony's judiciary that made it easier for the colonists to conduct their business and for the magistracy--in the counties as at Jamestown--to contend with the legal affairs of a population of increasing size and complexity.[58]

And there was more. The 1642 Remonstrance named some but not all of the specific legislation completed at that session. The extension of jury trials to civil cases, for example, was not named in the Remonstrance. The language of the Remonstrance was vague and general: it declared that "the inhabitants . . . have recorded the birthright of their mother nation"; it applauded "the near approach which we have made to the laws and customs of England in proceedings of the court and trials of causes"; and it alluded to "greater motives to . . . take the opportunity of establishing our liberties and privileges and setling our estates . . . and of preventing the future designs of monopolizers contractors and preemptors." It is impossible to determine how many other specific reforms, like the changes in jury trials, were not explicitly mentioned in the Remonstrance. A substantial collection of other evidence suggests, however, that about June 1642 a decision was taken that the councillors and the burgesses were to meet separately in the General Assembly of Virginia, after the manner of the English parliament.[59]

In March 1643, for the first time in any English colonial assembly, an elected member, burgess Thomas Stegg of Charles City County, was named as Speaker. For the first time, the evidence suggests, the burgesses sat as a lower house and the council sat as an upper house. The presence of a Speaker in 1643--as in late-fourteenth-century England, Massachusetts Bay in 1644, or Maryland in 1650--corresponds with the beginning of bicameralism: the lower house needs a presiding officer and spokesman. By 1648 the supporters of a new proprietary colony could point to Virginia and Massachusetts as precedent for their "Politique and Civill Government": the governor, secretary of State, and councillors comprised "the Councell of State or upper House," and "thirty Burgesses, or Commons," formed the lower house in annual meetings of the "Parliament or Grand Assembly, . . . and without full consent of Lord [i.e., governor], upper and lower House nothing is done."[60]

Another bit of evidence to support the assertion that the General Assembly of Virginia became bicameral in the 1640s is found in the roster of clerks. From the mid-1640s there were two clerks in attendance at assembly sessions, one to serve the House of Burgesses and one to serve the governor and Council: John Corker was "Clerk of the Assembly" in 1640 when the body was unicameral, but in 1646 he was "Cler[k] to the Burgesses," and during the 1650s he used a Latin title, "Cl[ericus] Dom[us] Com-[munis]." While the presence of a Speaker of the House of Burgesses and of clerks for the upper and lower houses may be the most convincing evidence for the existence of a bicameral assembly after 1643, an unusually revealing description of assembly procedure also is found in a passage from the Council minutes that was copied into the records of Lower Norfolk County.[61]

According to this account, the recently established House of Burgesses reviewed the accounts of an outgoing sheriff and issued its certificate to the governor and Council, who discharged the sheriff from office:

> At a quarter court holden at James City
> the 13th of March anno Dom 1645
> present Sir William Berkeley,
> Knight, Governor, etc. . . . .

> Upon certificate from the House of Commons that Capt. John Sibsey, high Sheriff of Lower Norfolk County hath produced his accounts and perfected the same and made payment and collection according to the trust of his office, It is therefore ordered that he be hereby discharged from the said office and this order to be his quietus.

Another recorded entry, this one concerning Christopher Burroughs, a burgess for Lower Norfolk County, tells a similar story. Burroughs evidently had committed an offence for which the lower house thought the punishment was to severe, but "upon the Intercession of the House of Commons" in his behalf, the governor and Council agreed to "mitigate" Burrough's penalty. Finally, the act adjourning the assembly of 1647 left no doubt about its bicameral structure: on 1 October 1648 "all members of both houses" were to "give their attendance." In short, there is much scattered evidence that, when gathered and examined, demonstrates that one element of the reform of 1639-1643 in Virginia was the division of the assembly into upper and lower houses, and that the first meeting of

Virginia's bicameral General Assembly--the first meeting of a House of Burgesses--occurred in March 1643.[62]

When in the 1660s, Secretary Thomas Ludwell wrote a description of Virginia and described Sir William Berkeley as "the sole author of the most substantial parts of [the government], either for Lawes or other inferior Institutions," he was essentially correct. No contemporary comment about bicameralism survives from Virginia, but the evidence suggests that the establishment of separate upper and lower houses of assembly was Berkeley's doing. Berkeley alone had compelling reason to want bicameralism: for him bicameralism had both practical and theoretical attractiveness. Berkeley was not about to be thrust from office.[63]

Berkeley recognized the existence of four political groups in Virginia. One was the Mathews-Claiborne faction; they were the men who had ousted Harvey and who sought to control the colony and its trade. A second group, which was rapidly disintegrating, consisted of the handful of men who had supported Harvey. The third and fourth groups were important; the first consisted of members of the merchant-planter elite whose trading interests rivalled the London-Virginia axis of the Mathews-Claiborne faction. Argoll Yeardley, Charles and Edmund Scarborough, and the Custis and Thoroughgood families formed no faction, but

their trading interests, especially with Dutch ports, conflicted regularly with the objectives of Mathews and Claiborne.[64]

Berkeley perceived that this third group of prominent merchant-planters were potentially useful allies. He also recognized that they represented a merchant-planter interest in continued free trade with the Dutch that was popular with the lesser Virginia planters who lacked--this is important--the means to export their tobacco in their own vessels. It is the voice of these lesser planters, the fourth political category, that one hears in many of the General Assembly's resolutions against monopolies. The prohibition of foreign traders, they said in 1647, was "the invention of some English merchants on purpose to affright and expell the Dutch, and make way for themselves to Monopolize not only our labours and fortunes, but even our persons." For the colonists who could not ship their crops to European markets, competition between wholesalers was the only protection against exploitation. "Wee must . . . provide for our owne safeties and subsistence," the assembly resolved, "in Order whereupon, wee doe againe invite the Dutch Nation, and againe publish and declare all Freedom and libertie to them to trade within the Collony." The common interest of the third and fourth groups--the free-trade merchant-planters and the lesser planters-at-large--was well put in the General Assembly's 1642 Declaration against the Company: "the freedom of our trade . . . is the blood and life of a commonwealth." The assembly warned that there were some Virginians who "with most secret reservation and most subtility argue for a company," but that their hidden goal was "propriety to the land and power of managing the trade, which word managing in any sence we can no ways interpret, then a convertable [i.e., synonymn] to monopolizing."[65]

These two groups were particularly important to Sir William Berkeley, who recognized the danger that the Mathews-Claiborne "Aristocracie"--entrenched in the Council of State --posed to his effectiveness, and to his survival, as governor of Virginia. By allying himself with the planters who traded with the Dutch and with the planters-at-large, Berkeley successfully exploited the division of commercial interests in order to protect himself from domination or ouster. A surviving list of bills and debts owed to Richard Glover, an English merchant trading out of Amsterdam, reads like a partial roll call of the Virginians who stood outside the London-connected faction of Mathews and Claiborne. Save for George Menefie's widow Mary, not one of Glover's transactions had involved an associate of Mathews or Claiborne, but among the nineteen persons named in addition to Berkeley and Mrs. Menefie were the following additions to the group of independent, or free-trade, merchant-planters: George Ludlow, who joined the Council in 1642; Bridges Freeman and Ralph Wormeley, who were appointed to the Council in 1650; Robert Holte, who was a burgess in 1656 and again from 1666 to 1676; Stephen Gills, who was a burgess in 1652; Richard Lee I, who joined the Council in 1651; and John Chew, who was a burgess on many occasions between 1624 and 1644. Glover seems not to have traded to the Eastern Shore, where the Yeardleys, Scarboroughs, and Custises lived, but his list reveals independent merchant-planters of nearly equal prominence: the amounts due from the twenty-one individuals are torn from the edge of the page, but the total survived and the average was twenty-seven hundred pounds of tobacco per person.[66]

Had he described the pragmatic political benefit of bicameralism, Governor Berkeley probably would have used familiar--indeed commonplace--political theory. From Aristotle to Charles I, and from the Roman *senatus* to the the Stuart's House of Lords, political observers recognized the upper house as the fit representative of the wealthy few, of society's better, wiser elements. Stuart politicians saw the bicameral structure of Parliament as the institutional mirror of the "distinctions of family and merit" without which a well-ordered state fell inevitably, in Charles I's foreboding words, into a "dark, equal chaos of confusion."[67]

As the Civil War approached, astute politicians witnessed the commons's readiness to invade both the king's prerogative and the traditional rights of the lords. The leveller tracts of the mid-1640s were yet to be published, but anxious observers at court could foresee arguments that might be used in favor of the Commonwealth. Sir William Berkeley's brother, John, sat on the Privy Council. Berkeley himself sailed for Virginia shortly after a series of constitutional reforms were made in August 1641, but before the issuance of Charles I's classic defense of mixed government, his Answer to the Nineteen Propositions, on 21 June 1642. If all power were "vested in the House of Commons," Charles warned, the number of members of Parliament would make it "incapable of transacting affairs of state with the necessary service and expedition." As a result, the common people would "call parity and independence liberty, devour that estate which had devoured the rest, destroy all rights and proprieties, and distinctions of families and merit, and by this means," Charles concluded, "this splendid and excellently distinguished form of government [will] end in a dark, equal chaos of confusion, and the long line of our many noble ancestors in a Jack Cade or a Wat Tyler."[68]

Recent events in Virginia suggested that the balance there had been tipped toward the "Aristocracie" of merchant-councillors who, as Harvey had complained, turned the General Assembly toward mutiny. From the governor's viewpoint, "the ill of aristocracy is faction and division, the ills of democracy are tumults, violence and licentiousness," and a mixed government cured both. If Berkeley had not already recognized the merchant-councillors' potential threat, or discovered that conflicting interests separated the Mathews-Claiborne faction from the rest of the colonists, he must have learned much at the April 1642 meeting of the assembly. Two councillors (Claiborne and Stegg) did not sign the Declaration against the Company, and several others (such as Mathews, Peirce, Bennett, and Wyatt) signed it but may have been those "who with most secret reservation and most subtility," as the Declaration put it, sought "power of managing the trade."[69]

Berkeley seems to have chosen his allies among the burgesses and some few councillors, such as Argoll Yeardley, who supported the Dutch trade and who opposed all monopolies. While the merchant-councillors who had thrust Harvey from office and sought to establish monopolies for themselves concurred in public with the Declaration Against the Company, they also prepared themselves for political conflict. They dispatched one of their number to manage the newly formed

House of Burgesses. Thomas Stegg, Sr., was "one of the ablest merchants in the Colony" and the Virginia factor of Maurice Thompson and Mathew Craddock. He was also a partner of William Claiborne, and he was a member of the Council at the beginning of Berkeley's administration. Stegg last attended a meeting of the Council on 1 August 1642, immediately following the 1642 session of the assembly, but then he apparently resigned. Charles City County elected Stegg to the assembly of 1643, where he was chosen Speaker of the new House of Burgesses.[70]

It is impossible to determine how the burgesses and the populace may have reacted to the adoption of bicameral procedure. Possibly the establishment of upper and lower houses of assembly was seen as one of the "benefits redounding" to the colony from the consultations acclaimed in the 1642 Remonstrance. Possibly the model of Parliament suggested that bicameralism be seen as "the birthright of their mother nation," or a "near approach . . . to the laws and customs of England." Yet, not until the mid-1650s did the House of Burgesses fully grasp and exploit the fact of its independence, and then it opposed Mathews, Claiborne, and their allies, not Sir William Berkeley and the crown.[71]

There is evidence of political manuevering during 1642 and 1643, and some evidence to suggest a *quid pro quo*. Berkeley gave up the annual collection of four pounds of

tobacco from each colonist and recognized the assembly's
sole authority to levy taxes. In return he got: "the
orchard with two houses . . . as a free and voluntary gift
in consideration of many worthy favors manifested toward
the collony"; and a special levy of "2 shillings a head
for every tithable person in the collony" in lieu of his
annual salary of one thousand pounds sterling, which was
suspended "through unkind differences now in England";
as well as passage of a tax of nine pounds of tobacco per
poll to be expended according to the assembly's order.
The Remonstrance described the bargain in laudatory terms:

> In gaining a firm peace to ourselves and our
> posterity and a future immunity and ease from
> taxes and impositions . . . we have thought
> it seasonable for us liberally and freely to
> open our purses[,] not doubting but all well
> affected persons will with all zeal and good
> affection embrace the purchase.

Berkeley, it seems, arranged to complete Wyatt's reforms
so that they protected his office, and also managed to get
the burgesses cheerfully to double the tax rate and brag
about it to their constituents.[72]

The beginning of bicameralism in Massachusetts Bay
offers a revealing contrast to these constitutional developments in Virginia. For ten years prior to the 1644 separation of the upper and lower houses of assembly in the Bay
Colony, puritan politicians engaged in bitter dispute over

the negative voice. In Massachusetts Bay, as in Virginia, the mercantile men were more strongly represented in the upper house. The establishment of the House of Deputies finally occurred as the result of a suit brought by Mrs. Richard Sherman against Robert Keayne, one of the Bay Colony's richest merchants, over the ownership of a white sow with a ragged ear and a shilling-sized black spot under its eye.[73]

Goody Sherman's suit failed in a jury trial, but popular sentiment held her to be "an 'oppressed goodwife' who in her attempts to restore her 'rightful property' had been cheated and mercilessly fined for her efforts." Keayne was the just the man to fit the role of "a hard man and a usurer," for he had been convicted and fined earlier for sharp dealing. When Sherman's case came before the Bay Colony's unicameral legislature, the General Court, on appeal, the magistrates, although fewer in number than the elected deputies, used their negative voice to deadlock the appeal. This confirmed the jury's decision in Keayne's favor. The deputies took Mrs. Sherman's side, and when they found themselves stymied by the magistrates' veto, moved for the separation of the appointed and elected members of the General Court to be henceforth two houses of assembly.[74]

In the rancorous debates that followed, Governor John Winthrop argued that the deputies threatened the foundation of ordered society and government. Massachusetts Bay, he feared, was about to "change from a mixt Aristocracy to a

meere Democratie . . . which is . . . among most Civile
nations, accounted the meanest and worst of all formes of
of Government." This far, both Winthrop and Berkeley, for
all their other differences, shared the vision of a well-
ordered, hierarchical society, and both men admired mixed
government. It was the prospect of a bicameral assembly
in Massachusetts Bay that troubled Winthrop.[75]

Massachusetts Bay professed to be more than a civil
polity, it professed to be a model for Christendom in its
age of crisis, a commonwealth engaged on a holy errand with
its magistrates and people "united in love and affection."
The theoretical premise of bicameralism, however, was that
permanent social or political heterogeneity needed to be
accomodated within the structure of the legislature. It
recognized and institutionalized division. Winthrop lamented
that the deputies, who were unwilling docilely to follow
their society's natural leaders, thought that Massachusetts
Bay "should rather be divided in factions etc: If this past
for good doctrine," Winthrop concluded, "then let us no
longer professe the Gospell of Jesus Christ, but take up
the rules of Matchiavell and the Jesuits, for Christ sayethe
Love is the band of perfection, and a Kingdome or house
devided cannot stand but the others teache (or rather the
Devill teacheth them) divide et imperia etc." For John
Winthrop, who saw in it the ugly face of democracy and the
disappointing failure of unanimity among God's chosen ones,

bicameralism was a threat to his colony's perfectionist goals. For Sir William Berkeley, who faced the power of the Mathews-Claiborne "Aristocracie" entrenched in the Council of State and intolerant of the economic interests of the planters-at-large, divide et imperia was sound policy, and bicameralism was a means to preserve in Virginia the well-ordered society and government then being threatened by doctrinaire zealots in England. It is perhaps also characteristic of the two political traditions, that in Winthrop's case one focusses on his words, and in Berkeley's case one must study actions.[76]

A WELL-TEMPERED CAVALIER:

Sir William Berkeley

and Institutional Maturation

during the Civil War, 1643- 1652

The reform of 1639-1643, and particularly the establishment of the House of Burgesses within a bicameral General Assembly, formed institutional mechanisms that sustained the delicate balance of political interest groups in Virginia, even as England and nearby Maryland were beset with civil war. Until after the execution of Charles I on 30 January 1649, power was balanced between Governor Berkeley and the Mathews-Claiborne faction, a situation that allowed significant accretions of authority to settle in the hands of the burgesses, the county court commissioners, and the vestrymen. After the passage c the Navigation Act of 1651 on 9 October of that year, the balance tipped toward the merchant-councillor faction, but by then the House of Burgesses had transcended its initial role as a pawn of gubernatorial-conciliar politics and become the principal institutional expression of an increasingly stable political community. Governor Berkeley seems to have intended that the lower house would buttress the proper social order and

protect him and his office--and in this he was successful.
But during the 1640s the groundwork also was laid for the
eventual domination of Virginia colonial government by the
counties and the legislature.

"Dangerous tymes"

Scarcely more than one year after the dissolution of
the General Assembly of 1643, which had enacted sweeping
political reforms in its revisal of the colony's laws, the
aged Opechancanough ordered a surprise attack upon the
colonists. This time, on the day before Good Friday, 18
April 1644, some five hundred settlers, mostly residents of
outlying plantations, were killed. The attack had far less
debilitating effect than the uprising of 1622, and politically
Opechancanough's 1644 attack drew the colonists together
just as certain centrifugal elements had been ready to pull
them apart. On 1 June 1644, the assembly recorded "to
Posterity" its intention "for ever [to] abandon all formes
of peace and . . . to the uttmost of our power pursue and
root out those which have any way had theire hands in the
shedding of our blood and Massacring of our People."
Provisions for war--men, shot, boats, powder, and "Cotton
Coats to the Number of 50"--were pressed for the campaign,
which was led by the arch merchant-councillor himself,
William Claiborne. Berkeley was given letters of credit
for one-hundred fifty pounds sterling, to be "satisfyed in

tob[acc]o at the next Cropp," so that he could "repaire for England and Implore his Majesty's gracious assistance for our Releife." That September *The Court Mercurie*, of London, reported "that the Governor of Virginia is now with his Majesty and has related the desperate condition the poor Christians are in there." *The Court Mercurie* lamented that England's "owne dangers are so great it is our greife we cannot help them."[1]

Although Governor Berkeley returned to Virginia without the weapons for which Virginians had hoped, during his absence William Claiborne's actions at the head of the Virginia forces apparently strengthened the governor's hand. By June 1645 it had become obvious that Claiborne had diverted Virginia's forces away from the colony's intended purpose of relentless pursuit of Indians so that he could pursue his own lifelong quest for the repossession of Kent Island. As Claiborne recaptured Kent Island, Richard Ingle overran Saint Mary's City, the capital of Maryland. Baltimore's authority in his colony was overthrown in the name of Parliament and Protestantism.[2]

Recognizing that Claiborne's personal vendetta against Baltimore was not the colony's intended object, on 6 June 1645 (according to notes taken by Conway Robinson from original records destroyed in 1865) the Virginia Council of State resolved "concerning the government of the isle of Kent" that Claiborne was "not to intermiddle with the government." The next day marked the "sudden arrival of Sir William Berkeley," who vigorously carried the war to the Indians. According to oral tradition recorded by Robert Beverley in 1705, Berkeley pursued the aging chief Opechancanough until, "hearing that he was at some Distance from his usual Habitation, [Berkeley] resolved at all Adventures to seize his Person. . . . With a Party of Horse he made a speedy March, surprized him in his Quarters, and brought him Prisoner to James-Town; where, by the Governour's Command, he was treated with all the Respect and Tenderness imaginable," until he was treacherously killed by a guard.[3]

A treaty ended the two-year-long war in 1646 and brought the colony three decades of peace with the area's Indian tribes, but the war had had important political ramifications in Virginia. "We are at peace among our selves, and have been so ever since the massacre," a Virginia puritan wrote in 1644, but without the war it could easily have been otherwise.[4]

Scarcely anything could be as divisive in a mid-seventeenth-century English-speaking society as controversy over religion. Both English and Continental experience during the sixteenth century was taken as proof that religious uniformity was necessary for civil peace, and events in England were proving the accuracy of Archbishop Laud's observation that those who would overthrow "the seats of ecclesiastical government, will not spare (if they get power) to have a pluck at the Throne of David." In Virginia, Governor Berkeley's first instruction was to "be carefull Almighty God may be duly and daily served according to the forme of Religion Established in the Church of England," and to "Suffer no Invasion in matters of Religion." Berkeley's second instruction embodied the political assertion of religious uniformity: "Administer the Oaths of Allegiance and Supremacy to all such as come thither, with intention to Plant themselves in the Country which if he shall refuse he is to be returned and shiped from thence home, . . . the same Oath is to be Administered, to all other persons when you shall see fitt as Mariners, Merchants, etc. to prevent any danger of Spyes."[5]

Few Virginians had strenuous objections to Berkeley's first instruction and its enactment as the first act of the assembly of March 1643, confirming the powers of the vestries even as it admonished the vestrymen to maintain religious orthodoxy, but the assembly's sixty-fourth act provided for "the preservation of the puritie of doctrine and unitie of the church" by requiring that ministers conform to the practices of the Church of England, and that the governor and Council compel "all non-comformists upon notice . . . to depart the collony with all conveniencie." Virginia's non-conformists (whose very existence is sometimes forgotten, or obscured by remnants of nineteenth-century Cavalier mythology) were disgruntled when Governor Berkeley expelled several dissenting clergymen during the mid-1640s, but it was the attempt to enforce religious and political allegiance by oath that met with extensive resistance. A revealing assembly order of 3 June 1644, passed shortly after Berkeley sailed for England, tells us that compliance with an earlier order, which required county commissioners to administer oaths of allegiance, had lacked "dispatch." Berkeley and the assembly of 1644 considered the administration of the oath to be "a matter of noe meane Consequence in these dangerous tymes," but the new order probably was as ineffectual as the first, for the governor sailed off to England and the colonists occupied themselves with the Indian campaign.[6]

Circumstance tempered policy, and Virginia was spared the division that would have followed an attempt to enforce doctrinal conformity and political allegiance to Charles I. An anonymous Virginia puritan was right when he wrote that the massacre of 1644 "did divert a great mischiefe that was growing among us by Sir William Barclay's courses; for divers of the most religious and honest inhabitants, were mark't out to be plundered and imprisoned for

the refusall of an Oath that was imposed upon the
people, in reference to the King of England. It was
tendered at mens houses, the people murmured, and most
refused to take it: Those few that tooke it did it more
for feare then affection; so that it is the opinion of
judicious men that if the Indians had but forborne for
a month longer, they had found us in such a combustion
among our selves that they might with ease have cut of[f]
every man." Subsequent events suggest that Berkeley
arrived at the same judicious opinion.[7]

Berkeley's campaign against Opechancanough enhanced
his popularity among the colonists. More importantly,
Berkeley altered his tactics after returning from England,
where a first-hand look at the violent conflict over
politics and religion perhaps led him to reconsider his
policy of force and compulsion. Force is a crude and
expensive technique for the maintenance of order.
Berkeley's commitment to the Church of England never
wavered, but after 1645 his strategy changed from coercion
to inducement.

In 1646 and 1647 the assembly passed laws requiring
ministers to conform to the established church and "duely
upon every Sabboth day read such prayers as are appointed
and prescribed unto them by the . . . booke of common
prayer." Instead of a Laudian tactic of enforced compliance, however, Berkeley's new approach was similar to the

Edwardian act of uniformity with which the first English prayer book had been introduced in 1549. Ministers who failed to "preach in the forenoon and catechise in the afternoon of every Sonday" were to forfeit five hundred pounds of tobacco "to be disposed off by the vestry for the use of the parish," and parishioners were exempted from the payment of "any manner of tythes or dutyes to any unconformist." Once the less ardent and more parsimonious vestrymen and parishioners took advantage of this provision, the reasoning went, puritan ministers would be forced to leave the colony for lack of support. And, since clergymen frequently had had to resort to court to collect their tithes, orthodoxy could be maintained with scarcely any exertion by local officials, and with no further action by the governor. Rather than incurring the difficulty and expense of forced oaths and reaping only resentment and resistance, after his return from England Berkeley simply had seen the law rewritten to induce vestrymen and parishioners to accomplish his objectives for him.[8]

Ultimately this delegation of ecclesiastical responsibilities to the vestries "brought about the predominance of the laity in determining church policy" and thwarted later attempts to impose an Anglican hierarchy within the colony. But for the moment Berkeley's new moderate and decentralized measures in support of religious uniformity made Virginia unattractive to politically agressive puritans without coercing moderate non-conformists (or low church Anglicans accustomed to de facto local autonomy) and inciting the very social discord that uniformity of religion was intended to prevent.[9]

As the anonymous puritan had written, the massacre of 1644 had diverted a great mischief by interrupting Berkeley's repressive religious policy of oath-taking: the key to Berkeley's post-1645 religious policy is the same realization that had led him to court the vestries, the county courts, and the burgesses--to have done otherwise he would have forfeited the goodwill and popularity he had won through his political reform, his opposition to companies or monopolies, and his victory over Opechancanough. To have done otherwise he would have risked disaster at the hands of his rivals. The memory of Harvey's Thrusting Out was scarcely a decade old, and the prominent merchant-councillors, such as Claiborne, Mathews, and Bennett, were openly sympathetic to puritanism and parliament. Charles I, whose own plight might not have been so desperate had he recognized the occasional utility of goodwill and popularity, could offer his governor no support, and Berkeley's rivals and their transatlantic allies were formidable.

Parliamentary Rivals

When Charles I dismissed Algernon Percy, tenth earl of Northumberland, from the office of lord high admiral on 1 July 1642, Parliament appointed Robert Rich, second earl of Warwick, to command the fleet in its behalf. Warwick had been the largest stockholder in the Bermuda Company, one of the largest investors in the Virginia Company, and a prominent investor in other joint and private ventures: "for forty years," J.H. Hexter has observed, Warwick "had a hand in every important overseas enterprise, Puritan or not, legitimate or not; . . . so long as it was a trans-Atlantic affair Warwick was in on it." On 2 November 1643, Parliament named him "Governor in Chief and High Lord Admiral of all those Islands, and other Plantations inhabited, planted or belonging to any [of] His Majesty's the King of England's Subjects," and head of a commission of five other peers and twelve M.P.s responsible for the government of the plantations. Very little has been written about this Warwick commission, but it is clear that it was dominated by Warwick and others whom Hexter characterized as the "middle group" in English politics during the early years of the Civil War, including Lords Manchester, Say and Sele, Wharton, and Robartes, and Sir Arthur Haselrig, Sir Gilbert Gerard, and John Pym.[10]

With the parliamentary fleet occupied in actions against the king's forces, the Warwick commission allowed Virginia to remain aloof during the 1640s. Nevertheless, it claimed power to do "all Things which they shall from Time to Time find most fit and advantageous to the well-governing . . . and chiefly to the Preservation and Advancement of the true Protestant Religion amongst the said Planters," and power to appoint and remove colonial governors as it saw fit "for the better governing and preserving the said Plantations and Islands from open Violence and Private Disturbance and Distractions." Neither Sir William Berkeley or his principal rival, Samuel Mathews, could mistake the commission's position. When the war had been won, Charles I executed, and the power of the moderates eclipsed, Parliament did send a fleet to subdue Virginia; in the meantime, Warwick, who favored colonial self-government, took no action to unseat Berkeley. His policy toward Virginia, a policy informed by circumstance and disposition, was described in three extant letters.[11]

In the first, which is undated but seems to have been written before news of the April 1644 Indian attack had reached him, Warwick announced his appointment by Parliament and explained that the commission had "taken into Consideration how to dispose the government in Virginia," but that he did not know "the State thereof at present." Therefore, he continued, the commission "resolved it to be most comodious to authorize you the Inhabitants to make election of such Governor as you shall conceive most fitt, whereby you are left at libertie to chouse the present Governor if you shall see Cause. If not," he wrote, "we have recomended to your respecte Captain [Samuel] Mathews a man of approved affection to the good of that plantation against whom if you shall except you may use your owne freedome."[12]

Warwick's first letter, addressed to "Virginia," concluded with his admission that he knew "not how the matter as now offered unto your Priviledges will be entertained by some of you." But he promised that the commission's object was only "(next to the honor of God and his Majestie) the advancement of your Condition, and the makeing of you serviceable with most advantage to your selves and the Countrey," and that he stood ready to hear all the Virginians' addresses with "a minde very ready to lerne you."[13]

Warwick's second letter was written, evidently soon after the first, to Samuel Mathews. Although sympathetic to Mathews in tone and substance, Warwick's public and private letters were similar. After announcing his own appointment and describing the commission's decision to leave the choice of their governor to the Virginians but to recommend Mathews "as a man of Integrity . . . very capable of that charge," Warwick cautioned Mathews that his letters might occasion "dispute amongst some whether a submission to our authority may not be interpreted [as] a desertion from dutie."[14]

Warwick gave Mathews an opportunity to take over the government of Virginia in the name of Parliament if he could, but the rest was up to Mathews. "I have heard so much of your Ingenuity and Candor," Warwick said, but "the maine thing considerable is the manner of manageing the busines now proposed which must be left to your owne discretion, who are best able to observe opportunities and to judge of persons to whom the same is in the first place properly comunicable, that a good foundation being laid you may proceed toward a transaction with most safety and successe," Mathews was then in England, and evidently Warwick entrusted the public, first letter to his custody.[15]

Warwick assured Mathews that he had "willed my desire to the ships in harbor to be assistant," and that if Mathews thought the time was not yet "fitt for publication" of the letter he might "suspend it as you shall see Cause." Finally, Warwick reminded Mathews that the commission's intention was to render the colony "plentifull in it selfe, so honorable in the eyes of others, that it may be a flourishing Commonwealth." In short, although the Warwick commission endorsed Mathews if the Virginians desired, or could be brought to desire, a change in government, they did not seek Berkeley's removal at the expense of "open Violence and private Disturbance and Distractions."[16]

Warwick's attitude toward Berkeley changed when he learned of the massacre of April 1644 and of Berkeley's policy of requiring oaths of allegiance and of threatening confiscation of property to those who refused. "We perceive that the distractions which have opprest these parts of the world," Warwick wrote in the third letter, "have extended themselves even to you partly through the treachery of the Natives and partly through the cunning and malice of some of our owne Nation amongst you, who under color of duties have laboured to divide your affections from your parliaments with no other designe how specious soever they pretend, but to subjugate to theire owne wills your estate and liberties." Nevertheless, Warwick maintained an even-handed perspective and, almost with a slight sense of disappointment, recalled that the commission had offered the colonists an opportunity "to elect one that had learned to overlooke his owne Interest and to attend to the peace and advancement of the Colony, . . . but [that] these good intentions were interrupted by some that sought themselves not you."[17]

For the immediate future Warwick saw no prospect of intervention in Virginia because his commission was too busy with the "great affaires attending their Care for preservation of this Kingdome." All he could send was his encouragement. "Although you be remote in scituation, Yet you be neare our Care and memorie," he wrote, and "you shall upon all occasions find us earnestlie desirent of your flourishing and advancment toward which we hope the Parliament will shortly be able to set apart some serious thoughts. God having of late by many glorious providences in the Success of theire Armies given good grounds of confidence that his power and wisdome will release them from those pressures which have attempted in the ruine of them, to ruine Religion, libertie, and all the dearest Concernments of this Nation in the fruites of which mercy you may expect your portion." The Warwick commission gave Mathews and the merchant-councillors authorization to rule Virginia in the name of Parliament if they could--but Claiborne chose to recapture Kent Island and Mathews chose to stay in England. It was Berkeley who defeated the Indians, moderated his religious policies, and continued to govern.[18]

Institutional Maturation

Political strategy was an inducement to the increased

delegation of routine powers to the local administrative and judicial officials, but a preeminent fact that forced this development was population growth. The colony's population, estimated at about eight thousand in 1640, climbed to about fourteen thousand in 1653 and to more than twenty-five thousand in 1662, and after the peace of 1646 the pattern of settlement was increasingly dispersed. "As the Old Dominion grew," Warren Billings has observed, "the Assembly turned over to the county court increasing responsibility for local affairs. What began in 1634 as agencies of regional administration with narrowly prescribed powers emerged by 1662 as the units of government whose wide authority touched the colonists' lives far more immediately than did that of the Assembly or the governor."[19]

This development had three stages: 1) experiment-- between 1634 and 1641 monthly courts were set up in an attempt to cope with the legal needs of the growing population; 2) delegation--during the 1640s genuine county courts were established with specific powers subject to the oversight of the governor, Council, or General Assembly; and 3) autonomy--after 1652 the county commissioners and burgesses assumed powers that had been reserved to governor and Council, for after the surrender to Parliament in 1652 the county commissioners and burgesses found that they could control the provincial government. During the 1640s, however, Governor Berkeley delegated powers without surrendering control and, conversely, consolidated control by delegating specific powers.

The delegation of specific ecclesiastical powers to the county courts and vestrymen was, as we have seen, carefully in accord with Berkeley's goal of religious orthodoxy. In temporal matters, too, provincial oversight of local administration was maintained and local officials were employed in the administration of provincial policies. Thus, sheriffs were given power to distrain a debtor's goods in order "to collect the fees of the Secretary and the Clerks of the Counsell." Sheriffs also were made subject to fines of 100 pounds of tobacco if they failed to bring defendants before the General Court or to serve quarter court executions signed by the governor and attested by the secretary. Another act stipulated that "in case the commissioners do not take a strict care in takeing accompt of the constables in the execution of this act, that then the said commissioners shall be fined at the discretion of the Governor and Council." The act requiring ordinary keepers to have "the approbation of the court of the county" also required them to be "licensed from the Governour."[20]

Perhaps the most effective measure of central control was the requirement that the county clerk, who was appointed

by the governor, "bring up a true copy of all your
proceedings at every Quarter Court unto the Governor
and Council." This requirement sometimes was inherent
in subsequent acts of assembly--as when the county clerk
was required to keep "an exact register" of orphans'
estates, or "records of the proceedings of all actions
and causes" heard in chancery by the county commissioners--
and sometimes explicitly prescribed--as in the provision
that county courts were "to give certificate to the
secretaries-office at James Citty for a quietus est . . .
and likewise that all such [probate] administrations
being granted and made" in the county courts "be sent up
to the said office to be exemplified under the seale of
the collony." Finally, although a provision to have
councillors sit with the county commissioners as senior
justices or as circuit riders eventually proved unworkable,
in it, too, is evidence of the intention to delegate a
measure of authority without relinquishing provincial
power. One should not fail to admit the long-range
significance of the counties' acquisition of these and other
powers, with or without limitations, during the course of
the seventeenth century. Nevertheless, during the 1640s
the increasing competence of the county courts was not
won at the political expense of the governor--not yet.
Before the colony's surrender to Parliament, the governor

and Council retained considerable power to direct local affairs and to control county appointments.[21]

The emergence of the county as the principal basis of representation in the newly established House of Burgesses, and the emergence of the House as a self-reliant institution and as the expression of a cohesive political community, were the chief institutional legacies of the 1640s. Prior to 1634 representation in the assembly had had no formal connection with any agency of local administration. In 1633, for example, burgesses had been elected, in varying numbers, from twenty-one geographically defined areas of settlement: four men represented the Eastern Shore and two the settlers between Harrop and Martin's Hundred along the James River, for example, but York, Kiskyake, and Nutmegg Quarter sent one burgess each. In 1640, the burgesses were listed according to counties, but again the number of representatives varied, from two to seven, and the seven burgesses from James City County were identified as representatives of particular geographical precincts within the county.[22]

Occasionally it is possible to distinguish between those burgesses who were elected and paid by the counties and those, fewer burgesses who were chosen and paid by parishes within the counties, even though no distinction is recorded in extant assembly records and no parochial records from the early years survive. On 18 October 1639,

for instance, the Lower Norfolk County Court, having
received an order from the governor and Council directing
that "the Commissioners of every County, with the consent
of all the freemen should choose Burgesses for their county,"
decided "with the consent of the freemen therein, that Mr.
Henry Seawell and Mr. John Hill should be Burgesses for
this county." Evidently the two other burgesses named in
the assembly records, John Sibsey and John Sidney, came to
the assembly as parochial burgesses representing Elizabeth
River Parish (which was coterminous with the county until
divided into four parishes in 1643). Similarly, in 1642
Accomack County elected two burgesses and the third evidently
was sent by Accomack Parish (which was coterminous with the
county until divided into two parishes the next year).
Other known examples, in Lancaster County in 1653 and Lower
Norfolk again in 1659, might be cited as well.[23]

A county court paid only for the county's burgesses.
Parochial burgesses, who often were also county court commissioners, were to be paid by the parish. Of course, no
matter whether a burgess represented the county or a parish
(some parishes were coterminous with the counties and in
other places, as in James City County, a county might have
had as many as eight parishes during the 1640s), a burgess's
charges, which were not inconsiderable especially during
long meetings, were borne by the residents. A 1643 act of
assembly directed "that the inhabitants of the several

counties and precincts shall be assessed in the defraying of the Burgesses charges." A 1659 act of assembly refers to "many disputes and controversies . . . about the defraying of the charge of paroachiall Burgesses," and in March 1662 the General Assembly eliminated parochial representation. As Warren Billings has observed, the county courts' post-1662 monopoly of House membership marks the counties' emergence as "the base for Virginia's ruling elite."[24]

These changes in the composition of the House of Burgesses also demonstrate the increasing sense of institutional self-consciousness (which is evident throughout the records of the 1640s and 50s) through which the members of the House of Burgesses came to see themselves as spokesmen, participants, and leaders in an evolving political community. When, for instance, in November 1645 the assembly decided to limit to four the number of burgesses from any one county (except "James Cittie onely, which shall elect 5 Burgesses for the said county and one for James Citty"), the action was taken because the number of burgesses had fluctuated "without any certain rule for the same." Throughout the 1640s, sustained by Berkeley's strategy of securing his position by fostering the evolution of well-ordered political institutions, the General Assembly--like the courts and the vestries--defined its certain rules and customs.[25]

The burgesses provided that they should be free from arrest from the time of their elections until ten days after the dissolution of the assembly in which they served. The General Assembly provided that "no act of court [i.e., the Council] or proclamation" was to stand "contrary to an act of Assembly unless in manner of seating of new plantations," and that no "refractory person" was to refuse obedience to an act of assembly "under any pretence whatsoever." Provisions for the payments of burgesses' charges were enacted; power to collect them was given to the sheriffs. Colonial officials were protected from being "molested or troubled in their persons or estates for the due performance and execution of any act or law." The channel of appeals was settled: from the county courts to the quarter sessions of the General Court to the General Assembly. Sheriffs were required to hold elections for burgesses "in those places where the county courts be held," and to give inhabitants at least six days notice before conducting elections. The assembly claimed sole authority to levy taxes within the colony. Viva voce election of burgesses was required instead of the "disorderly and illegal election of Burgesses, by subscribing hands," and all freemen except indentured servants were required to vote or be fined one hundred pounds of tobacco. In sum, the General Assembly defined its legislative and judicial functions, codified its formal relationships with the governor, Council, counties, and parishes, and established the House of Burgesses as the representative element in a stable, mixed constitution.[26]

As to the internal organization of the House of Burgesses, unfortunately little genuine parliamentary evidence survives from which to determine how the new lower house of assembly fashioned itself into a body capable for asserting and jealously sustaining its prerogatives after the colony's surrender to Parliament. Clearly, one important part of the House's development was its leadership. The Speaker at the first bicameral assembly session, Thomas Stegg, was closely allied with the merchant-councillors who had dominated Virginia politics throughout the 1630s, but during the mid-1640s Captain Stegg seems to have preferred the quarterdeck to the chair, as he captured royalist ships by virtue of a commission from the earl of Warwick. At the next two assemblies, in March 1644 and February 1645, the Speaker was Edward Hill, of Charles City County. Hill, too, had trading interests, especially in the upper Chesapeake, and leaned toward a puritan religious outlook; nevertheless he adopted a more moderate political stance than William Claiborne and was willing to cooperate with Governor Berkeley. Early in 1646, the assembly sent Hill and Thomas Willoughby to Maryland to secure the return of certain unnamed Virginians. Finding Maryland in great disorder after the invasions of Claiborne and Richard Ingle in 1644, Hill, under instructions from Berkeley and the Virginia Council of State,

declared himself governor of Maryland, called an assembly
there, and tried to restore order; then Leonard Calvert
returned from England, and, again with Berkeley's assistance,
mounted an expedition to end the rebellion and restore
proprietary authority. Thus, the House's second Speaker
seems to have been somewhat more independent of the merchant-
councillor faction than its first.[27]

The third Speaker of the House of Burgesses, Edmund
Scarborough, was entirely independent of the merchant-
councillors. An often cantankerous royalist from the Eastern
Shore, Scarborough owned his own fleet, traded where and
with whom he would, and won himself a swash-buckling reputation for his assaults against Indians and Quakers. Scarborough was prosecuted by the merchant-councillors soon
after they took over Virginia's government in 1652, but in
the mid-1640s, immediately after Claiborne's attack at Kent
Island and amid the post-massacre Indian warfare, his election
as Speaker may be attributed to his reputation as an Indian
fighter and to the burgesses' unwillingness to be led by an
ally of the Mathews-Claiborne faction. Little is known of
the fourth Speaker of the House of Burgesses, Ambrose Harmer,
of James City County, save for his part in a controversy
with Governor Harvey during the 1630s over the custody of
Benoni Buck, "Ideott, and his Estate." Governor Wyatt had
seen Harmer appointed to the Council about January 1640, but
he had not continued on the Council into Berkeley's admini-

stration. Harmer presided over the House at the assembly of 1646 and died soon thereafter.[28]

Probably neither Harmer nor the fifth Speaker of the House of Burgesses, Thomas Harwood, of Warwick County, was inclined toward either a royalist or a roundhead extreme. Governor Harvey had hamed Harwood as "one of the chieff of the Mutinous Burgesses" in 1635; Harwood's commercial interests seem to have been closely linked with those of Mathews and Claiborne; and after the surrender to Parliament he did become a member of the Council. Yet Harwood presided at the assemblies of 1647-1648 and 1649, whose expressions were firmly royalist.[29]

The difficulty of categorizing Harwood's political position reveals a larger problem: from the scant evidence that survives it is impossible to determine what factional alliances may have been present in the House of Burgesses, and except in a few instances it is also impossible to know how important contemporary English political divisions were in Virginia. Governor Berkeley, a former courtier and part-time playwright, never wavered in his loyalty to the king, and no doubt there were others equally firm at his side in Virginia, and still others as steadfast for Parliament. But the evidence will not allow us to know who was who, or, more significantly, whether the categories of Roundhead and Cavalier had any important meaning in Virginia's internal politics. There is enough evidence to suggest that, except for Thomas Stegg, the Speakers of the House of Burgesses during the 1640s probably were not tools of either the governor or the merchant-councillors. Rather, they were the elected officers of a House of Burgesses that was self-consciously establishing itself as an institution within a maturing political community.[30]

A Careful Surrender

On 15 January 1648 the English Parliament took the staggering decision, for such it must have seemed to the Virginians, of renouncing allegiance to the king. The second Civil War immediately began. Charles I was defeated and captured; the Rump Parliament resolved that legislative power rested solely with the commons; and Charles I was tried, sentenced to death, and beheaded at Whitehall on 30 January 1649. This whirlwind of distant but close-felt events brought severe intellectual and political crisis to Virginia. In the emergency, the royal governor and Council assumed increasingly complete responsibility for the colonial government while the assemblies progressively departed from their usual procedure. At first the changes were only verbal--affirmations of the sweeping emergency powers inherent in the office of the king's governor--but in time, as a parliamentary fleet threatened Virginia's coast, "Assemblies of Burgesses were discontinued" and the governor and

Council ruled alone. The March 1651 and March 1652 assemblies were so brief and crisis-pressed that the burgesses did not organize themselves or elect a Speaker at either. But the real accomplishments of the 1640s were demonstrated when the House and its Speaker emerged intact after Virginia surrendered to Parliament on 12 March 1652.[31]

In October 1648, the assembly enacted the first program of emergency legislation, which endorsed the governor and Council's power to act swiftly and forcefully in the crisis. Motivated either by prudence or paranoia, or both, the assembly gave Governor Berkeley a ten-man bodyguard to protect him against either "treacherous attempts threatened by the salvages" or "disaffections to the government from a schismaticall party, of whose intentions our native country of England hath had and yet hath too sad experience." The reference to a "schismaticall party" is difficult to interpret. The colonists may have thought that there was a possibility of an Indian plot against Berkeley, as five hundred people had been killed in the uprising four years earlier, but this seems unlikely. Probably the merchant-councillors did not plot anything so desperate as an assassination, but we do know that Mathews had Warwick's support, and that the Thrusting Out of Governor Harvey had been supported by at least a show of force, and that (given the state of the evidence) Berkeley and the assembly knew more than historians ever shall. Probably Berkeley was allaying anxiety by taking precautions.[32]

In a second, carefully worded act, the assembly of 1648 affirmed, but did not presume to create, the governor's power to rule: it was "thought fitt not by law to establish, but to declare the judgement of this Assembly uppon perusall of his Majesty's commission and instructions that by vertue of the said commission and instructions full and ample power is derived from his Majesty to the Governor and Council to make peace or warr, and as a necessary consequent to levy or presse men or other provisions for the warr upon any emergent occasion." This was not a grant of emergency power by the people's representatives, but rather a firm statement acknowledging that the king's lieutenant already possessed such authority. The burgesses could not "presume to conceive that any act of Assembly can add strength or vigor" to the power of the governor and Council.[33]

In effect the General Assembly was saying four things: first, that they concurred in the governor and Council's assumption of control during the crisis; second, that there was no basis upon which any colonist could challenge that authority except "out of a mistake in opinion"; third, that the governor and Council could declare war, levy taxes, and press troops into service without any further reference to the assembly; and finally, that it was indeed wise and necessary for the governor and Council to act without again calling the burgesses into session because the emergency did

not allow "delay of time nor those slow motions of great
counsells." The phrasing of the assembly's act of adjournment to 10 February 1649 was significant, too: instead of
requiring "that all members of both houses do then give
their attendance," as it had previously done, the assembly
declared only that "the council are all enjoyned to be then
present to attend there his Majesties service and the affairs
of the country." In short, the burgesses acknowledged that
Berkeley and the Council possessed full emergency power--
derived directly from the king--wrote a carte blanche endorsement of executive government, washed their hands, and
adjourned.[34]

Even so, news of the execution of Charles I reached
Virginia a few months later and threatened to undermine the
basis of order and government and to throw the colony into
civil and intellectual chaos. Berkeley, therefore, summoned
an assembly in October 1649 to contradict an opinion,
which we are told was held by "divers out of ignorance, [and]
others out of malice, schisme and faction," that the authority of his commission had been nullified by the regicide--
"all magistracy and office thereon depending to have lost
their vigor and efficacy." It seems unlikely that Berkeley's
genuinely formidable rivals, the Mathews-Claiborne faction,
would have been inclined to raise this question until the
time was right--until they had a fleet and some forces behind

them. From the texts of the 1649 legislation we learn
that the king's death made it possible for some Virginians
to assert, or at least for the assembly to worry that
people might assert, "arguments easily and naturally deduced from . . . cursed and destructive principles" that
the commission that transmitted royal authority to the
governor and Council was void. Were this true, the colony
was literally in anarchy, and chaos was sure to follow.[35]

The assembly of 1649 declared that it was treason
to defend the regicide, to asperse the memory of Charles I,
or to doubt the legitimate succession of Charles II. Anyone who did was declared "accessory post factum, to the
death of the aforesaid King." The assembly's other declaration had greater political importance: it was declared
treasonable to advocate, or to repeat except as testimony
in court, "any thing tending to change of government, or
the lessening of the power and authority of the Governor or
government." The assembly of 1649, summoned because the
king's death had raised doubts about the legitimacy of
Berkeley's authority, reaffirmed its earlier proclamation
that the governor and Council possessed legitimate power
derived from the crown, and declared it treason to disagree.[36]

Berkeley's recourse to the General Assembly for endorsement of his authority was, in fact, a recognition of the
genuine political importance that the House of Burgesses had
assumed. But the almost abjectly servile acknowledgment of
royal authority written into the 1649 legislation enabled

the royal governor to accept popular approbation without
surrendering the intellectual, spiritual, and legal bases
of order and society that had been challenged by the
king's enemies. Once again, Berkeley, reaping a bountiful
harvest from his earlier seeds of goodwill, shrewdly used
the General Assembly to sustain his government and rally
the colonists to his support, even as he allowed them to
deny that their endorsement was necessary.

Virginia's future had become Berkeley's sole
responsibility, and for seventeen months Berkeley and the
Council--which seems often to have styled itself a council
of war--governed Virginia without summoning another
assembly. Then came news of Parliament's 3 October 1650
Navigation Act, which prohibited trade with Virginia,
Barbados, Bermuda, and Antigua, the four English colonies
still loyal to the king. It was the fit moment to summon
the burgesses and rally the colony again with an eloquent
and defiant speech against the "men of Westminster."
On 17 March 1651 the assembly met for one day. The
burgesses did not organize themselves or elect a Speaker.
Rather, the whole assembly--governor, Council, and "House
of Commons"--met together to hear Berkeley's address,
adopt a stirring answer to "the pretended Act of Parliament,"
and reaffirm the colony's allegiance to the king and to his
lieutenant. No other business seems to have been conducted, and after the meeting ended Berkeley resumed
his conciliar government.[37]

Later that year Parliament dispatched five commissioners to seek Virginia's surrender to the Commonwealth. Several of their names are, by now, familiar: William Claiborne, Richard Bennett, and Captain Edmund Curtis sailed on the _Guinea_; Thomas Stegg and Captain Robert Dennis sailed on the _John_, which was lost at sea. On 24 March 1652 Claiborne, Bennett, and Curtis reported that in Virginia "immediately upon the coming in of that Act prohibiting Trade, &c., which came hither about a year since [i.e., March 1651], the Governor began more than ever to strengthen himself." Berkeley, the commissioners continued, poised "the whole Country" for resistance. But, in January 1652, after publishing broadsides that "gave great satisfaction to the People," the commissioners had sent a communication to the governor and Council of War. "Assemblies of Burgesses were discontinued," the report said, "and the Country wholly so governed." The Council's answer to the commissioners was "somewhat milder than expected," and they sent the Council another dispatch, which "produced the calling of an Assembly" and the cessation of hostility and dispersal of forces before blood had been shed. On 12 March 1652, this unicameral assembly (for again the burgesses did not organize themselves or elect a Speaker) met for one day and accepted articles of surrender negotiated with the commissioners, two of whom were Virginians prominent in the merchant-councillor faction. One of the articles provided that "the Grand Assembly as formerly shall convene and transact the affairs of Virginia," provided that nothing be "done contrarie to the government of the common wealth of England and the lawes there established."[38]

Although no blood was shed, it would be incorrect to assume that the surrender came easily. All the familiar trappings of royal authority--all the traditional bases of social order--had been dismantled and replaced by allegiance to "the Commonwealth of England as it is now Established, without Kinge or howse of Lords." Backed by a fleet, which Berkeley had not had when he had attempted to enforce allegiance by oath eight years earlier, agents of Parliament enforced allegiance to the Commonwealth by oath (copies of which survive in the records of Northampton and Northumberland counties, the latter with the individual subscribers' signatures). Evidence of popular attitudes throughout the Civil War years is disappointingly scarce. In 1643 a colonist had been dragged into court for allegedly disturbing the peace by proposing a toast "To the damnation of Pymms God and the Confusion of the Parliament," and in 1652 a resident of Lower Norfolk County went to court to secure protection against Berkeley's former councillor Francis Yeardley, whom the colonist feared would do him "boddily harme" or burn his houses.

At the next assembly, which met from 26 April to 6 May 1652, the House of Burgesses, which seems to have experienced no unusual changes in membership as a result of the surrender, chose not only a Speaker but a governor and Council as well. The principal commercial objective of the Mathews-Claiborne faction, the exclusion of the Dutch from Virginia's tobacco trade, had been enacted by Parliament in the Navigation Act of 1651. In the main, Parliament's authority rested lightly upon Virginia during the 1650s, and the approach outlined in the earl of Warwick's letters to Samuel Mathews seems to have been followed. On 30 April 1652, "after long a serious debate and advice taken for the settleing and governing of Virginia," the General Assembly appointed a governor, Richard Bennett, a secretary, William Claiborne, and thirteen councillors to serve for one year or until the next meeting of the General Assembly, with "such power and authorities and to act from time to time, as by the Grand Assembly shall be appointed and granted to their severall places respectively for the time abovesaid." Two days later the burgesses reserved to themselves the power to name county commissioners, and on 6 May, on the question "whether the Governour and Council shall be members of this Assembly or no," the House "generally voted they shall be, taking the oath the

Burgesses take." Berkeley, who had been allowed to retire to his Green Spring plantation, must have been pleased to see that the stable institutions he had fostered had emerged intact, and that, despite the colony's surrender to a Commonwealth without king or House of Lords, his vision of a proper, mixed constitution had been endorsed by majority vote in Virginia's lower house.[40]

5
THE BURGESSES ASCENDANT:
1652 -- 1660

The passage of the Navigation Act of 1651 was an economic victory for the London interloping merchants who long had sought the exclusion of foreign, and particularly Dutch, shipping from the colonial trades in tobacco and other commodities. Virginia's surrender to the Commonwealth was a political victory for the Mathews-Claiborne faction of merchant-planters. Between the surrender and the Restoration, Virginia's governors were affiliated with the merchant faction: Richard Bennett, Edward Digges, and Samuel Mathews, Jr. With both ends of the transatlantic trade empire secure in friendly hands, Bennett, Mathews, Digges, and Claiborne sought to achieve the final objective of their 1630s program: the discontinuance of Lord Baltimore's patent and his "popish monarchical government," which Mathews and Bennett, in lengthy papers for the Committee of Trade, argued was inconsistent "to the liberty and freedom of English subjects" under the Protectorate, not to mention inimical to their commercial interests. Toward this end, Mathews spent most of the decade in England, leaving his son behind to assume the governorship in 1656, when Digges joined Mathews and Bennett in England.[1]

Probably if the surrender had occurred a decade earlier, during the immediate aftermath of the Thrusting Out of Governor Harvey and before the countless little events and relationships of a decade of political life firmed the colony as tendrils infix a dune, violence and upheaval might have occurred, as they did in Maryland. There was tension and uncertainty in Virginia, but no civil war. There was political change, but the leading royalists remained in Virginia, unmolested, during the 1650s. Some offices changed hands as a result of the surrender, but there is no evidence of institutional discontinuity: the governorship, Council, House of Burgesses, counties, and vestries continued to exist. Having gained control of Virginia's government at the same time that their principal objective became, by virtue of the Navigation Act of 1651, the law of the empire, the Mathews-Claiborne faction had no cause to change Virginia's governemnt. The major development in Virginia politics during the 1650s was the series of minor skirmishes through which the House of Burgesses discovered its strength, asserted that strength, and in 1658, somewhat reluctantly, came of age.

"Politick Proviso's"

Governor Sir William Berkeley had been ready to meet Cromwell's emissaries with armed resistence when their fleet had appeared off Virginia in 1652, and the emissaries themselves had been empowered, in case the Virginians would not "submit by fair means[,] to use all acts of Hostility to enforce them." And, the commissioners had a fleet. After an exchange of communications that were "somewhat milder than was expected, though mixt with some such politick Proviso's" (which eventually became the terms of surrender), Berkeley and his Council of War had summoned an assembly. The assembly disbanded the defensive forces (which the commissioners claimed had numbered about a thousand men-in-arms at Jamestown) and completed the surrender, thereby sharing responsibility for the end of resistence, "though not without divers difficulties yet without damage or harm to any, or the loss of a drop of blood."[2]

The treaty between the commissioners and the assembly is, in at least one respect, a curious document, for the commissioners used the occasion of Virginia's surrender to push anew toward their faction's remaining objective: to extend Virginia's boundaries to "the antient bounds and lymitts granted by the charters of the former Kings," and to confirm those boundaries with a charter from Parliament "against any that have intrencht upon the rights

thereof"--that is, against Lord Baltimore and his colony
of Maryland. The commissioners also promised that no
taxes, customs, or impositions whatsoever would be imposed
in Virginia "without the consent of the Grand Assembly."
Both these clauses in the articles of surrender, and a few
minor matters of wording, were challenged in the House of
Commons that August, and there seems to be no evidence
that Parliament ever formally acceded to the articles
that its commissioners had negotiated. Certainly Baltimore's
colony and charter remained secure despite the best
attempts of Mathews, Bennett, and Claiborne against the
proprietary. Bennett and Claiborne may have represented
Parliament in the surrender negotiations, but they seem
to have been careful to press a congenial vision of Virginia's,
Parliament's, and their faction's common interest. Having
won their fight with the Dutch traders in the committee
rooms of Parliament, where the victory was not subject
to the scrutiny of the lesser planters, the Mathews-
Claiborne faction probably found most Virginians ready to
support this final element in their program.[3]

The other terms of the articles of surrender are
familiar: Virginia acknowledged that its surrender was
voluntary and "not forced nor constrained by a conquest
upon the countrey." This was an important ideological
point, for an act of conquest would have threatened the

logical basis of the colony's claim (and the commissioners' promise) "that they shall have and enjoy such freedomes and priviledges as belong to the free borne people of England."[4]

Other items in the document declared void the authority of the former royal government and its "commissions and instructions," and authorized the General Assembly to meet "as formerly" and to "convene and transact the affairs of Virginia." Full indemnity for "all acts, words or writeings done or spoken against the parliament of England" was assured. The document confirmed existing land patents and existing procedures for headrights and quitrents, and gave assurance that title to cattle or recently imported goods would not be challenged. Use of the Book of Common Prayer was permitted for one year (there is no subsequent evidence that the prayer book ever was prohibited), and the colony was assured that it would not bear the cost of the commissioners' fleet. Two clauses in the articles of surrender were less congenial. Item seven promised Virginia "free trade as the people of England do enjoy to all places and with all nations according to the lawes of that commonwealth"--phrasing that put the best possible face on the fact that, despite their previous reliance on Dutch merchants to keep the tobacco trade free from monopolists, Virginians were to comply with the new navigation acts, which were the embodiment of the Mathews-Claiborne faction's program. Item ten required that all inhabitants were to subscribe the Engagement, and that those who refused to sign this statement of allegiance to Parliament had "a yeares time if they please to remove themselves, and their estates out of Virginia." As with the clause about the prayer book, item ten seems to have been more rigid on paper than in practice.[5]

Commissioners Claiborne, Bennett, and Curtis had been instructed to "give liberty to those who have taken the Engagement to choose Burgesses for regulating and governing affairs" in Virginia. Accordingly, three dozen burgesses, their names returned by the county sheriffs as usual, gathered in Jamestown in April 1652. This assembly established the new government and undertook a complete revisal of the legal code, the third such revision in the colony's history. The election of thirty-seven-year-old Edward Major, of Nansemond (formerly Upper Norfolk) County, as Speaker of the House of Burgesses suggests that the commissioners' and merchants' influence in the assembly was strong, for Major was a puritan and a neighbor of Richard Bennett; he had come to Virginia in 1635 as a headright of Bennett's brother Robert. In general, it is correct to conclude that the 1652 revisal of the laws "demonstrates a marked continuity with the past" in such matters as the regulation of land and property, Indian affairs, local government, and agriculture, for in matters such as these the revisal of 1652 did not attempt "any major alteration in Virginia's provincial or local government."[6]

In three main respects, however, the assembly of 1652 did change Virginia's laws. First, of course, all references to royalty (except those in an act dealing with tributary Indian tribes, which were quietly retained "for manye Reasons of State") were expunged from the code. Second, existing statutes requiring conformity to established doctrine, oaths of allegiance or supremacy, and a close approximation to "the orders and constitutions of the church of England," were repealed and replaced by a congregationalist statute stipulating "that all matters concerninge the Vestrye, . . . and other things Concerninge the parrishes or parrishoners Respectively be Referred to theire owne orderinge and dispossall from time to time, as they shall thinke Fitt." Third, a number of mercantile laws that had regulated trading vessels, prevented engrossing of commodities, required merchants to pay the cost of tobacco casks, limited the sale of wine and liquor, prohibited the export of hides and leather, and encouraged free trade with the Dutch, were repealed. Virginia had been surrendered into the hands of the merchants.[7]

The assembly of April 1652, however, had made sure that their hands were not too strong. Bennett and Claiborne were elected governor and secretary, respectively, for one year "or untill the next meeting of the Assembly," and with thirteen councillors given power "to execute and do right and equall justice to all the people" according to any instructions they might receive from Parliament "and according to the knowne laws of England; And the acts of Assembly here established." Their authority derived not from God and king, as had Berkeley's, nor it seems from Parliament, but rather from "the Burgesses the representative[s] of the people." The House itself began to choose commissioners for the county courts--a prerogative the royal governor had exercised--but a few days later, apparently weary of the task, decided to trust the new governor and Council with the appointment of "all officers not already constituted," cautioning them that this procedure was "not precidental to any succeeding Assembly." On what may have been the last day of the assembly, 6 May 1652, the House of Burgesses resolved not to follow in Virginia the pattern of the House of Commons, which had dispensed with king and lords. The burgesses determined to continue the bicameral constitution Berkeley had promoted a decade before: even though by virtue of its representative sovereignty the House was in the position to constitute the other two estates, the governor, Council, and House of Burgesses were to comprise the bicameral assembly just as they had before 1652.[8]

Although Henry Read McIlwaine's assertion that the assembly of April 1652 "seems to have been unicameral throughout" is correct, because the situation and evidence

are easy to misunderstand, it is important to show
precisely what that statement means and how the evidence
supports it. The spring 1652 assembly was a constitutive
body meeting in the aftermath of the colony's surrender to
Parliament. Royal authority, the aegis under which previous
assemblies had met, could no longer be invoked. The assembly's formal claim to legitimacy was that Parliament had
instructed the commissioners to hold elections open to those
colonists who had professed allegiance to the Commonwealth.
But throughout the 1650s the Virginians--and the commissioners
were Virginians also--tacitly recognized that government
could not be conducted without the support of the elected
burgesses, and that the sense of legitimacy associated with
the election of burgesses derived from something more than
Parliament's prescription that elections be held. References to a more radical basis of authority were, at first
perhaps, inchoate, but by 1658 events drew Virginia's
inherent admission of popular sovereignty into open expression. Sixteen-fifty-two's brief allusions to burgesses as
representatives of the people became, within a few years,
forthright assertions that "the supreme power of this
country of Virginia"--in a word, sovereignty--was "resident
in the Burgesses." Close attention to the language that
the assembly used in 1652 suggests that this latter position
already was recognized as valid, although it was not aggres-

sively asserted.[9]

At the beginning of the assembly on 26 April 1652, two sorts of persons--and only two sorts of persons had any claim to office since the extinction of royal authority in the colony--were present: the elected burgesses and the parliamentary commissioners. The assembly organized itself as a House of Burgesses with a Speaker and a "Cl[ericus] Dom[us] Com[munis]," or clerk of the House, as had been the practice throughout the 1640s. The difference between this and any previous assembly was that, until 30 April, no governor or Council existed. Prior to 1643 Virginia's unicameral assemblies had been enlarged meetings of the governor and Council, but the unicameral assembly of April 1652 was a meeting of the House of Burgesses alone, convened to negotiate for the colony with commissioners who represented Parliament. Only after four days of "long and serious debate" did the burgesses and commissioners agree to appoint a governor, secretary, and Council for one year. Commissioners Bennett and Claiborne were chosen governor and secretary, and a thirteen-man Council was named.[10]

The day after the assembly of 1652 had decided that Virginia's government should continue to be comprised of "the Governor, Council and Burgesses," it took up the ancillary question: whether, like the constitutive spring 1652 assembly itself, future General Assemblies were to consist of the House of Burgesses alone, or whether the gover-

nor and Council were to have some constitutional role in
them. The proposition had two important dimensions. First,
because Governor Bennett's appointment ran only for one year
"or untill the next meeting of the Assembly," as did the
secretary's and the councillors' terms of office, the proposition implied a general question of whether the governor
and councillors were to hold office during the meetings of
future assemblies, or whether they were merely to serve as
an interim steering committee between assemblies. Second,
if they were to continue in office, then were the governor
and Council to have a deliberative role in future assemblies?
Again, the House affirmed the general bicameral structure
that had been instituted in 1643: [11]

> Whether the Governor and Council shall be members of this Assembly or no: Generally voted
> they shall be, taking the oath the Burgesses
> take.

Meeting in 1652, then, as a constitutive body at least
to some degree aware of the democratic basis of its authority,
the House of Burgesses endorsed a bicameral constitution and
rejected the viewpoint that the governor and Council should
be excluded from participation in the assembly as the contemporary king and lords had been excluded from Parliament.
Virginia's principal institutional legacy of the 1640s was
this stable, conservative, bicameral constitution within

which the lower house of assembly learned to become
jealous of its independence and its power as "representative of the people." The House was cautious when considering anything that might prove "precidential" in the future.
At the next assembly, in November 1652, with Thomas Dew as
Speaker and John Corker again as clerk, the House expelled
two members for scandalous and mutinous conduct--an action
that indicated, as Mary Patterson Clarke wrote, "that here
was a body that took parliamentary government very seriously
indeed." A year later, in July 1653, the governor and
Council presumed to challenge the House of Burgesses' choice
of its Speaker and precipitated a constitutional conflict
in which the House began to define its institutional independence in more forceful terms.[12]

The cases of Speakers Chiles and Hill

Walter Chiles, a prominent merchant who had come to
Virginia in 1638 and had served on Berkeley's Council in
1651, was elected to the House of Burgesses in 1653 by the
residents of Jamestown, where Chiles apparently lived in
the brick house he had bought from Berkeley in 1649. "By
plurality of votes," Chiles was elected Speaker on 5 July
1653, and upon learning of the House's choice Governor Bennett and the Council dispatched a letter to the burgesses
questioning the advisability of Chiles's election as
Speaker. The ensuing controversy is important in three

respects: It demonstrates the burgesses' institutional jealousy and independence. It reveals the working constitution of the assembly. And it shows how Parliament's attempt to drive the Dutch out of the colonial trade affected politics in Virginia, where the Dutch rivals to the Mathews-Claiborne faction had been the lesser planters' guardians against de facto monopoly.[13]

The Commonwealth first had attempted to regulate Virginia's trade in September 1650, when, as an act of war, it had prohibited all trade with the royalist colonies of Antigua, Barbados, Bermuda, and Virginia (with the provision that English merchants might obtain special license from the Council of State for trade with these colonies). London merchants involved in the colonial trade, notably Maurice Thompson, Claiborne and Mathews's ally and sometime partner, had protested the law and secured a requirement that prohibited future trade by foreign vessels to any English colony except by special license. In the year that followed these initial steps, Thompson and his circle of interloping merchants made "great strides," wrote the Venetian ambassador from London, "as government and trade are ruled by the same persons." Thompson himself became the guiding spirit behind the Navigation Act of 1651, enacted on 9 October, although scholars have not unanimously agreed that Thompson was the principal author of the act.[14]

Virginia still had been a royal colony on 24 January

1652 when Walter Chiles had set out for Rotterdam in his
Fame of Virginia. Whether he had been aware of Parliament's
latest navigation act is moot, because Virginia had consistently denied Parliament's claim to regulate colonial
commerce, and because the 1651 act concerned foreign ships.
Since the assembly of 1651 had expressly resolved to defy
Parliament's restrictions on royalist colonies' commerce,
however, Chiles clearly knew that he risked capture by
parliamentary vessels on the high seas.[15]

When the *Fame of Virginia* returned to Virginia waters
in June 1652 and anchored off the Eastern Shore, the colony
had surrendered to Parliament. On 13 June Chiles sailed for
Jamestown, but en route he was stopped and boarded by Captain
Richard Henfield. Henfield claimed that because Chiles
lacked a license from Parliament (as required by the 1650
act) the *Fame of Virginia* was subject to seizure, and Henfield reported his capture to his superior, Richard Husband,
captain of the *Hopeful Adventure*. Chiles, meanwhile, protested to the Northampton County Court that Henfield's
action violated the terms of Virginia's surrender to the
Commonwealth, which had provided "that the people of Virginia have free trade as the people of England do enjoy
to all places and with all nations." Chiles's argument was
firm insofar as its reference to the terms of surrender was
based on the act of 1650, and Henfield apparently was
convinced.[16]

Henfield's superior, Richard Husband, however, declared the *Fame* *of* *Virginia* to be his prize on different grounds. The Navigation Act of 1651, which was designed to cripple the Dutch colonial trade, required that cargo be transported in English bottoms owned by English merchants and manned by English seamen. Husband, therefore, claimed that the *Fame* *of* *Virginia* was his prize because Chiles did not own it: the ship, its master, and its crew, he alleged, "belonge to the [Dutch] West Indya Companye." Further, Husband alleged that when seized Chiles's *Fame* *of* *Virginia* had not been homeward bound to Virginia, but outward bound from Rotterdam, and that its intended voyage was to trade with Brazil and return to Holland. The members of the Northampton County Court, who stressed that their "Knowne Experience both in the course of Trade from us to Holland and soe backe againe doth fully informe us," dismissed this allegation as nonsense.[17]

Convinced that he had a lawful prize from which he and his crew stood to benefit, Husband evaded the directions of the Northampton County Court, which held him in custody. He pretended to cooperate by agreeing to submit to the decision of Nathaniel Littleton and Argoll Yeardley. The two arbiters, who were members both of the county court and of the Council of State, ruled that Chiles was to have his ship and that Husband was to be released from custody and from threat of suit for his actions. Husband wrote his crew ordering them to return the _Fame of Virginia_, and he was released. Once aboard the _Hopeful Adventure_, however, he reneged on his promise and, on 18 June 1652, the day he was released, he wrote a letter to the Northampton County Court claiming that the _Fame of Virginia_ was his rightful prize for the reasons he had earlier alleged. Husband refused to surrender the ship, and, after receiving another court order to do so, sailed off with both Chiles's _Fame of Virginia_ and his own _Hopeful Adventurer_ on 19 June.[18]

During the months that followed, rumor swept through the Eastern Shore that the county would be held responsible for its court's mistake in allowing Husband to escape with the ship, which Chiles valued at two thousand pounds. The incensed Northampton justices resolved to prosecute Husband in English courts, and they demanded Governor Bennett's assistance: "Wee expect from your selfe (As the Representative power of the Countrye)," they wrote Bennett, "Such wrightings as shalbe by you drawne to that purpose, And (as you shall think fitt to give Evidence of his abuse) which Wee shall second with all our power And, by Mr Edmund Scarburgh prosecute to the uttermost." County inhabitants, many of whom had signed a bitter protest against the "arbitrarye and illegall" tax levy of forty-six pounds per poll just months before the maritime incident, came to fear "that a great summe of money is to be paid to satisfye for a shipp taken here by Capt Rich Husband and restored by a Court unto Mr Walter Chiles."[19]

"Instigated thereunto merely through the Effects of feare," county residents gathered in angry meetings. At one such gathering, Stephen Horsey, one of the first six signators of the county protest against taxation, "revile[d] against some of the Magistrats of this County (sayeinge) The County would be ruinated by a company of Asses and villayns." A "scandalous and seditious" paper was drawn and circulated, largely by the effort of Edmund Scarborough, the former Speaker, who had lost ships under the new navigation acts himself and been barred from office by the assembly of 1653 for his part in the Northampton protest.[20]

Chiles and Scarborough, meanwhile, each had resolved upon a new plan to recoup his loss: each determined to exploit the very law under which he had suffered. In March 1653 Captain Peter Wraxall gave "Mr Scarburgh a Coppie of his Commission from the Admiraltye" with which Scarborough set out "for the Dutch to surprise some of their vessells." He captured the Dutch merchant ship Hopewell.[21]

Chiles, however, was less swashbuckling in his exploitation of the new navigation act. Late in October 1652 he had sold eight hundred thirteen acres of land near the Appomattox River. When a Dutch ship was captured and "adjudged Forfeit," Chiles was ready to buy. According to witnesses' testimony, on 6 June 1653, "Mr Gunnell and Mr Reade masters of London Shipps" boarded the Dutch vessel <u>Leopoldus of Dunkirk</u> in Virginia waters. Their attempted capture was unsuccessful, but after the Londoners left, a party of Virginians boarded the ship. "The Skipper Said to Coll. [William] Clayborne and others Who then came aboard, if they were Prize they would be Prize to the Country [i.e., to Virginia not to the London shipmasters], And if they [i.e., the Virginians] pleased to send fifty men on board they Should be Welcome."[22]

Chiles saw the capture of the <u>Leopoldus of Dunkirk</u> as an opportunity to recoup his earlier loss of the <u>Fame of Virginia</u>, and other Virginians evidently saw an opportunity to satisfy Chiles's claim for damages against the county without incurring further public expense. Arrangements were made that seem to have involved at least Chiles, Bennett, Claiborne, Littleton, and Yeardley (the last two were councillors who had served as the arbiters, but who also exercised admiralty jurisdiction on the Eastern Shore). The package seems to have been this: Chiles got the <u>Leopoldus</u> for four hundred pounds, a price that looked reasonable but was probably a bargain for the three-hundred-ton vessel "with her guns, tackle, apparel and furniture and whatsoever belongeth or appertaineth to the said shipp [i.e., her cargo]." Bennett signed an order authorizing the surprise and capture of Dutch ships on 11 July; the next day Chiles's bill of sale for the <u>Leopoldus</u> was signed. From its terms we discover the other part of the package arrangement. Chiles's four hundred pounds went to appropriate pockets: Claiborne got one hundred, Samuel Mathews got two-hundred fifty, Speaker William Whitby got thirty, and two others got ten pounds each. The assembly of 1653 ratified the entire agreement in July, the terms being set forth in the bill of sale signed by three representatives of each house of the assembly: Governor Bennett, Secretary Claiborne, and Robert Huberd, "Cl[ericus] Counsilli," for the Council; and George Fletcher, a Northumberland County burgess, William Whitby, Speaker, and John Corker, "Cl[erk] to the House of Burgesses."[23]

Governor Bennett and the Council probably were concerned about the apparent conflict of interest if Chiles continued as Speaker of the House of Burgesses that ratified this agreement, and although the House was concerned about the propriety of allowing the governor and Council to influence its choice of Speaker, probably the burgesses (and Chiles) saw merit in the Council's reservations. It is impossible to know exactly how the selection of the Speaker of the House of Burgesses occurred. Probably during the 1640s and again after the Restoration the burgesses chose their Speakers after being told to do so by the governor, then presented their candidate to the governor for formal approval, at which time the Speaker made the traditional

Speaker's petition for the House's traditional privileges. During the 1650s, however, because gubernatorial authority derived from the assembly rather than the reverse, it seems unlikely that the governor had any role in the selection of the Speaker--unless, of course, a precedent were to be established. The evidence about the election of Speaker in 1653 is susceptible to somewhat more speculation than often is the case, however.[24]

Chiles was elected "by plurality of votes" (that is, probably by a majority of votes, for the American usage of *plurality*, as distinguished from *majority*, dates only from the 1820s). Probably (if English practice was followed in the 1650s as it was later in Virginia) two or three men--the persons named in the committee to inform the governor of the House's choice--had been nominated. The candidacies of former Speaker Edward Major, Governor Bennett's friend from Nansemond County, and, perhaps, William Whitby, of Warwick County, who succeeded Chiles when he resigned, are suggested from the membership of that ad hoc committee. If Major was Chiles's principal opponent for Speaker, then Bennett's interference in the elections had political implications beyond the question of conflict of interest, for Major was allied with the merchant-councillor faction while Chiles had been extensively engaged in the Dutch trade.[25]

Whatever the circumstances of the election may have been, upon learning of the House's choice, Bennett and the Council addressed this letter to the burgesses:

> Gentlemen:
>
> Not to entrench [or in another source, "incroach"] upon the right of Assemblies in the free choice of a speaker, nor to undervalue Lefft. Coll. Chiles, but onely by way of advice, It is my opinion, the Council likewise concerning [i.e., concurring] therein, That it is not so proper nor so convenientt att this time to make choice of him for that there is something to be agitated in this Assembly concerning a shipp lately arrived, in which Left. Coll. Chiles hath some interest, for which and for some other reasons we conceive it better at present to make choice of some other person amongst you whom you shall agree upon.
>
> Your reall servant,
>
> July the 5th, 1653   RICH. BENNETT

The House then sent a committee composed of Edward Major, George Fletcher, William Hockaday, and William Whitby to request the governor and Council's "reasons, wherefore they cannot joyne with us the Burgesses in the busines of this Assembly, about the election of Lev't. Coll. Walter Chiles for Speaker of this Assembly."[26]

The procedural implications of the burgesses' statement is unclear. Did they think it necessary that the governor and Council "joyne with" the House and formally concur in its selection of the Speaker? or did they only think it desirable that the governor and Council "joyne with" them in congenial support of their duly elected presiding officer? Although the sense of the House may have been closer to the latter position, the answer is not clear because Chiles requested, and the House granted him, leave to resign. On 6 July Chiles explained "to the house his extraordinarie occasions in regard of the dispatch of some shipping . . . in which he is much interested and concerned, [and] The house upon his desire . . . [gave] him leave to follow his private affairs notwithstanding the election aforesaid." Conscious of its independence, of the important role that precedents played in the definition and maintenance of that independence, and of the truth in Governor Bennett's advice, the House accepted Chiles's resignation and then passed over Bennett's friend and neighbor Edward Major and elected William Whitby to succeed Chiles.[27]

The next day, Captains Abraham Read and Edward Gunnell, who first had attempted to capture the Leopoldus, acknowledged their offenses before the House and petitioned for pardon, and on 12 July the episode ended when Bennett, Claiborne, and Huberd for the Council, and Whitby, Fletcher, and Corker for the House, signed Chiles's bill of sale for the <u>Leopoldus</u>. Few other laws were passed at the assembly of 1653, although more than a dozen orders were issued: the House agreed to Sir William Berkeley's request for an extension of the time allowed him to leave the colony, and provided that "the governor Councell and [county] Commissioners togeather with the Sherrifes . . . bee and remaine in their power and places respectively untill the next Assembly."^{28}

At the next assembly, in November 1654, the House having voiced but not forcefully pressed its privilege of electing a Speaker independent of gubernatorial or councilliar influence, the burgesses demonstrated that they demanded respect from all Virginians, and that they would countenance no aspersions of the House or its officers. Sometime prior to the November meeting of the assembly, an allegation had been made that Edward Hill, who had been Speaker of the House in 1644 and 1645 and a member of Berkeley's Council in 1651, was an atheist and blasphemer. Religious controversy and plain libel were always of concern to seventeenth-century Virginia civil authorities, for even if the disputants were obscure servants, their petty quarrels disrupted the public peace. Hill was prominent. At the last quarter session before the November meeting of the assembly, the governor and Council had considered the allegations raised about the former Speaker's conduct or sentiments and had "cleared the said Coll. Edward Hill."[29]

Convening on 20 November 1654, the burgesses unanimously elected Hill as their Speaker, whereupon sharp-tongued William Hatcher, a former burgess from Henrico County, "maliciously reported" and circulated the old charge that Hill was "an atheist and blasphemer." Although "he had notice given him of the Governour and Councills pleasure therin and of the said Coll. Hill's being cleered as afforesaid," Hatcher also said, "That the mouth of this house was a Devil." The affair now was serious; Hatcher had committed both breach of privilege and contempt, and had flagrantly affronted the House's claim to authority—without which all was chaos. Following standard English practice, the House summoned Hatcher to the bar "upon his knees, [to] make an humble acknowledgement of his offence unto the said Coll. Edward Hill and Burgesses of this Assembly." Then, after paying an unspecified amount in "fees," Hatcher was dismissed.[30]

Traditions and Privileges

Throughout the Interregnum, the House of Burgesses demonstrated its concern for privilege, precedents, and procedures. Surviving evidence shows that it used committees extensively and effectively. Its committee for private causes, for example, considered appeals that came to each meeting of the assembly from the General Court. Operating according to the appellate system as it was defined in the revisal of 1643, the committee for private causes was comprised of ten to twelve burgesses and two or three councillors named by the upper house. Thus, as William Fitzhugh forcefully argued in the 1680s, when the appellate system of 1643 was discontinued, the appellate jurisdiction of the entire General Assembly was committed to members of both houses.[31]

Another regularly appointed committee apportioned the country levy, assigning proportionate amounts to each county. In 1655, an act concerning markets was referred to an ad hoc committee of four burgesses, and the next year, in December 1656, another four-man committee was assigned the task of reviewing the acts of the assembly, digesting them into one volume, and attesting to the accuracy of that volume--a task that continued after the assembly itself had risen and was completed before the meeting of the General Court in March 1657. Robert Huberd, clerk of the Council, was "given license to carry the originall booke of records home to his owne house to copie them out by." Clearly, the House had become both conscious of the importance of its records and careful to retain control over them.[32]

The House of Burgesses was equally careful about the proper conduct of elections. A 1655 law prescribed the procedure in detail: Within ten days after receiving the writ ordering elections to be held, the sheriff publicized the forthcoming election "by giving notice of the same from howse to house," announcing the day on which elections would be conducted "for all accustomed places in the Counties and parishes respectively." On election day the county sheriff oversaw the voting, which was now "by Subscription of the Major part of the hands of the Electors." Prior to the date of the assembly's meeting, the sheriff returned to the secretary at Jamestown the writ on which he had written the names of those persons duly elected. Neglect of this duty or submission of a false return was punishable by a fine of ten thousand pounds of tobacco. Only twenty-one-year-old heads of households ("whether freeholders, Leasholders, or otherwise tenants") "of knowne Integritie and of good Conversation" could vote. Ineligible persons who tried

to vote were subject to fines of four hundred pounds of
tobacco, payable to the county, for contempt. This restriction of the franchise was loosened at the next
assembly because it was thought "something harsh and unagreeable to reason, that any person should pay Equal
Taxes, And yet have noe Votes in Ellections." The data
will not support any estimate of the percentage of adult
males who had, or exercised, the vote, but the assembly
of 1656 agreed that the restrictions had "exclude[d]
Freemen from Votes," and they were repealed "provided
allwayes that they fayerlye give their Votes by Subscriptions and not in a tumultuous way." No disputed elections
are recorded for this period, although in several instances for political or religious reasons the House refused
to seat a person returned by his county. Both the conduct
of elections and the control of members of the House fell
within the House's purview.[33]

In part it may be correct to assert, as Michael
Kammen has, that the relative infrequency of colonial
laws about procedure is evidence that early American
legislators were concerned about "institutional forms
and stability, . . . [but] feared to put in print anything
that might smack of deviation from English norms, or be
offensive to executive forces." The earliest extant orders
for floor procedure in the Virginia House of Burgesses

were recorded in March 1659, but their general similarity
to procedural rules adopted by the Maryland assembly
as early as 1642 suggests that both were based upon
contemporary perceptions of English practice, probably
enunciated in parliamentary handbooks, and that similar
rules had been in effect in Virginia well before 1659.[34]

A burgess was expected to be present and attentive
to the business of the House, and in debate to "àddresse
himselfe to Mr. Speaker in a decent manner, And not
entertaine any private discourse, while the publique
affairs are treated off." Absent members were fined
twenty pounds of tobacco "to be disposed of by the major
part of the house upon every Saturday in the afternoon."
A graduated scale of fines (one hundred, two hundred, and
one thousand pounds of tobacco for successive offenses)
suggests that the House had a chronic problem with members
being "disguised with overmuche drinke." The Speaker's
presidential role in the House included formulating
questions for the House's consideration, and Virginia's
rules, like the rules of the House of Commons, required
that "upon debate of any thing proposed by the Speaker,
The party that speaketh shall rise from his seate and be
uncovered [i.e., bareheaded] dureing the time he speaketh,
wherein no interruption shall be made untill he have
finished his discourse, upon penalty of one hundred
pounds of tob'o." The rules prohibited irreverent or
disgraceful speech by any burgess against another, and

penalized offenders five hundred pounds of tobacco.[35]

Continuity of membership in the House of Burgesses was characteristic of the assembly during the 1650s. Between 1656 and 1660 an average of four of every ten members had had experience in at least one previous assembly. Available data suggest that as the crisis of the 1658 session passed and the crisis of the Restoration approached, the percentage of experienced burgesses rose from about 30 percent in 1656 to about 45 percent in 1660. About one of eight burgesses had served in three or more previous assemblies, and institutional continuity was further enhanced by the presence of men who had personally witnessed the House's actions before, during, and immediately after the colony's surrender to Parliament. In many counties, a member of the county bench might serve in the assembly one year, skip a year or two, and then return to the House in the third or fourth. Since his colleagues on the county bench frequently had the same pattern of House membership, and since they all had common interests in knowing what went on at Jamestown, even burgesses who attended occasionally or intermittently probably were well aware of the House's past, its procedures and precedents. These members were a reservoir of experienced leaders from which the House could draw sustenance for its vision of its authority

Table one: Continuity of membership in the House of Burgesses, 1656-1660					
ASSEMBLY:	1656	1658	1659	1660	Averages
Total number of members known	41	44	37	47	169*
Members not known to have served in previous assemblies	29 70.7%	29 65.9%	20 54.1%	25 53.2%	103 60.9%
Members of the immediately preceding assembly	5 12.2%	8 18.2%	10 27.0%	16 34.0%	39 23.1%
Members of any one previous assembly (or more)	12 29.3%	15 34.1%	17 45.9%	21 44.7%	65 38.5%
Members of two or more previous assemblies	8 19.5%	9 20.5%	6 16.2%	10 21.3%	34 20.1%
Members of three or more previous assemblies	3 7.3%	4 9.1%	5 13.5%	4 8.5%	16 9.5%
Members of five or more previous assemblies	1 2.4%	1 2.3%	1 2.7%	2 4.3%	5 3.0%
Members who had served in assemblies prior to Virginia's surrender to Parliament in 1652	8 19.5%	5 11.4%	5 13.5%	3 6.4%	21 12.4%

*This statistic does not measure specific individuals, but seeks to supply data for the average assembly of this period; e.g., John Sidney had experience in two previous assemblies by 1656, three by 1658, and four by 1659, hence is counted at several places in order to make the average percentages accurate.

Table two: Profile of composite experience in the House of Burgesses, 1656-1660

ASSEMBLY	1646	1647-1648	1649	1651-1652	Apr. 1652	Nov. 1652	1653	1654-1655	1656	1658	1659
1656	1	4	4	3	3	5	3	5	—	—	—
1658	0	3	3	1	2	4	5	4	8	—	—
1659	0	1	3	1	2	1	2	6	7	10	—
1660	0	2	1	2	0	0	1	3	5	6	13

The figures in the body of this table represent the number of burgesses in each of the assemblies identified at left who had been present at the earlier assembly identified above each column.

and privilege.

The House's committee structure increased the influence of the experienced burgesses. The eight members of the 1656 committee for private causes, for example, included Moore Fauntleroy, who had been a burgess in 1648, 1651-1652, and 1653; William Harris, who had served in 1652 and 1653; and William Whittaker, who had attended five previous assemblies since 1649. Committees expanded the experienced members' influence: In 1656 less than 20 percent of the burgesses had two years of experience, but more than 35 percent of the committee for the private causes did. In 1658 about 20 percent of the House had two years of experience, but almost 30 percent of the committee to draft a "vindication of the Assembly's power" did, and these members had experience in the House that preceded the surrender to Parliament. The House's traditions, precedents, and procedures were matters of living memory, not abstract privilege. Two of the six committeemen charged to prepare the revisal of 1658 had begun their careers in the House in the 1640s. A sizeable minority in any meeting of the House of Burgesses had first-hand experience with the traditions and privileges of the assembly, and the experienced member's influence is always greater than a statistic suggests. When the House of Burgesses stood up for itself and its constituents, it

did so as a stable, self-conscious institution--a whole
generation of recent assertions about the chaotic nature of
early American politics to the contrary notwithstanding.
By the mid-1650s the House of Burgesses was a representative body capable of quashing the claims of Governor Samuel
Mathews, Jr., and Secretary William Claiborne, and of
surviving the Restoration fully intact.[37]

"We have in our selves the full power"

One of the provisions of the 1652 articles for the
surrender of Virginia had been "that Virginia shall have
and enjoy the antient bounds and lymitts granted by the
charters of the former Kings," and that efforts would be
made to "seek a new charter from the parliament to that
purpose against any that have intrencht upon the rights
thereof." The assembly of 1652 had agreed with commissioners
Bennett and Claiborne to support this program--the last
unfinished item in the merchant-councillors' program--
and to challenge Lord Baltimore's proprietary colony in
Maryland. But the House of Commons had refused to agree,
and Samuel Mathews, Sr., who had more powerful connections
in London than any other Virginia merchant, had gone to
England to press Virginia's claim to rightful possession
of Maryland. In March 1655 Governor Bennett vacated his
office and the assembly sent him to assist in the lobbying
effort, and in December 1656 the assembly had elected

Governor Edward Digges with the provision that he would "retaine the reines of government in his hands" until he was able to sail and "join with our friends colonel Mathews and mr. Bennett."[38]

The same assembly chose Samuel Mathews, Jr., the wealthy son of the colony's principal agent and leading merchant, as "Governour elect." The young man was in his twenties and had represented Warwick County in the House from 1652 to 1655, but as governor, as Richard L. Morton wrote, he "was inclined to assert his authority beyond the limits set . . . in 1652." Mathews seems to have been something of a pawn in the hands of William Claiborne and other members of the Council. He assumed the office when Digges sailed for England in March 1657 and, according to a cryptic note made by Conway Robinson, in April the Council denied a "petition for assembly the 10th of May." When the assembly next convened, on 13 March 1658, the Council and the House of Burgesses quickly fell into dispute over the House's claim to sovereignty. The burgesses won, and enforced their claim with words and actions that could not be mistaken.[39]

The 1656 assembly had directed Virginia's agents in England to "desist from all manner of farther proceeding" in their efforts to undermine Lord Baltimore's claim to Maryland. William Claiborne, whose desire to repossess

Kent Island and to oust Baltimore had become the overarching focus of his considerable talents, could not have concurred with this decision. As the secretary of the colony, Claiborne long had been second in rank to the governors. But, as Claiborne's friendly biographer observed, the assembly of 1656 "not only did not name him to the Governorship but took care that he was now in no position to assume that office in the absence of others. . . . Richard Bennett assumed the next place in Council," even though he was absent. The House knew its rival--some burgesses remembered what he had done with the army he had commanded in the 1640s.[40]

The first recorded disagreement between the House and the Council in the assembly of 1658 occurred when the House solicited the Council's views on its proposal to revive an earlier law prohibiting paid attorneys from practicing in any of the colony's courts. On 23 March Secretary Claiborne sent a curt "answer . . . to the House's Message about the lawyers": "The Governor and Council will consent to this proposition so farr as it shall be agreeable to Magna Charta." Unimpressed by Claiborne's reference to Magna Charta (or, perhaps, as puzzled by the precise meaning of the reference as the twentieth-century reader), the House resolved that a reply "be drawn upp by the committee." "Wee have considered Magna Charta," the House replied firmly in its committee's letter, "and wee cannot discerne any prohibition conteined therein but that these propositions may pass into lawes." But the Council's bluff took an unexpected turn, for the House committee cited the actions and records of "former Assemblyes" and observed that the burgesses "have no less power nor cause to make the like laws." The next day, on the question of whether to regulate or totally eject lawyers, the House "resolved, By the first vote. An ejection."[41]

A few days later the House resolved that the councillors be denied their usual allowance of two hundred pounds of tobacco for attendance at assemblies and quarter sessions, that the burgesses be paid out of the county levies, and that officers of the government be paid from the receipts of a two-shilling-per-hogshead export tax on tobacco rather than continuing "the inequality of raiseing taxes per poll." These provisions transferred some of the burden of taxation to the merchants from the populace at large, and made the councillors, governor, and secretary dependent for their salaries upon the effective collection of the export tax on tobacco, while charging the burgesses' salaries to the colony--where they were sure to be paid-- rather than to the individual counties. The House also reclaimed the authority of appointing members of the county court, which previous assemblies had repeatedly delegated to the governor and Council with the claim that the delegation was "not presidentiall to any succeeding Assembly."[42]

On 1 April 1658 (the day after a committee of burgesses had taken their revisal of the laws to the governor "to advise with him and his councill about the explanation or altering of any seeming difficulties or inconveniencyes, Yet with this lymitation not to assent to any thing of consequence without the approbation of the House") the governor and Council threw down the gauntlet. Mathews, Claiborne, and eight councillors sent this letter to the House:

> The Governour and Councill for many important causes do think fitt hereby to declare, That they do now dissolve this present Assembly, And that the Speaker accordingly do dismiss the Burgesses.

The burgesses' reply was firm, but polite: "The House humbly presenteth, That the said disolution as the case now standeth is not presidentall neither legall according to the lawes, now in force." "Therefore," the reply continued, "wee humbly desire a revocation of the said declaration, especially seeing wee doubt not but speedily to finish the present affaires to the satisfaction of your honour and the whole country."[43]

The House of Burgesses gave the governor and Council a face-saving opportunity to abandon their effort to dissolve the House--a last chance to avoid confronting the constitutional issue they had raised. Having met with principled resistance from the House of Burgesses, the governor and Council might have agreed that since the business of the assembly was nearly complete they would withdraw their order to dissolve the House. Such a course would have left the constitutional issue nicely muddled so that it might be raised another day when it might be asserted and carried: ripeness is all. Had the governor and Council retreated under cover of a vaguely evasive statement, they might have lost no ground. Instead, they refused to let the constitutional question go unanswered and, refusing to bend, they were crushed.

On 2 April Mathews and Claiborne sent the Council's reply to the House. It began with words of conciliation: "Upon your assurance of a speedy issue to conclude the acts so near brought to a confirmation in this Assembly, wee are willing to come to a speedy conclusion." The fact that the reply did not stop here suggests that someone of the Council was angry and wanted to press the issue. The remaining phrases of the reply smack of an ill-considered compromise reached, probably, after a long debate between some angry and assertive councillors (such as Claiborne) and some reticent or cautious ones. Probably the sides

were evenly matched, and the young governor and his
councillors were unable to agree whether to press or drop
the issue. "And," the Council's reply concluded, "to
referre the dispute of the power of disolving and the
legality thereof to his Highnesse the Lord Protector."[44]

Of course, it is possible that the Council's suggestion
was not an ill-considered, last-minute attempt to find a
compromise. It may have been an attempt to trick the
House into recognizing another--Cromwell's--external
limitation on its claim to independence so that the
House's decision to call off the activities against Baltimore
could be rescinded. Instead, the burgesses stood their
ground and declared themselves "unanimously of opinion
that the answer returned is unsatisfactory." They proposed
another moderate course, "That the Governour and Councill
please to declare[:] The House remaines undissolved that a
speedy period may be putt to the publique affaires."[45]

Mathews and the Council had failed to recognize the
House's jealousy about its claims of independence and
sovereignty. Although, like Bennett and Digges, Mathews
was allied with the merchant-councillor faction led by
Claiborne and his father, unlike his interregnum predecessors,
Mathews and his council had attempted to push their authority farther than it was likely to go. And the members
of the House were somewhat more likely to resist than their
predecessors may have been. Virginia's political alignments

were defined by factors other than the allegiances of the
Civil War, but English politics had a place in the colony.
If the choice of Speakers suggests something about the
complexion of the House, then the election of Francis
Moryson in 1656 and Francis Dade (who used the alias John
Smith) in 1658 suggest that the House of Burgesses no longer supported the interregnum governors as it had when
Edward Major and Thomas Dew had presided over the assemblies
in 1652. Smith, whose name appears on all the House's
replies to Mathews and Claiborne in 1658, is thought to
have come to Virginia early in the 1650s and taken his
alias in order to escape prosecution for his participation
in an unknown royalist plot. Land records associate his
name with other royalist immigrants such as Sir Henry
Chicheley, Colonel Richard Lee, and Jenkin Price (the trader
whom Berkeley had sent to rescue royalist officers Francis
Moryson and Henry Norwood after they had fled England in
1649 and shipwrecked off the Eastern Shore). It is difficult
to imagine a Speaker less likely to agree to the Council's
suggestion to refer the question--any question--to Cromwell.[46]

But the House's stand in the face of the Council's
challenge derived, at bottom, neither from English politics
or personal animosities. Regardless of how the conflict
had begun, the issue had become nothing less than the
constitution of the colony and the place of the House of
Burgesses in that constitution. As early as the constitutive

assembly of 1652, the House of Burgesses had described itself as "the representative of the people." The crisis of 1658 tested that claim of popular sovereignty, and the House's conduct during the crisis demonstrated the strength of its traditions--the mature resiliance of a self-consciously English lower house of assembly.[47]

The House of Burgesses had been prepared for battle from the beginning. At the same time that it had made its first answer to the Council's order to dissolve, the House had resolved "unanimously, That no Burgess [leave the House] and if any shall depart, That he shall be censured as a person betraying the trust reposed in him by his country." The burgesses had also agreed "to act in all things and to all intents and purposes as a whole and entire house, And Further, That Mr. Speaker signe nothing without the consent of the major part of the house." Finally, all the burgesses swore an oath of secrecy, vowing not to "repeate nor discover the present or future transactions, debates or discourses . . . in the House to any person or persons whatsoever except to a Burgesse of this Assembly. . . . So help you God and the contents of this Booke."[48]

When the House of Burgesses received Mathews and Claiborne's second message (the 2 April letter revoking the dissolution but claiming to refer the dispute to Cromwell) its response was sweeping and forceful.

"Unsatisfied with these answers," the House appointed a seven-man committee "to draw up a report for manifestation and vindication of the Assembly's power," and authorized the committee to prepare "all such propositions as any way tend to concerne the settling the present affaires of the country and government." First, the committee determined that, "by the records, The present power of government" was held in trust by "such persons as shall be impowered by the Burgesses (the representatives of the people) who are not dissolvable by any power now extant in Virginia, but the House of Burgesses." Perhaps the words <u>now extant</u> were meant to call the king to mind; in any event the committee recommended that Mathews be retained as governor and that a "Councill be nominated, appointed and confirmed by the present Burgesses."[49]

The House's first step was to expand its committee's report. Pointing to "the many letts [i.e., hindrances] and obstructions in the affaires of this Assembly" as evidence "that some persons of the present councell endeavor by setting up their own power to destroy the apparent power resident only in the burgesses, representatives of the people, as is manifest by the records of the Assembly," the burgesses issued their declaration

> That we have in our selves the full power of the election and appointment of all officers in this country untill

> such time as wee shall have order
> to the contrary from the supreme
> power in England, All which is
> evident upon the Assembly records.

But mere words—even the strong words of a public declaration backed by the weight of demonstrable precedent—were not enough.[50]

Accordingly, the House's second step was "for the better manifestation thereof." The House declared, in a proclamation signed by its Speaker, "that we are not dissolvable by any power yet extant in Virginia but our owne," and—to prove their claim—"that all former election of Governour and Councill be void and null." The governor and Council had made illegitimate claims of authority, so the burgesses threw the bastards out. The conflict, however, turned on questions related to legitimate constitutional authority and sovereignty, however, and the House's objective was only to win that confrontation, not to conduct a palace revolution. Furthermore, the House recognized that Claiborne and other councillors, not the young governor, had been responsible for the Council's conduct. Therefore, the House's declaration conferred "the power of governour for the future" on Mathews, "who by us shall be invested with all the just rights and priviledges belonging to the Governour and Capt. General of Virginia." Finally, the declaration announced the House's intention to appoint a Council, and stipulated that "for the future none bee admitted a councellor but such who shall be nominated, appointed and confirmed by the house of Burgesses as aforesaid." By nightfall on 2 April 1658, Virginia had no councillors.[51]

But again, of course, mere words in a declaration were not enough. The House's third step was the issuance of private orders (probably dispatched at the same time as the public declaration was made) to enforce its position. One order, "in the name of his Highnesse the Lord Protector," directed Captain Robert Ellison, high sheriff of James City County and sergeant of arms of the assembly, "not to act or execute any warrant, precept or command directed to you from any other power or person then the Speaker of this hon'ble House." Another directed William Claiborne, "late secretarie of state forthwith [to] surrender and deliver the records of the country into the hands of the Speaker." Sergeant at arms Ellison went to command Claiborne's compliance, and burgesses John Carter and Warham Horsmenden (who had been members of the committee appointed to search the records in order to vindicate the assembly's power) were authorized to receive the records in behalf of the House, "and for such records as they shall receive to give . . . Claiborne a full receipt and discharge."[52]

The next day, 3 April, Carter and Horsmenden's committee delivered to Governor Mathews the oath that he and the members of the new Council were to take, and Mathews presented the House of Burgesses "a list of those he desired to be of his Councill." Nathaniel Bacon and Francis Willis, both of York County, were denied seats on the reconstituted Council. Claiborne (as secretary), Thomas Pettus, of James City, Obedience Robins, of Northampton, William Bernard, of Isle of Wight, and George Reade, of York, were reappointed to the Council after they swore to uphold "the knowne laws of England or acts of Assembly which are or shall be in force." Seven other councillors were appointed by the House, but evidently not present to take the oath. Finally, three members of the House--the two committeemen Carter and Horsmenden, and Anthony Elliott, of Gloucester County--also were named to the Council, with the provision that they were "not to be sworne untill the dissolution of the Assembly."[53]

Carter, Horsmenden, and Elliott served as watchdog members of the Council until the next meeting of the House of Burgesses, at which time they returned as burgesses and were active in the affairs of the House. That they did not simultaneously continue as councillors is evident from the House's resolution of 15 March 1659, that their continuation as watchdog councillors was subject to "a new election." As the records of the assembly of 1659 are incomplete, we have evidence only of the House's intention to confirm these members by a new election. Presumably the three burgesses returned to the Council after the assembly of 1659 had risen, and presumably their continuation demonstrates the House of Burgesses' concern lest the 1658 victory be subverted.[54]

The House's jealousy appears in the records of the assembly of 1659, too. When news of Oliver Cromwell's death and Richard Cromwell's succession as Lord Protector was announced in a letter from Henry Lawrence, president of the Protector's council, the letter was read in the chamber of the House of Burgesses in the presence of Governor Mathews and the Council on the afternoon of 8 March 1659. When the House resolved to take time to consider the letter, "the Governor and Councill departed." The burgesses then agreed to the portions of the letter that required obedience to Richard Cromwell and adjourned until the next morning.[55]

On the ninth the House again summoned Mathews to its chamber, "to be satisfied from the Governour's owne expressions," that "he acknowledged the supream power of electing officers to be by the present lawes resident in the Grand Assembly, And that he would joyne his best assistance with the countrey in makeing an addresse to his Highnesse for confirmation of their present privileges, And that for this reason, That what was their privilege now might be his or their posterities hereafter." The 1659 assembly also reminded Secretary Claiborne of his rightful place: after requiring him to acknowledge that he had "received [his office] from the Assembly," the House of Burgesses confirmed his appointment until its next meeting.[56]

Thus, the constitutional crisis of 1658 had forced the House of Burgesses to make a clear declaration of its institutional privilege and a forceful political affirmation of its sovereignty, both of which derived from the House of Burgesses' role as "the representative of the people." During the 1650s the House of Burgesses had come to terms with its own history and found vitality in its own precedents. The House had learned to be jealous of its own privilege and independence, and it had forced its rivals to recognize its claims and to share its vision "that what was their privilege now might be . . . their posterities hereafter." No matter what theoretical changes might come, such lessons in practical politics were not forgotten when a king replaced a lord protector.[57]

Epilogue

THE RESTORATION, AND AFTER

Sixteen fifty-nine drew to a close with perhaps twenty-seven thousand inhabitants living in seventeen Virginia counties. The colony's General Assembly was four decades old. Compared to Maryland or England, Virginia's experience during the two decades since the beginning of Wyatt's second administration in 1639 had been relatively calm. The basic institutional pattern that had emerged early in the 1640s--governor, bicameral assembly, county courts, and parish vestries--was intact and generally stable. Power had changed hands without bloodshed, and authority had been redefined with the pen. Within a year Virginians would be able to see that they had successfully avoided chaos, and within a few years a Virginian would be able to look back with confidence and write "that the strings of Government are always kept in tune."[1]

For the moment, however, most of Virginia's inhabitants --like most of their contemporaries in England and on the Continent--saw only more danger before them. The words of a sermon delivered to the House of Commons in 1643 still jangled: "these are days of shaking . . . and this shaking is universal." Lord Protector Oliver Cromwell had died on 3 September 1658, leaving his son Richard as his successor. But after a short-lived period of popularity the new protector's limitations became evident to all. "He was fearful and unresolved," Sir Richard Baker wrote, "of a spirit unbecoming the quality he assumed; and many of those about him were as irresolute as he . . . and, as it happens in the consultations of fearful people, they debated many things fit to be done, till the time was past to put them into execution." He abdicated in May 1659, and word of his abdication probably reached Virginia early in summer. None in England could predict what would happen--and when it did, word would travel slowly across the Atlantic to Virginia where, perhaps, distance compounded uncertainty. By January 1660 Virginians had probably learned of the unsuccessful royalist rising led by Sir George Booth and of the expulsion of the Rump by John Lambert and the army officers. They probably knew that Charles Stuart was yet on the Continent and that George Monck was yet in Scotland, and perhaps they had heard the newly coined facetious adage, "as certain as England."[2]

Then came the death in January 1660 of Governor Samuel Mathews, Jr. Surely Mathews's death and the vacancy it caused were unsettling, but there is no surviving evidence from which to reconstruct the events of February 1660. By an act of the last assembly, the quarter court was not scheduled to meet until 20 March. Surviving land records, which seem to be relatively

complete, give no evidence of patents or grants issued
between 24 September 1659 and 22 March 1660, and in the
General Court records he examined in 1830 (now lost)
Conway Robinson found "no entry of later date" than 12 June
1658 during the Interregnum. Robinson found evidence
that Sir William Berkeley "was acting as governor Augt 4.
1660" on page 64 of the "book marked No 2 1660 to 1664,"
but left only cryptic notes of what he may have seen on
pages 1 through 63.[3]

An assembly met on 13 March 1660, perhaps having been
convened according to one or another of the means
described by the 1659 statute "concerning conveneing of
Assemblies"--perhaps in February the secretary had issued
writs for the elections of burgesses, or, failing that,
perhaps each county sheriff had "by his owne power to
convene the people (by the 20th of February)" conducted
elections. In any case, forty-seven burgesses met on
13 March at Jamestown.[4]

In the crisis of 1658 the House of Burgesses had
declared itself to be "the supreame power of this country
of Virginia," but had also referred occasionally to "the
supreame power in England." But now it was impossible
for anyone to know whether there was a sovereign power
in England. The assembly of 1660 lamented that "by
reason of the late frequent distractions," England had
"noe resident absolute and gen[era]ll confessed power."

What was to be done when, as Sir William Berkeley phrased it, the English lacked any person or institution with "a publiquely confessed politique capacity to be a Supreame power"? These questions were carefully and fretfully worded concerns voiced by men who sought, for the moment, neither to raise a parliamentary nor a royal pennant, but merely to stay afloat amid a political gale in which they knew not' whither the winds would blow. In fact, of course, one senses in these questions the concerns of one's fellow citizens in the post-medieval West.[5]

Not choice, the Virginians agreed, but "necessitie forceth us (during these distractions) to declare some power, Under which this collonie may be settled." Few anywhere in the English-speaking world of 1660 countenanced anarchy, and one does not overstate the case to observe that the difference between the burgesses' declarations of 1658 and those of 1660 were profound. In 1658 they were confident in the face of a known adversary that they claimed practical supremacy in Virginia, but in 1660 they were desperate in their recognition that events had forced them to become, for themselves and their neighbors, the supreme temporal authority in the universe. In outward respects, of course, the burgesses spanned this intellectual chasm with a pragmatic structure of political institutions and familiar practice, but one cannot have understood the structure or the builders until one paused at the abyss.[6]

Having agreed "to take the government into their owne power . . . till such lawfull comission or comissions appear to us as we may dutifully submit to," and to punish any disaffected persons whose idle words or actions might threaten civil order, the House of Burgesses asked former governor Sir William Berkeley to return to office on these terms: First, he was to govern according to the laws of England and Virginia. Second, all writs were to issue in the name of the "Grand Assembly of Virginia." Third, he was to convene the assembly at least biennially. Fourth, he was allowed to choose his secretary and Council "with the approbation of the Assembly." And fifth, he was not to dissolve the assembly "without consent of the major part of the House."[7]

Documents related to Berkeley's election to the governorship were carefully preserved, probably by the Speaker and a committee of the House, and survive in the form of seventeenth-century manuscript copies once owned by Thomas Jefferson and now preserved in the Library of Congress.[8] After the House had offered the governorship to Berkeley, he sent a long and eloquent letter to "Mr. Speaker, and the rest of my Hon'd Friends the Burgesses." Dated "from my House March 19th," Berkeley's letter formally declined the honor in terms that had, at once, similarities to the familiar disabling speech of a Speaker-elect of the House of Commons and a sense of genuine caution and doubt about his own abilities and about the situation that faced Virginia. In the end, Berkeley said, "What I am truly, is thine and my poor country's to command."[9]

"He that is not transported with soe high honours as you have showne me," Berkeley's letter began, "doth not deserve them; and indeed they have bin soe great that they are able to make a soberer and modester man then I, proud, but I have this allay to qualify that riseing passion, to believe that it is rather a mercifull aspect on my former endeavors to serve you than a strict intuition and contemplation of my present abilities." After rehearsing the occurrences since he had first come to Virginia in 1642 and reminding the burgesses that he had "lived most resigningly submissive" under the Interregnum government, Berkeley reviewed the desperate problem that his beloved colony faced: "If you had told me, Mr. Speaker, what this Supreame power was, or had denoted to me the Ensignes by which I might know him, you had quickly had my assent or negative. But indeed I want the Spirit of Prophecy to offitiate to me what this Supreame power in time may bee, which for ought I know, is as indefinite as the persons of booth sexes in England are."[10]

Berkeley wanted three doubts resolved before he

would accept the office and reenter public life in the colony. First, he worried about what would happen if the forces of Parliament regained control of England, "under whose displeasure and power," he said, ". . . I should never voluntarie put my selfe." Second, he worried about how Charles II, should he resume the throne, would take news of his return to office: "To assume a power under a Spirituall Supreame power," he said in a careful reference to Charles Stuart, "without his assent" was dangerous. "Wee may think, Mr. Speaker, we act innocently and necessarily in many of our emergencies," but if Charles II, "the power we once acknowledged," returned to the throne and on the basis of an unfriendly report meted out severe punishment to the disaffected, Berkeley wondered, "in what condition are we that the Difference of an independent partie even to extremitie is much more justifiable than the resistance of an acknowledging subject for a short time"?[11]

Third, Berkeley doubted that if he were to accept the office he would have the support of all the Council-- could he long survive in office if the House were to pass over Bennett? or Claiborne? "Show me but an honorable path," he suggested, "and if . . . I walke not in it, exclude me forever from your good opinions." Then he backed off a little before returning to the point: "Mr. Speaker, since you have thought me worthy . . . I presume to interpose my advice to you, which is, that you make choice of one, who hath more vigorous qualities to manage and support your affaires, and who hath more dexteritie to untie those knotts which I can neither unloose nor break amongst the Councill." Although he doubted his old merchant-planter rivals on the Council, he praised the House. "There are many in your own body," he continued, "which I dare not name, because it were an injury to give to any (soe equally worthie) precedence, though it were but in the Catalogue of their names." The letter is a masterpiece of statecraft; it closed by giving "the honorable House most humble Thanks for their intended munificence," and by declining the office in words that invited the House to meet his terms: "I should be worthily thought hospitall mad, if I would not change povertie for wealthy,--contempt for honor: But many urgent reasons obstruct the way of thos desired assents. But it is now time to begg pardon for troubling you thus long. Your Most Humble and Affectionate Friend and Servant, William Berkeley."[12]

Berkeley knew that he was negotiating from strength and that the House could force the Council to comply. The pragmatic political utility of a bicameral constitution was as useful to the governor in 1660 as it had been in 1642, and his letter had the desired effect. The House had the councillors sign a statement of support on

21 March--"Wee do unanimously concurr in the Election of
Sr. William Berkeley to be the present Governour of this
Colony"--and then ordered that Berkeley have the "free
liberty of treating with them, And that his letter and
their subscription approving his election be recorded."
The House's concern for precedents and record-keeping as
tools of order and stability brought, in effect, a
contractual agreement: the negotiations in which Berkeley
accepted the office of governor were fixed in writing
and copied into records that were used throughout the
seventeenth and early eighteenth centuries.[13]

Probably it was on 21 or 22 March that Sir William
Berkeley formally accepted election as governor, in two
speeches that he asked to have recorded along with the
other documents. "Wee have all had great and pressing
feares of offending a Supreame power which neither by
present possession is soe, nor yet has a publiquely
confessed politique capacity to be a Supreame power," he
told the House of Burgesses. "I alsoe, Mr. Speaker,
have my pressing feares too, and am seriously afraid to
offend him, who by all Englishmen is confessed to be in
a naturall politique capacity of being a Supreame power.
I have bin once already outed by a Supreame power; I
doe therefore in the presence of God and you make this
safe protestation for us all, that if any Supreame settled
power appeares, I will imediately lay down my comission."

In the 1640s Berkeley had promoted the establishment of a bicameral assembly in order to protect himself, now with the House of Burgesses firmly behind him, Berkeley addressed the Council, eloquently requesting their support. "You have given me a great Treasure but in vaine," he said, "except you help me carry it to a place of safetie; you have raised a high expectation of me, but you must instruct and prompt me how to satisfye it; you have layd high honours on me, but except you helpe to supporte me under them, they will sink me into disgrace." He asked them to join in his own deeply felt prayer "that this admirable Harmony of consents . . . may be ominous and exemplary to our nation, that peace may at last returne to our long afflicted, miserable, distracted Country: and let every one say, Amen."[14]

Berkeley's Amen echoed in many hearts that spring, on either side of the Atlantic. In May the Convention Parliament proclaimed Charles II and he returned to London. On 17 June Charles issued his warrant for a commission, and on 31 July he signed letters patent granting Berkeley as full and ample power "as any Governour and Councill there resident at any time within the space of thirty yeares now last past, had or might perform." Nothing was changed--but everything was changed: Virginians quickly looked away from the void they had surmounted, quickly abandoned the dizzying claims of sovereignty with which the House of Burgesses had bridged the chasm, when word of the Restoration reached them early that fall. Charles II was proclaimed king amid great celebration. One county paid 500 and another 800 pounds of tobacco for trumpeters. York County celebrated with volleys that consumed a barrel of powder, and healths that required 176 gallons of cider. Probably even the merchant-councillors had cause to rejoice--their navigation acts became the basis of English mercantilism. In October the General Assembly revised Virginia's code to eliminate all references to the Protectorate, and to replace them with the name of the king.[15]

Save for the restitution of royal authority as the basis of order in place of the ad hoc popular sovereignty of the 1650s, Virginia's mixed constitution, born in 1643 and matured in the decades since, continued without change. Virginia, as John Ogilby reported in 1671, was governed by a royal governor and Council, and her laws were made "by the Governor, with the consent of a General Assembly, which consists of two Houses, an Upper and a Lower; the first consists of the Council and the latter of the Burgesses chosen by the Freemen of the Countrey." In the half century that separated Sir William Berkeley from Captain John Smith--the half century that stands at the beginning of American political history--Englishmen created a society and a political system and a province called Virginia. They created, both through acts of will and through the countless day-to-day events that weave the fabric of a society, a social order, a strong system of local government, a mature and sophisticated House of Burgesses, a sagacious civilian governor, and a stable Council. Virginia's "verie maine matter" had been to discover a successful form of government and by 1660 it had done so. The desperate outpost had survived what Captain John Smith called "the infancy of a common-weale," and had become the king's "auntient Collonie of Virginia."[16]

SHORT TITLES
and Abbreviations

Adventurers — Annie Lash Jester and Martha Woodroof Hiden, comps., *Adventurers of Purse and Person: Virginia 1607-1625*, 2d ed. [Princeton, N.J.], 1964).

Andrews, *Colonial Period* — C. M. Andrews, *Colonial Period of American History*, 4 vols. (New Haven and London, 1934-1938).

Bemiss, *Three Charters* — Samuel M. Bemiss, ed., *The Three Charters of the Virginia Company of London With Seven Related Documents: 1606-1621*, Jamestown 350th Anniversary Historical Booklets (Williamsburg, 1957).

C.O. — Colonial Office, Public Record Office, London. Material in the Public Record Office and other British repositories as compiled on microfilm in the Virginia Colonial Records Project.

Craven, *Dissolution* — Wesley Frank Craven, *Dissolution of the Virginia Company: The Failure of a Colonial Experiment* (New York, 1932).

Craven, *Southern Colonies* — Wesley Frank Craven, *The Southern Colonies in the Seventeenth Century,1607-1689*, Wendell Holmes Stephenson and E. Merton Coulter, eds., *A History of the South* (Baton Rouge, 1949, 1970).

General Assembly Register	Cynthia Miller Leonard, comp., *The General Assembly of Virginia, July 30, 1619-January 11, 1978: A Bicentennial Register of Members* (Richmond, 1978).
Hening, *Statutes*	William Waller Hening, ed., *The Statutes at Large: Being a Collection of all the Laws of Virginia, from the First Session of the Legislature in the Year 1619* . . . (Richmond, Philadelphia, and New York, 1809-1823).
JHB	Henry Read McIlwaine, ed., *Journals of the House of Burgesses of Virginia, 1619-1659/60* (Richmond, 1915).
MCGC	Henry Read McIlwaine, ed., *Minutes of the Council and General Court of Colonial Virginia*, 2d ed. with supplementary material and introduction by Jon Kukla (Richmond, 1979).
Morgan, *American Slavery--American Freedom*	Edmund S. Morgan, *American Slavery--American Freedom: The Ordeal of Colonial Virginia* (New York, 1975).
Morton, *Colonial Virginia*	Richard L. Morton, *Colonial Virginia* (Chapel Hill, 1960).
OED	*Oxford English Dictionary*
Van Schreeven and Reese, *Proceedings*	William J. Van Schreeven and George Reese, eds., *Proceedings of the General Assembly of Virginia, July 30-August 4, 1619, Written & Sent from Virginia to England by Mr. John Pory, Speaker of the First Representative Assembly in the New World* (Jamestown, 1969).

Va. Co. Recs.	Susan Myra Kingsbury, ed., <u>Records of the Virginia Company of London</u>, 4 vols. (Washington, D.C., 1906-1935).
VMHB	<u>Virginia Magazine of History and Biography</u>
VSL	Virginia State Library
WMQ	<u>William and Mary Quarterly</u>

NOTES

PREFACE

1. The bibliography of early Virginia is extensive. For printed material a student should consult E. G. Swem, John M. Jennings, and James A. Servies, A Selected Bibliography of Virginia, 1607-1699, Jamestown 350th Anniversary Historical Booklets (Williamsburg, 1957); Donald Haynes, ed., Virginiana in the Printed Book Collections of the Virginia State Library (Richmond, 1975); Wesley Frank Craven's essay on authorities in his Southern Colonies in the Seventeenth Century, 1607-1689, Wendell Holmes Stephenson and E. Merton Coulter, eds., A History of the South (Baton Rouge, 1949, 1970); and the Virginia Magazine of History and Biography (1893-) and William and Mary Quarterly [title varies] (1892-).
   For manuscript material a student should exhaust the resources of the Virginia Historical Society, Richmond; the Manuscript Department and Rare Book Room of the Alderman Library of the University of Virginia, Charlottesville; the Virginia State Library, Richmond; and the Virginia Colonial Records Project. The last is a microfilming project described in The British Public Record Office: History, Description, Record Groups, Finding Aids, and Materials for American History, with Special Reference to Virginia, Virginia State Library Publications No. 12 (Richmond, 1960); the microfilm is available to researchers at the three repositories mentioned, as well as the Research Department of the Colonial Williamsburg Foundation, Inc., and by loan from the Alderman and Virginia State libraries. Important manuscript material, much of which has been published, is also in the Library of Congress, Washington, D.C.; see especially E. Millicent Sowerby, Catalogue of the Library of Thomas Jefferson.

2. Pierre Goubert, "Historical Demography and the Reinterpretation of Early Modern French History: A Research Review," in Theodore K. Rabb and Robert I. Rotberg, eds., The Family in History: Interdisciplinary Essays (New York, 1973), 16-27.

3. Wesley Frank Craven, White, Red, and Black: The Seventeenth-Century Virginian (Charlottesville, 1971), 77; Winthrop D. Jordan, White Over Black: American

Attitudes toward the Negro, 1550-1812 (Chapel Hill, 1968).

4. Larry R. Gerlach and Michael L. Nicholls, "The Mormon Genealogical Society and Research Opportunities in Early American History," WMQ, 3d ser., 32(1975): 625-629; British Public Record Office. . . With Special Reference to Virginia. For an antebellum inventory of Virginia General Court records lost in 1865 see my preface and appendix A to H. R. McIlwaine, ed., Minutes of the Council and General Court of Colonial Virginia, 2d ed. (Richmond, 1979), vii-viii, 537-544.

5. Craven, Southern Colonies, 427; Craven, "And so the Form of Government Became Perfect," VMHB 77 (1969): 131-145.

6. Wertenbaker, Patrician and Plebeian in Virginia; or, the Origin and Development of the Social Classes of the Old Dominion (Charlottesville, 1910), 220-228; Wertenbaker, Give Me Liberty: The Struggle for Self-Government in Virginia (Philadelphia, 1958). See also David Levin, History as Romantic Art: Bancroft, Prescott, Motley, and Parkman (Stanford, Calif., 1959).

7. The fullest examination of McIlwaine's colonial scholarship is my preface to McIlwaine, ed., Legislative Journals of the Council of Colonial Virginia, 2d ed. (Richmond, 1979). See also Craven, "And so the Form of Government Became Perfect."

8. Thomas Nelson Page quoted in L. C. Helderman, "A Satirist in Old Virginia," American Scholar 6 (1937): 490. Barbour, The Three Worlds of Captain John Smith (Boston, 1964); Lee Congdon, "The Hungarian Pocahontas: Laura Polanyi Striker," VMHB 86 (1978): 275-280. Darrett B. Rutman, "The Virginia Company and Its Military Regime," in Rutman, ed., The Old Dominion: Essays for Thomas Perkins Abernethy (Charlottesville, 1964), 1-20; Rutman, "The Historian and the Marshall: A Note on the Background of Sir Thomas Dale," VMHB 68 (1960): 284-294. Craven, Dissolution of the Virginia Company: The Failure of a Colonial Experiement (New York, 1932), 1-23, quoted at 15, 20, 21; Craven, "And so the Form of Government Became Perfect." Wilcomb E. Washburn, The Governor and the Rebel: A History of Bacon's Rebellion in Virginia (Chapel Hill, 1957), 1-16,

153-166; Jane Carson, Bacon's Rebellion, 1676-1976 (Jamestown, Va., 1976).

9. Craven, Southern Colonies, 138-182, 224-309; Greene, The Quest for Power: The Lower Houses of Assembly in the Southern Royal Colonies, 1689-1776 (Chapel Hill, 1963), 26-28.

10. Charles McLean Andrews, The Colonial Period of American History; 1 (New Haven and London, 1934): 150-213; cf. below, 182n12.

11. Morton, Colonial Virginia (Chapel Hill, 1960), 1-199. Thornton, "The Thrusting Out of Governor Harvey: A Seventeenth-Century Rebellion," VMHB 75 (1968):11-26. Washburn, Virginia Under Charles I and Cromwell, 1625-1660 (Williamsburg, 1957), 21-29.

12. Billings, "Growth of Political Institutions in Virginia, 1634 to 1676," WMQ, 3d ser. 31 (1974): 225-242.

13. J. R. Pole, The Seventeenth Century: The Sources of Legislative Power, Jamestown Essays on Representation (Charlottesville, 1969), 64. This and other insights are discussed at greater length in Pole's important Political Representation in England and the Origins of the American (London, 1966). Washburn, Virginia Under Charles I and Cromwell, 17; Sigmund Diamond, "From Organization to Society: Virginia in the Seventeenth Century," American Journal of Sociology 63 (1958):457-475; Edmund S. Morgan, American Slavery--American Freedom: The Ordeal of Colonial Virginia (New York, 1975), 143. Morgan's brief account of the founding of Virginia's General Assembly will not bear close scrutiny; at a critical point in his argument (ibid., 144) chronology and actors are shuffled, unwittingly, in a passive-voice construction.

14. Bernard Bailyn, "Politics and Social Structure in Virginia," in James Morton Smith, ed., Seventeenth-Century America: Essays in Colonial History (Chapel Hill, 1959), 90-115. Probably some of the enormous influence of this essay is attributable to its tidy fit with Bailyn's Origins of American Politics, The Charles K. Colver Lectures, Brown University, 1965 (New York, 1968) and his Ideological Origins of the American Revolution (Cambridge, Mass., 1967).

15. Bailyn, "Politics and Social Structure," 90, 108. Apparently Bailyn relied on Annie Lash Jester and Martha Woodroof Hiden's Adventurers of Purse and Person: Virginia 1607-1625 ([Princeton], 1956, 2d ed., 1964) without fully realizing that the strict genealogical criteria used to determine the inclusion of individual sketches could leave a false impression of the second generation. The book was published by the Order of First Families of Virginia, 1607-1624. Descent from late-comers such as the Byrds, the Carters, the Custises, the Lees, the Tayloes, the Tuckers, or the Wormeleys is not sufficient for membership, and the ancestors of these distinguished eighteenth-century families do not appear in the Order's book. On the other hand, biographical information about these third-generation ancestors is readily available in studies of the eighteenth-century elite such as Louis B. Wright, The First Gentlemen of Virginia: Intellectual Qualities of the Early Colonial Ruling Class (San Marino, Calif., 1940). Brief biographical sketches of a number of second-generation leaders will be available in my pamphlet Speakers and Clerks of the Virginia House of Burgesses, Virginia State Library Publications No. 48 (Richmond, forthcoming).

    The full implications of Bailyn's essay are evident in the exchange between Bailyn and Jack P. Greene in the American Historical Review 75 (1969): 337-367 in which both agree that it is not necessary to look before the 1670s for the American roots of American politics. See also Greene, "Changing Interpretations of Early American Politics," in Ray Allen Billington, ed., The Reinterpretation of Early American History: Essays in honor of John Edwin Pomfret (San Marino, Calif., 1966), 167-177; and Jon Kukla, "Politics and Society in Virginia, 1630-1650" (Paper delivered at the Ninety-fourth Annual Meeting of the American Historical Association, New York, 29 December 1979).

16. Bailyn, "Politics and Social Structure," 100; cf., Louis B. Wright, ed., Letters of Robert Carter, 1720-1727: The Commercial Interests of a Virginia Gentleman (San Marino, Calif., 1940), vi-vii.

17. Hobbes, English Works, ed. Sir William Molesworth (London, 1843), 8: viii; R. G. Collingwood, Idea of History (Oxford, 1946).

18. The summary of the consensus of recent scholarship is in George Dargo, Roots of the Republic: A New

Perspective on Early American Constitutionalism (New York, 1974), 146-147. The literature of New England puritanism and of early American republicanism is vast; one might begin with Perry Miller, Errand Into the Wilderness (Cambridge, Mass., 1956); Bailyn, Ideological Origins of the American Revolution; and Gordon S. Wood, Creation of the American Republic, 1776-1787 (Chapel Hill, 1969). On Madison's recovery of an inherently Aristotelian viewpoint from David Hume see Douglass G. Adair, "That Politics May Be Reduced to a Science: David Hume, James Madison, and the Tenth Federalist," Huntington Library Quarterly 20 (1957):343-360. Winthrop's comment is in Allyn Forbes, ed., Winthrop Papers (Boston, 1929-1947), 4:360; see also below p. 92. Reinhold Niebuhr, The Children of Light and The Children of Darkness: A Vindication of Democracy and a Critique of its Traditional Defence (New York, 1944, 1960), 119-152 (quoted at pp. 124, 152); see also C. Vann Woodward, "The Irony of Southern History," in his The Burden of Southern History (Baton Rouge, 1960).

19. The debate over the crisis interpretation of early modern European history is described in Theodore K. Rabb, The Struggle for Stability in Early Modern Europe (New York, 1975). Perry Miller recognized the place that Virginia's General Assembly occupied in the colonists' minds in his "Religion and Society in the Early Literature of Virginia," WMQ, 3d ser., 6 (1949):41: "In a world where the ancient landmarks were fading, where the will of God was becoming ambiguous to man's reading, the one remaining certainty, the one institution which could plead at least the excuse of utility, was the organized rights of Englishmen, exercised and protected in an elective assembly."

CHAPTER 1

1. Robert Gray, A Good Speed to Virginia (London, 1609); Bemiss, Three Charters, 1.

2. Gray, Good Speed to Virginia.

3. Louis B. Wright, "Elizabethan Politics and Colonial Enterprise," North Carolina Historical Review 32 (1955):254-269.

4. David B. Quinn, "Sir Thomas Smith (1513-1577) and the Beginnings of English Colonial Theory," American Philosophical Society, Proceedings 89:543-560;

Howard Mumford Jones, "Origins of the Colonial Idea in England," ibid., 85:448-465.

5. Bemiss, *Three Charters*, 1, 14.

6. Philip L. Barbour, ed., *Jamestown Voyages Under the First Charter, 1606-1609* (London, 1969), 1:46, 54. An instance of the express use of Aristotelian categories in Virginia is John Rolfe's *A True Relation of the State of Virginia Lefte by Sir Thomas Dale Knight in May Laste 1616* (Charlottesville, 1971), 3-4: "Maie you please to take notice; that the begunning of this *Plantacion* was gouerned by a *President & Councell Aristocratycallie*. . . . This government lasted above two yeres: in which tyme such envie, dissentions and iarrs were daily sowen amongst them, that they *choaked* ye *seedes* and *blasted* the *fruits* of all mens labors. . . . Afterward a more absolute gouernment was graunted *Monarchally*, wherein it still contynueth." The Englishman's intellectual debt to Aristotle is evident, for example, in Sir Thomas Smith, *De Republica Anglorum* (1st ed., London, 1565), chap. 1 and ff.; and Sir Walter Raleigh, *Maxims of State* (London, 1650), 2-3 and ff. Sir Robert Filmer, arguing that classical authors had been ignorant of the Bible and therefore unaware that "the first government in the world was monarchical," lamented of his contemporaries that "what cannot be found in scripture, many do look for in Aristotle; for if there is any other form of government besides monarchy, he is the man best able to tell what it is, and to let us know by what name to call it. . . . The usual terms in this age of aristocracy and democracy are taken up from him to express forms of government most different from monarchy: we must therefore make inquiry into Aristotle touching these two terms"; Peter Laslett, ed., *Patriarcha and Other Political Works of Sir Robert Filmer* (Oxford, 1949), 187, 193. See also Corinne Comstock Weston, *English Constitutional Theory and the House of Lords, 1556-1832*, Columbia Studies in the Social Sciences, no. 607 (New York and London, 1965), 1-43; and J. G. A. Pocock, *The Machiavellian Moment: Florentine Political Thought and the Atlantic Republican Tradition* (Princeton, 1975), 3-30, 506-552.

7. Morton, *Colonial Virginia*, 7-31; Barbour, "Captain George Kendall: Mutineer or Intelligencer?" *VMHB* 70 (1962):297-313.

8. Morton, *Colonial Virginia*, 19-27; Morgan, *American*

Slavery--American Freedom, 78.

9. Barbour, Jamestown Voyages, 1:233; Darrett B. Rutman, "The Virginia Company and Its Military Regime," in Darrett B. Rutman, ed., The Old Dominion: Essays for Thomas Perkins Abernethy (Charlottesville, 1964), 4-9.

10. Rutman, "Military Regime," 4-10; Rutman, "The Historian and the Marshall: A Note on the Background of Sir Thomas Dale," VMHB 68 (1960):284-294; Dutch documents concerning Dale and Gates are printed in E. B. O'Callaghan, ed., Documents Relative to the Colonial History of the State of New-York (Albany, 1856), 1:1-21.

11. WMQ, 2d ser., 7 (1927):42-46, 207-208; Henry Hartwell, James Blair, and Edward Chilton, The Present State of Virginia, and the College, ed. Hunter Dickinson Farish (Charlottesville, 1940), 21, 34.

12. Va. Co. Recs., 3:13. On Machiavelli's use of the term lo stato as the pivotal concept in The Prince see J. H. Hexter, The Vision of Politics on the Eve of the Reformation: More, Machiavelli, and Seyssel (New York, 1973), 162-163, 224-228.

13. William Strachey's "A True Reportory of the Wreck and Redemption of Sir Thomas Gates, Knight," is printed in Louis B. Wright, ed., A Voyage to Virginia in 1609 (Charlottesville, 1964), 63-64.

14. Ibid., 77-87.

15. Ibid., 80-81.

16. Martin Wight, The Development of the Legislative Council, 1606-1945 (London, 1947), 23-40.

17. OED, s.v., governor, governor-general, president, and vice-gerent.

18. Ibid.; James I used vicegerent in several speeches, although in his written statements he more frequently used lieutenant; Political Works of James I, ed. Charles Howard McIlwain (Cambridge, Mass., 1918), 61, 151, 158, 281, 307, 327.

19. Alexander Brown, Genesis of the United States (Boston and New York, 1890), 1:376-384.

20. Bemiss, *Three Charters*, 58; Rutman, "Military Regime," 10.

21. For the social and political importance of ceremony, see Rhys Isaac, "Dramatizing the Ideology of Revolution: Popular Mobilization in Virginia, 1774 to 1776," *WMQ*, 3d ser., 33 (1976):364-367. See also *Va. Co. Recs.*, 3:13, 25-26; Wesley Frank Craven, "An Introduction to the History of Bermuda," *WMQ*, 2d ser., 17 (1937):202-205.

22. David H. Flaherty, ed., *For the Colony in Virginea Britannia Lawes Divine, Morall and Martial, etc. compiled by William Strachey* (Charlottesville, 1968), 4.

23. *Va. Co. Recs.*, 4:76; Timothy H. Breen, *The Character of the Good Ruler: A Study of Puritan Political Ideas in New England, 1630-1730* (New Haven and London, 1970), 1-34.

24. J. Frederick Fausz and Jon Kukla, eds., "A Letter of Advice to the Governor of Virginia, 1624," *WMQ*, 3d ser., 39 (1977):113; *OED*, s.v., wisdom; James 3:15 (AV). A useful survey of the advice-to-courtiers literature is John E. Mason, *Gentlefolk in the Making: Studies in the History of English Courtesy Literature and Related Topics from 1531 to 1774* (Philadelphia and London, 1935), chap. 8, "Seventeenth-Century Treatises on Policy." On the extent of sermon literature see Godfrey Davies, "English Political Sermons, 1603-1640," *Huntington Library Quarterly* 3(1939-1940):1-2.

25. "Politick religion" was the principal point at which Englishmen were likely to part company with Machiavelli; see Fausz and Kukla, "Letter of Advice," 109-110, and especially Felix Raab, *The English Face of Machiavelli: A Changing Interpretation 1500-1700* (London, 1964). For the language in which Englishmen did adopt Machiavelli's ideas see especially Napoleone Orsini, "'Policy' or the Language of Elizabethan Machiavellianism," *Journal of the Warburg and Courtauld Institutes* 9 (1946): 122-134, and also George L. Mosse, "The Assimilation of Machiavelli in English Thought: The Casuistry of William Perkins and William Ames," *Huntington Library Quarterly* 17 (1953-1954):315-326. *Works of Francis Bacon*, ed. James Spedding, Robert Leslie Ellis, and Douglas Denon Heath, 12(New York, 1872): 95-96. R. Dallington, *Aphorismes Civill and Militarie:*

Amplified with Authorities, and exemplified with Historie, out of the first Quarterne of Fr. Guicciardine 2d ed. (London, 1629), 227, 183.

26. Va. Co. Recs., 4:76; Fausz and Kukla, "Letter of Advice," 127, 113.

27. Good narrative accounts of the military regime include Morton, Colonial Virginia, 19-51; Andrews, Colonial Period, 1:107-116, 123-140; and Darrett B. Rutman, "A Militant New World, 1607-1640. . ." (Ph.D. diss., University of Virginia, 1959), 125-231.

28. Morgan, American Slavery--American Freedom, 82, 94; Andrews, Colonial Period, 1:124-125.

29. Craven, Dissolution, 44; Craven, Southern Colonies, 116-117; Irene W. D. Hecht, "The Virginia Colony, 1607-1640: A Study in Frontier Growth" (Ph.D. diss., University of Washington, 1969), 79.

30. Hecht, "Virginia Colony," 166, 186-188, 194.

31. Craven, Dissolution, 45-46.

32. Bemiss, Three Charters, 95.

33. Craven, Dissolution, 46-104.

34. Bemiss, Three Charters, 98.

35. J. P. Kenyon, Stuart England (London, 1978), 40.

36. Theodore K. Rabb, Enterprise and Empire: Merchant and Gentry Investment in the Expansion of England, 1575-1630 (Cambridge, Mass., 1967), 35-97; Ralph Hamor, A True Discourse of the Present State of Virginia (London, 1615), Virginia State Library Publications No. 3 (Richmond, 1957), 25.

37. John Rolfe, A True Relation of the State of Virginia Lefte by Sir Thomas Dale Knight in May Last 1616 (Charlottesville, 1971), 3; Edmund S. Morgan, "The Labor Problem at Jamestown, 1607-18," American Historical Review, 76 (1971):608; Sigmund Diamond, "From Organization to Society: Virginia in the Seventeenth Century," American Journal of Sociology 63 (1957-1958):459.

38. Howard Mumford Jones, O Strange New World: American

Culture: The Formative Years (New York, 1952), 125.

39. Morgan, American Slavery--American Freedom, 110-111.

40. Hecht, "Virginia Colony," 203.

41. Morton, Colonial Virginia, 144-145; Dallington, Aphorismes, 183.

42. T. H. Breen, ed., "George Donne's 'Virginia Reviewed': A 1639 Plan to Reform Colonial Society," WMQ, 3d ser., 30 (1973):458, 460.

43. A Description of the Province of New Albion, Peter Force, ed., Tracts and Other Papers (Washington, D.C., 1836), 2:38.

44. Northampton County Deeds and Wills, 4, 1651-1654 (VSL), 188; Hening, Statutes, 1:502.

45. Peter Force, ed., "The Colonial History of Virginia," Southern Literary Messenger 11 (1845):1-2.

CHAPTER 2

1. Bemiss, Three Charters, 95.

2. Adventurers, 375-378.

3. Craven, Dissolution, 49; idem., Southern Colonies, 124; Theodore K. Rabb, "The Early Life of Sir Edwin Sandys and Jacobean London" (Ph.D. diss., Princeton Univ., 1961); idem., Enterprise and Empire: Merchant and Gentry Investment in the Expansion of England, 1575-1630 (Cambridge, Mass., 1967), 35-92; idem., "Sir Edwin Sandys and the Parliament of 1604," American Historical Review 69 (1963-1964):661-669.

4. Craven, Dissolution, 78-79, 94-97; idem., Southern Colonies, 126.

5. Craven, Dissolution, 78-79.

6. Bemiss, Three Charters, 95; VMHB 16 (1908):121.

7. Alexander Brown, Genesis of the United States (Boston and New York, 1915), 1:380.

8. OED, s.v., council, council of state; Bemiss, Three

Charters, 122-123.

9. Martin Wight, Development of the Legislative Council, 1606-1945 (London, 1946), 30.

10. Perry Miller, "Religion and Society in the Early Literature of Virginia," WMQ, 3d ser., 6 (1949):41; Derek Hirst, Representative of the People? Voters and Voting in England under the Early Stuarts (Cambridge, London, New York, and Melbourne, 1975), 105.

11. Craven, Dissolution, 71-80; Bemiss, Three Charters, 127; Arthur Percival Newton, ed., "A New Plan to Govern Virginia, 1623," American Historical Review 19 (1914-1915):561-562.

12. Newton, "New Plan," 561, 567; Craven, Dissolution, 78.

13. Newton, "New Plan," 561, 562; Bemiss, Three Charters, 128.

14. Van Schreeven and Reese, Proceedings; Edward Arber and A. G. Bradley, eds., Travels and Works of Captain John Smith (Edinburgh, 1910), 540-541; Hirst, Representative, 105.

15. JHB, xxvii; OED, s.v., burgess.

16. May McKisak, Parliamentary Representation of the English Boroughs during the Middle Ages (Oxford, 1932), 119-120; Van Schreeven and Reese, Proceedings, 13. The Bermuda Company, which was comprised principally of members of the Virginia Company, applied the same terminology to the assembly established in its colony in 1620.

17. McKisak, Parliamentary Representation, 119-120. Burke is quoted (at p. 163), and the American colonists' adoption of "medieval forms of attorneyship in representation" discussed, in Bernard Bailyn, Ideological Origins of the American Revolution (Cambridge, Mass., 1967), 161-175. A thoughtful survey of the connection between representation and community is presented in Helen M. Cam, Antonio Marongiu, and Günther Stökl, "Recent Work and Present Views on the Origins and Development of Representative Assemblies," in International Congress of Historical Sciences, Relazioni del X Congresso internazionale di Scienze Storiche, vol. 1,

Metodologia Problemi Generali (Firenze, 1955), 15-48.

18. Van Schreeven and Reese, Proceedings, 15.

19. Van Schreeven and Reese, Proceedings, 15-17.

20. OED, s.v., speaker; J. S. Roskell, The Commons and their Speakers in English Parliaments, 1376-1523 (Manchester, 1965), 4, 76. Pory did not petition for freedom of speech or from arrest or to be held blameless for the actions of the assembly, for the customary Speaker's petition was not appropriate to his situation, but since the commons debated the Speaker's role at length in the parliament of 1610 of which he was a member, surely he was not unaware of these procedures; Mary Patterson Clarke, Parliamentary Privilege in the American Colonies, Yale Historical Publications, Miscellany, 54 (New Haven, 1943), 61-92; Elizabeth Read Foster, Proceedings in Parliament, 1610, Yale Historical Publications, Manuscripts and Edited Texts, 22 (New Haven and London, 1966), 2:82-92; J. Henry Lefroy, comp., Memorials of the Discovery and Early Settlement of the Bermudas or Somers Islands, 1515-1685 (London, 1877), 1:214. On the relationship of the Bermuda and Virginia companies see Craven, Southern Colonies, 114-118.

21. In his report Pory generally described his actions in the third-person active voice (e.g., "the Speaker tooke exception"), as he did with many of Yeardley's actions (e.g., "the Governor himselfe alledged"), but in orders and acts he frequently used the passive voice; Van Schreeven and Reese, Proceedings, 17, 19, 77n8, and passim; Clarke, Parliamentary Privilege, 54. The bar did not need to be a physical barrier, its function might be served by any line defining the limits of the house; Josef Redlich, Procedure of the House of Commons: A Study of its History and Present Form, trans. A. Ernest Steinthal (London, 1908), 2:22-23. Members probably knelt to take the oath; Foster, Proceedings in Parliament, 1610, 1:99.

22. Van Schreeven and Reese, Proceedings, 15, 19, 77n9. The instructions that Yeardley had been given are in Va. Co. Recs., 3:105-106.

23. Van Schreeven and Reese, Proceedings, 19; a fine sketch of Martin is in Samuel Merrifield Bemiss,

Ancient Adventurers: A Collection of Essays (Richmond, 1964), 27-39, quoted at p. 37.

24. Va. Co. Recs., 3:105-106.

25. Van Schreeven and Reese, Proceedings, 21-23, 35; Clarke, Parliamentary Privilege, 132-134; Pasbahegh was on the east bank of the Chickahominy River at its confluence with the James, across the James from Martin's Brandon.

26. Van Schreeven and Reese, Proceedings, 25-27.

27. OED, s.v., committee. "In Elizabethan usage, one to whom a bill is committed is called a committee; i.e., an Elizabethan committee is a member of what we should call a committee"; G. R. Elton, The Tudor Constitution: Documents and Commentary (Cambridge, 1960), 248n.

28. Van Schreeven and Reese, Proceedings, 31-51. The Bermuda assembly of 1620 "satt only in the morneinges. . . , the afternoones being bestowed either in consultation with the Governour in his house, or upon some perticular committees to frame business against the next daye"; Lefroy, History of the Bermudas, 197. It is possible to identify the first book because Pory quoted the first line of the second, and to suggest the approximate extent of the third book from his mention of the clause for 10-mile limits between plantations, but since the committees made no objection to the Great Charter, determination of the contents of the four books is not essential. The laws were not numbered or clearly distinguished from each other in the twenty paragraphs of legislation recorded in Pory's report; the orderly numbering of laws in vol. 1 of Hening, Statutes, is not always found in the original manuscripts. Hening's pencilled editorial additions and omissions are found in the sources his compositor used, many of which are preserved in the Library of Thomas Jefferson Collection in the rare book room of the Library of Congress.

29. Van Schreeven and Reese, Proceedings, 51, 53.

30. Ibid., 53.

31. Ibid., 51, 53, 67, 63.

32. Ibid., 51, 53.

33. Ibid., 67-69; Helen M. Cam, "The Legislators of Medieval England," *Proceedings of the British Academy* 31 (1945):127-137; J. G. Edwards, "'Justice' in Early English Parliaments," *Bulletin of the Institute of Historical Research* 27 (1954):35-53; Frederick Clifford, *A History of Private Bill Legislation* (London, 1885), 1:270. This petition apparently was a written document "contained in one sheet" and signed by "nine of James citty"; Yeardley sent the petition to England; *Va. Co. Recs.*, 3:252; Van Schreeven and Reese, *Proceedings*, 67.

34. Pory reported that "the Governor sente into England in the Prosperous" Poole's sworn testimony late in July 1619; *Va. Co. Recs.*, 3:152, 218, 242, 252. The record does not sustain Van Schreeven's statements that "no testimony was presented" in Garnett's case or that "Spelman was sentenced on the testimony of one person"; Van Schreeven and Reese, *Proceedings*, 9, 63-67.

35. Van Schreeven and Reese, *Proceedings*, 63-65; Pory commented: that the assembly "might perhaps both speedily and deservedly have taken his life from him," that Spelman "had in him more of the Savage then of the Christian," and that he showed no "thankfulness to the Assembly for their so favourable censure." Pory's changed opinion of Poole and Spelman is in *Va. Co. Recs.*, 3:251-253, where he describes Spelman's conduct as "unadvised," and Poole as "a neutral person" who would have been called to account "for telling false tales" if that would not have jeopardized the colony's reconciliation with Opechancanough. John Rolfe's opinion of Poole was more harsh; ibid., 3:244-245.

36. Van Schreeven and Reese, *Proceedings*, 65-67.

37. Van Schreeven and Reese, *Proceedings*, 71; Jack P. Greene, *The Quest for Power: The Lower Houses of Assembly in the Southern Royal Colonies, 1689-1776* (Chapel Hill, 1963), 17-18; the company's promise is in *Va. Co. Recs.*, 3:484. Yeardley prorogued the assembly until 1 Mar. 1620, but shortly thereafter (before Pory prepared the fair copy of his report) "dissolved the same." McIlwaine's assertion (*JHB*, xxviii) that the assembly later reconvened cannot be sustained.

CHAPTER 3

1. Craven, Dissolution, 315; William S. Powell, "Aftermath of the Massacre: The First Indian War, 1622-1632," VMHB 66 (1958):44-61; Robert C. Johnson, ed., "Virginia in 1632," ibid., 65 (1957):462; Hening, Statutes, 1:126, 150-151, 190-192, 194-195, 215-217. The best succinct treatment of the founding of Maryland and its relation to Virginia politics is J. Mills Thornton III, "The Thrusting Out of Governor Harvey: A Seventeenth-Century Rebellion," VMHB 76 (1968):11-26; useful narratives include Andrews, Colonial Period, 2:274-324; Craven, Southern Colonies, 195-198; Morton, Colonial Virginia, 122-146; and the unsigned annotation in the Collections of the Massachusetts Historical Society, 4th ser., 9 (1871):81-101, 131-149.

2. This statement is based on all relevant material (available on Virginia Colonial Records Project microfilm) in Colonial Office classes 1 and 5; see also, T. H. Breen, "Looking Out For Number One: Conflicting Cultural Values in Early Seventeenth-Century Virginia," South Atlantic Quarterly 78 (1979):342-360.

3. C.O. 5/1354, 199; JHB, 40; Thomas Cary Johnson, ed., A Proclamation for Setling the Plantation of Virginia 1625 (Charlottesville, 1946), [29]; W. Stitt Robinson, Jr., Mother Earth: Land Grants in Colonial Virginia, 1607-1699, Jamestown 350th Anniversary Historical Booklets (Williamsburg, 1957), 29; Fairfax Harrison, Virginia Land Grants: A Study of Conveyancing in Relation to Colonial Politics (Richmond, 1925), 18-19; "Discourse of the Old Company, [1625]," VMHB 1 (1893-1894):306; OED, s.v., jealousy.

4. Johnson, Proclamation, [27]; commission to Sir Francis Wyatt, WMQ, 2d ser., 8 (1928):160; "'Propositions touching Virginia, 1625,' presented by Sir George Yeardley," ibid., 162.

5. Craven, Dissolution, 312; Thornton, "Thrusting Out of Harvey," 13-14; Nicholas P. Canny, "The Ideology of English Colonization: From Ireland to America," WMQ, 3d ser., 30 (1973):575-598. The right of conquest was not invoked in Ulster in 1609 nor would it have been necessary in Virginia. Escheat and the quo warranto decision were sufficient, and they avoided the moral and political implications

of the right of conquest; see Quentin Skinner, "History and Ideology in the English Revolution," Historical Journal 8 (1965):151-178.

6. George Louis Beer, The Origins of the British Colonial System, 1578-1660 (New York, 1908), 308-312; JHB, 43.

7. "Propositions touching Virginia, 1625," 161-163; the request for an act of Parliament is evidence that the Virginians wanted, technically, not a charter, which would have been subject to royal revocation at any time, but rather statutory recognition of their liberties that would have been enforceable in common law courts and secure from subsequent crown action; see Charles Howard McIlwain, The High Court of Parliament and Its Supremacy (New Haven and London, 1910), 364; and G. R. Elton, The Tudor Constitution: Documents and Commentary (Cambridge, 1972), 20-23; "The Virginia Charter of 1676, With Introductory Note by Thomas J. Wertenbaker," VMHB 56 (1948):263-266; Johnson, Proclamation, [27-29]. The parallel situations of Virginia and Ireland are striking, and when a group of dispossessed Ulster landowners went "to Dublin to complain of the treatment they had received, they were shipped off as slaves to Virginia"; George O'Brien, The Economic History of Ireland in the Seventeenth Century (Dublin and London, 1919), 24. The Stuarts' desire to implement tenures in capite, which were more lucrative for the crown and its seignorial lords, in Ireland, Virginia, and Maryland is discussed in Viola Florence Barnes, "Land Tenure in English Colonial Charters of the Seventeenth-Century," Essays in Colonial History Presented to Charles McLean Andrews by his Students (New Haven, 1931), 13-37. The earliest identified Irishman claimed as a headright in Virginia was listed in a patent issued to William Clarke on 29 September 1636; Nell Marion Nugent, Cavaliers and Pioneers: Abstracts of Virginia Land Patents and Grants (Richmond, 1934-1979), 1:50.

8. Johnson, Proclamation, [27-29].

9. Beer, Origins, 110-116, 134-139, 169-173; Neville Williams, "England's Tobacco Trade in the Reign of Charles I," VMHB 65 (1957):405-407; Bemiss, Three Charters, 89; Craven, Dissolution, 221-250.

10. Beer, Origins, 134; MCGC, 55-56; WMQ, 2d ser.,

8 (1929):57.

11. WMQ, 2d ser., 8 (1928):161.

12. McIlwaine (JHB, xxx, 43) and Andrews (Colonial Period, 1:194-197) attached great significance to the absence of the word General Assembly in their sources. The Wyatt Manuscripts (earl of Romney's deposit, Loan Collection 15, British Library) published in several segments in volumes 7 and 8 of WMQ, 2d ser. (quoted at 8 [1928]:56-57, 130-131), evidently escaped Andrews's notice. Craven (Southern Colonies, 154) and Morton (Colonial Virginia, 111-112) followed Andrews.

13. WMQ, 2d ser., 7 (1927):129-130; MCGC, 57-59, 62.

14. Beer, Origins, 140-148.

15. Lefroy, Memorials of the Bermudas, 1:439-440; Beer, Origins, 149.

16. C.O., 1/4, 85, 109; JHB, 45, 50-51; Beer, Origins, 150-151.

17. JHB, 57; W. L. Grant, James Munro, and Almeric W. Fitzroy, eds., Acts of the Privy Council of England, Colonial Series, vol. I, A.D. 1613-1680 (London, 1908), 128.

18. Hening, Statutes, 1:137-202.

19. Ibid., 139, 141, 142, 153, 154, 159, 161, 162, 179, 183.

20. Ibid., 139, 141, 142, 150.

21. Thornton did not address the constitutional issue. Peter C. Hoffer and N. E. H. Hull, "The First American Impeachments," WMQ, 3d ser., 35 (1978): 655-658, admit that "only in the Harvey case do the records furnish no direct evidence of specific knowledge of English impeachment proceedings," but they force a reading of the evidence without regard either to the structure of institutions in 1635 (the assembly was not yet bicameral) or the terms of Harvey's commission. E.g., they assert that, in "an impeachment prosecution without the terminology," the General Assembly petitioned the Council against Harvey; however, the "assemblies" mentioned in the

contemporary accounts were mass meetings at York and elsewhere, and the General Assembly did not convene until *after* Harvey's arrest.

22. Thornton, "Thrusting Out of Harvey," 18-19; C.O. 1/5, 65-67.

23. J. E. Farnell, "The Navigation Act of 1651, the First Dutch War, and the London Merchant Community," Economic History Review 16 (1963-1964):446; Andrews, Colonial Period, 4:43. The most extensive discussion of the interloping merchants in Robert Paul Brenner, "Commercial Change and Political Conflict: The Merchant Community in Civil War London" (Ph.D. diss., Princeton University, 1970); chapters 3 through 6 are especially important for the London-Virginia trade.

24. Thornton, "Thrusting Out of Harvey," 16, 20, 24; Brenner, "Commercial Change," 110-111, 124.

25. MCGC, 109, 110, 188; Nugent, Cavaliers and Pioneers, 1:2; Brenner, "Commercial Change," 127-129; Adventurers, 31, 248-249; C. M. MacInnes, The Early English Tobacco Trade (London, 1926), 154-157.

26. Brenner, "Commercial Change," passim; Farnell, "Navigation Act," 446.

27. Thornton, "Thrusting Out of Harvey," 18-19; C.O. 1/5, 65-67.

28. Thornton, "Thrusting Out of Harvey," 19-21.

29. Ibid.; C.O. 1/6, 93.

30. Grant et al., eds., Acts of the Privy Council, Colonial, 1:187-189; "Virginia in 1632-33-34," VMHB 8 (1900-1901):149-150; Johnson, "Virginia in 1632," ibid. 65 (1957):462-463.

31. Thornton, "Thrusting Out of Harvey," 21.

32. C.O. 1/8, 197-198; printed in VMHB 1 (1894):425-429 with minor errors in transcription.

33. Ibid., JHB, 45-50; Thornton, "Thrusting Out of Harvey," 11; Mathews to Sir John Wolstenholme, 25 May 1635, C.O. 1/8, 178-181; printed with minor transcription errors in VMHB 1 (1894):416-424.

34. C.O. 1/8, 178-181.

35. Mathews reported the dialogue in the language quoted in this and following paragraphs; ibid.

36. *Richard the Third*, act 3, sc. 4, lines 61-64, 68, 77-78.

37. Thornton, "Thrusting Out," 22-26.

38. Ibid.

39. C.O. 1/8, 178-181; Morton, *Colonial Virginia*, 137-143.

40. Harvey's declaration, C.O. 1/8, 197-198; Harvey to Windebank, 16 December 1634, ibid., 106-107; Mathews to Wolstenholme, ibid., 178-181; Morton, *Colonial Virginia*, 141-144.

41. Morton, *Colonial Virginia*, 141-146; Thornton, "Thrusting Out of Harvey," 22-26.

42. Morton, *Colonial Virginia*, 141-146.

43. Ibid.

44. Commission to Wyatt, 11 January 1639, C.O. 5/1324, or *VMHB* 11 (1903-1904):50-54.

45. T. H. Breen, ed., "George Donne's 'Virginia Reviewed': A 1638 Plan to Reform Colonial Society," *WMQ*, 3d ser., 30 (1973):450, 458-460; C.O., 1/8, 195-196.

46. Thornton, "Thrusting Out of Harvey," 23; C.O. 1/8, 195-196.

47. C.O. 1/8, 196.

48. Sigmund Diamond, "From Organization to Society: Virginia in the Seventeenth Century," *American Journal of Sociology*, 63 (1958):457-475; Edmund S. Morgan, *American Slavery--American Freedom: The Ordeal of Colonial Virginia* (New York, 1975), 133-136; Wesley Frank Craven, *White, Red, and Black: The Seventeenth-Century Virginian* (Charlottesville, 1971), 52-55; J. Frederick Fausz and Jon Kukla, eds., "A Letter of Advice to the Governor of Virginia, 1624," *WMQ*, 3d ser., 34 (1977):104.

49. Warren M. Billings, "The Growth of Political

Institutions in Virginia, 1634 to 1676," WMQ, 3d
ser., 31 (1974):228-230. Average prices are taken
from United States Bureau of the Census, Historical
Statistics of the United States: Colonial Times to
1970 (Washington, D.C., 1975), 1198; these averages
were derived from Russell R. Menard, "A Note on
Chesapeake Tobacco Prices, 1618-1660," VMHB 84
(1976):404-406.

50. George B. Curtis, "The Beginnings of a County Court:
Accomack County, Virginia, 1633-1639" (unpublished
M.A. thesis, University of Virginia, 1971), 1, 13,
35, 53-54, 59n28, 67; the percentage of debt-related
cases increased annually from 1633 to 1637, and during
the decade an estimated 87% of Accomack's population
were named in court proceedings of one kind or
another (ibid., 26). (Curtis's thesis is summarized
in his "The Colonial County Court, Social Forum and
Legislative Precident: Accomack County, Virginia,
1633-1639," VMHB, 85 [1977]:274-288.) Hening,
Statutes, 1:225-226; proclamation of Governor Wyatt
and the Council, 16 June 1642, in Lower Norfolk
County Court Records, 1637-1643, 1:159 (Virginia
Historical Society).

51. Hening, Statutes, 1: 125, 130, 133, 168-170, 224;
Lower Norfolk Records, 1:160; Jon Kukla, ed.,
"Some Acts Not in Hening's Statutes: The Acts of
Assembly, October 1660," VMHB 83 (1975):91.

52. Lower Norfolk Records, 1:175-176, 200-202.

53. Hobbes, English Works, ed. Sir William Molesworth
(London, 1843), 8:viii.

54. Fragment of the order book of Charles City County,
1642, 5, 11 (Virginia Historical Society); JHB,
xxxvii-xxxix, 60, 69, 70; Hening, Statutes, 1:230-238.

55. Stanley M. Pargellis, "The Procedure of the Virginia
House of Burgesses," WMQ, 2d ser., 7 (1927):73-86,
143-157.

56. Hening, Statutes, 1:230.

57. Susie M. Ames, ed., County Court Records of Accomack-
Northampton, Virginia, 1640-1645 (Charlottesville,
1973), 99; JHB, 69.

58. Hening, Statutes, 1:179-180, 239-240; Kukla, "Some
Acts," 79, 82-83.

59. Hening, Statutes, 1:237-238.

60. A Description of the Province of New Albion, Peter Force, ed., Tracts and Other Papers, 2 (Washington, D.C., 1836), 38.

61. WMQ, 1st ser., 4 (1895-1896):161; ibid., 12 (1903-1904):37; VMHB 17 (1909-1910):121, 124; Hening, Statutes, 1:383; JHB, 76, 78, 82, 83; Manuscript order, 29 June 1642, Archives Division, VSL.

62. Lower Norfolk Records, 2:126, VMHB 23 (1915):241; Hening, Statutes, 1:241.

63. "A Description of the Government of Virginia," VMHB 5 (1898):55.

64. I am grateful to Warren M. Billings for supplying lists of Dutch merchants engaged in the Virginia trade; fifty of the fifty-seven Dutch merchants traded to the Eastern Shore.

65. JHB, 66-67.

66. Breen, "Virginia Reviewed," 455, 460, 462; York County Records No. 2, Wills and Deeds, 1645-1649 (VSL), 95; Leonard, comp., General Assembly Register, xix-xxii, 3-38.

67. J. P. Kenyon, ed., The Stuart Constitution, 1603-1688: Documents and Commentary (Cambridge, 1966), 21-23.

68. Ibid.; Jane Dennison Carson, "Sir William Berkeley: Governor of Virginia: A Study of Colonial Policy" (Ph.D. diss., University of Virginia, 1951), 1-16.

69. Raleigh, Maxims of State (London, 1650), 20.

70. Jon Kukla, Speakers and Clerks of the Virginia House of Burgesses, Virginia State Library Publications No. 48 (Richmond, forthcoming).

71. Hening, Statutes, 1:236-238.

72. Ibid., 236-238, 244, 267, 279, 280-281.

73. Three accounts of the Massachusetts episode are: Andrews, Colonial Period, 1:442-461; Wall, Massachusetts Bay, 41-92; Perry Miller, Orthodoxy in Massachusetts, 1630-1650 (Cambridge, Mass., 1933), 220-262. Wall, Massachusetts Bay, 41-92, failed to

recognize the mercantile interests of his "great gentlemen," and argued for an internal geographical sectionalism that seems not fully convincing. See Bernard Bailyn, The New England Merchants in the Seventeenth Century (Cambridge, Mass., 1955), 42, 45-46.

74. Wall, Massachusetts Bay, 53; Andrews, Colonial Period, 1:450.

75. Allyn Forbes, ed., The Winthrop Papers (Boston, 1929-1947), 4:383; Wall, Massachusetts Bay, 80.

76. Forbes, Winthrop Papers, 4:360. J. R. Pole's observation that "the development of bicameralism in native American legislatures may be taken both as a token of the increasing sophistication of procedures and of the sense of actual difference of purpose between elected assemblymen and appointed councillors" is in his The Seventeenth Century: The Sources of Legislative Power, A. E. Dick Howard, ed., Jamestown Essays on Representation (Charlottesville, 1969), 64.

CHAPTER 4

1. Wesley Frank Craven, White, Red, and Black: The Seventeenth-Century Virginian (Charlottesville, 1971), 55-57, 70n45; Morton, Colonial Virginia, 152-156; "Acts, Orders and Resolutions of the General Assembly of Virginia at sessions of March 1643-1646," VMHB 23 (1915):229, 234, 237, 238; The Court Mercurie. Number 10. From Saturday the 7 of September, to Saturday the 14th 1644 (London, 1644) McGregor Collection, Alderman Library, University of Virginia, Charlottesville. Another newspaper account of the massacre, more notable as royalist propaganda than useful for historians of Virginia, is Mercurius Aulicus (Oxford, 25 August 1644), 1136-1137; Virginia Historical Society, Richmond.

2. Andrews, Colonial Period, 2:308.

3. MCGC, 501; Robert Beverley, The History and Present State of Virginia, ed. Louis B. Wright (Charlottesville, 1947), 61-63.

4. Joseph Frank, ed., "News From Virginny, 1644," VMHB 65 (1957):85.

5. William Laud, sermon at the opening of Parliament,

6 February 1626, in J. P. Kenyon, ed., The Stuart Constitution: Documents and Commentary (Cambridge, 1966), 153; instructions to Sir William Berkeley, August 1641, in Warren M. Billings, ed., The Old Dominion in the Seventeenth Century: A Documentary History of Virginia, 1606-1689 (Chapel Hill, 1975), 51.

6. Hening, Statutes, 1:240-243, 277; Morton, Colonial Virginia, 1:150-153; Babette M. Levy, "Early Puritanism in the Southern and Island Colonies," Proceedings of the American Antiquarian Society, n.s. 70 (1960):123-126; "Acts, Orders and Resolutions, 1643-1646," 237.

7. Frank, ed., "News From Virginny," 85-86.

8. Hening, Statutes, 1:342; A. G. Dickens, The English Reformation (London, 1964), 220; Levy, "Early Puritanism," 131 (another indication of Berkeley's post-1645 strategy may be the handling of his puritan chaplain, Thomas Harrison, whom he allowed three years' leeway "in the hope that such a brilliant preacher might be brought to conform" before he forced him to leave the colony; ibid., 127); Clara Ann Bowler, "The Litigious Career of William Cotton, Minister," VMHB (1978):281-294.

9. William H. Seiler, "The Anglican Parish in Virginia," in James Morton Smith, ed., Seventeenth-Century America: Essays in Colonial History, 127; Craven, Southern Colonies, 228-230.

10. J. H. Hexter, The Reign of King Pym, Harvard Historical Studies, 48 (Cambridge, 1941), 85; Andrews, Colonial Period, 1:167; DNB, s.v., Robert Rich; C. H. Firth and R. S. Rait, eds., Acts and Ordinances of the Interregnum, 1642-1660 (London, 1911), 1:331.

11. Firth and Rait, eds., Acts of the Interregnum, 1:332, 333; Andrews, Colonial Period, 1:232.

12. Warwick to "Virginia," n.d., Lord Warwick Correspondence, ca. 1646-1648, Stowe Manuscripts, British Library, 184, 124ro; internal evidence suggests that the earlier letters in this collection were written before Warwick had learned of the April 1644 massacre.

13. Ibid.

14. Warwick to "Cap. Mathews," n.d., ibid.

15. Ibid.

16. Ibid.

17. Warwick to "Virginia," n.d., ibid., 125-126.

18. Ibid.; Firth and Rait, eds., Acts of the Interregnum, 1:333. Other evidence of Warwick's moderate and tolerant religious and administrative policies is in J. H. Lefroy, comp., Memorials of the Discovery and Early Settlement of the Bermudas, or Somers Islands, 1515-1685 (London, 1877), 1:586-591, 600-603.

19. Warren M. Billings, "The Growth of Political Institutions in Virginia, 1634 to 1676," WMQ, 3d ser., 31 (1974):228.

20. Hening, Statutes, 1:266, 272, 287, 344.

21. Lower Norfolk County Court Records, 1637-1643, Virginia Historical Society, Richmond, 1:160; Hening, Statutes, 1:261, 303-304; Billings, "Growth of Political Institutions," 232-233.

22. The most comprehensive lists of burgesses for this period are those I compiled for Leonard, ed., General Assembly Register.

23. Compare the 1640 Lower Norfolk Burgesses in ibid., 18, with those named as county burgesses in Lower Norfolk Records, 1:36; the Accomack 1642 burgesses in Leonard, ed., Register, 20, with those named in Susie M. Ames, ed., County Court Records of Accomack-Northampton, Virginia, 1640-1645 (Charlottesville, 1973), 141; Hening, Statutes, 1:379 and 506, respectively, with Lancaster County Deeds, Etc., No. 1, 1652-1657 (VSL), 90-91, and Lower Norfolk County Wills and Deeds, D. 1656-1666 (VSL), 234.

24. Hening, Statutes, 1:267, 520, 2:106; Billings, "Growth of Political Institutions," 235. Explicit authorization for the election of parochial burgesses from three parishes was written into the acts creating or defining those parishes; Hening, Statutes, 1:250, 277; and in 1652 the Assembly confirmed the parishes' rights to "choose one, or two Burgesses Respectivelye provided they maintaine theire Charges," Billings, ed., "Some Acts Not in

Hening's Statutes: The Acts of Assembly, April 1652, November 1652, and July 1653," VMHB 83 (1975):46. For changes in parish boundaries south of the James see Charles Francis Cocke, Parish Lines: Diocese of Southern Virginia, Virginia State Library Publications No. 22 (Richmond, 1964).

25. Hening, Statutes, 1:299-300.

26. Ibid., 263, 264, 270, 272, 300, 320, 333-334.

27. Jon Kukla, Speakers and Clerks of the Virginia House of Burgesses, 1643-1776, Virginia State Library Publications No. 48 (Richmond, forthcoming).

28. Ibid.

29. Ibid.

30. Ibid.; the text of Berkeley's Cornelia, written before 1662, is lost; his The Lost Lady, written about 1637, was performed in London before and after the Civil War (Pepys saw it twice after the Restoration); R. C. Bald, "Sir William Berkeley's The Lost Lady," The Library, 4th ser., 17 (1937): 394-426.

31. "Surrender of Virginia to the Parliamentary Commissioners, March, 1651-2," VMHB 11 (1903-1904):33.

32. Hening, Statutes, 1:354-355.

33. Ibid., 355.

34. Ibid., 341, 355, 357.

35. Ibid., 359-360; Morton, Colonial Virginia, 166.

36. Hening, Statutes, 360, 361.

37. Morton, Colonial Virginia, 168-170; JHB, 75, 76.

38. Leo Francis Stock, ed., Proceedings and Debates of the British Parliaments respecting North America (Washington, D.C., 1924), 1:222, 226-232; "Surrender of Virginia to the Parliamentary Commissioners," VMHB 11 (1903-1904):32-34; Northampton County Deeds and Wills, 1651-1654, 4 (VSL), 80.

39. Hening, Statutes, 1:363; the oath to the Commonwealth is in Northampton County Deeds and Wills, 1651-1654, 188, and is printed in Northern Neck of Virginia

Historical Magazine 28 (1978):3089-3095, from the signed copy circulated in Northumberland County; Ames, ed., County Court Records, 1640-1645, 297; Norfolk County Wills and Deeds, C, Dec. 15, 1651 to Oct. 15, 1656 (VSL), 20.

40. Hening, Statutes, 1:371-372.

CHAPTER 5

1. Andrews, Colonial Period, 2:321-322.

2. "Surrender of Virginia to the Parliamentary Commissioners, March 1651-2," VMHB 11 (1903-1904):34, 38.

3. Hening, Statutes, 1:363-368; Leo Francis Stock, ed., Proceedings and Debates of the British Parliaments respecting North America (Washington, D.C., 1924), 1:229-232.

4. Hening, Statutes, 1:363; Quentin Skinner, "History and Ideology in the English Revolution," Historical Journal 8 (1965):151-178.

5. Hening, Statutes, 1:363-365.

6. "Surrender of Virginia," 39; Hening, Statutes, 1:369-373; Jon Kukla, Speakers and Clerks of the Virginia House of Burgesses, 1643-1776, Virginia State Library Publications No. 48 (Richmond, forthcoming); James Branch Cabell, The Majors and Their Marriages (Richmond, 1915), 13-27, 34, 37; Warren M. Billings, ed., "Some Acts Not in Hening's Statutes: The Acts of Assembly, April 1652, November 1652, and July 1653," VMHB 83 (1975):24-25.

7. Billings, "Some Acts," 26-27, 31, 34, 65; Hening, Statutes, 1:245-246, 258, 307, 319, 351-352. Of the 222 acts of Assembly passed between 1643 and 1651, only 67 were re-enacted in April 1652. Of the 155 acts allowed to expire, about one-third (54) had been of a one-time or temporary nature (e.g., to define a parish boundary or to appropriate money for a particular end). Another dozen related to Indians or defense. Of the remaining 89 non-military acts not re-enacted in April 1652, 19% (17) supported the Anglican position in religion, 56% (50) concerned matters of judicial administration, 17% (15) concerned trade, and 8% (7) dealt with agriculture.

8. Hening, Statutes, 1:371-373.

9. JHB, xliii; "Surrender of Virginia," 39; Hening, Statutes, 1:431.

10. Hening, Statutes, 1:371.

11. Ibid., 371-373.

12. Ibid., 372, 374-375; Mary Patterson Clarke, Parliamentary Privilege in the American Colonies, Yale Historical Publications, Miscellany, 46 (New Haven, 1943), 185.

13. [Lyon G. Tyler], "Lieut. Col. Walter Chiles," WMQ, 1st ser., 1 (1892-1893):75-77; W. B. Cridlin, "The Chiles Family in Virginia," VMHB 19 (1911): 104-106; Hening, Statutes, 1:377-378.

14. J. E. Farnell, "The Navigation Act of 1651, the First Dutch War, and the London Merchant Community," Economic History Review, 2d ser., 16 (1963-1964): 440-446 (quotations appear at page 443).

15. Both acts are printed in C. H. Firth and R. S. Rait, eds., Acts and Ordinances of the Interregnum, 1642-1660 (London, 1911), 2:425-429, 559-562. Virginia's defiance is in JHB, 75-78.

16. Northampton County Deeds and Wills 1651-1654 (VSL), 126-127; Hening, Statutes, 1:364.

17. Northampton Deeds and Wills, 128-129.

18. Ibid.

19. Ibid., 129; Jennings Cropper Wise, Ye Kingdome of Accawmacke, or the Eastern Shore of Virginia in the Seventeenth Century (Richmond, 1911), 139.

20. Northampton Deeds and Wills, 183; Hening, Statutes, 1:380.

21. Northampton Deeds and Wills, 130, 144.

22. "Historical and Genealogical Notes," WMQ, 1st ser., 26 (1917-1918):285; Hening, Statutes, 1:382; Norfolk County Wills & Deeds C, 1651-1656 (VSL), 52-53.

23. Hening, Statutes, 1:382-383, 385; Northampton Deeds and Wills, 144. The April 1652 act authorizing

two commissioners of each county court to hear maritime cases is in Billings, "Some Acts," 70.

24. Clarke, Parliamentary Privilege, 61-92.

25. OED, s.v., plurality; Hening, Statutes, 1:378.

26. Hening, Statutes, 1:377-378.

27. Ibid.

28. Ibid., 382-383; JHB, 87-88.

29. Hening, Statutes, 1:387; Kukla, Speakers and Clerks.

30. Hening, Statutes, 1:387.

31. Ibid., 272; JHB, 95; Jon Kukla, "Robert Beverley Assailed: Appellate Jurisdiction and the Problem of Bicameralism in Seventeenth-Century Virginia," VMHB (in press).

32. JHB, 95, 99, 101; Act 145, Laws of Virginia, 1657, Sloane Manuscripts, 1378, British Library, London.

33. Hening, Statutes, 1:411-412; Act 15 of March 1656, in Surry County Deeds, Wills, Etc., 1 (VSL).

34. Michael Kammen, Deputyes and Libertyes: The Origins of Representative Government in Colonial America (New York, 1969); Hening, Statutes, 1:507-508; 2:206-207. See also W. H. Browne, ed., Archives of Maryland, 1 (1883):131-132, 272-274; and J. Henry Lefroy, The Historye of the Bermudaes or Summer Islands (London, 1882), 197-198.

35. Compare Hening, Statutes, 1:507-508, with The Manner of holding Parliaments in England . . . (London, 1641), n.p., 2; Lefroy, Historye, 197-198; and Archives of Maryland, 1:273. I am indebted to Warren M. Billings for graciously supplying a photocopy of The Manner of holding Parliaments in England from his personal library.

36. The data in this paragraph, and in tables one and two, are compiled from Leonard, comp., General Assembly Register, 25-36.

37. Ibid.; Hening, Statutes, 1:422, 501.

38. Hening, Statutes, 1:364, 385, 425, 426; JHB, 104, 105,

128; Stock, Proceedings and Debates of the British Parliaments, 1:229-232; Minnie G. Cook, "Governor Samuel Mathews, Junior," WMQ, 2d ser., 14 (1934): 105-113; John Frederick Dorman, "Governor Samuel Mathews, Jr.," VMHB 74 (1966):429-432; Morton, Colonial Virginia, 178-180.

39. Hening, Statutes, 1:426; Morton, Colonial Virginia, 180; MCGC, 505.

40. Hening, Statutes, 1:425; Morton, Colonial Virginia, 180; Nathan C. Hale, Virginia Venturer: A Historical Biography of William Claiborne, 1600-1677 (Richmond, 1951), 301. (Hale's statement that Samuel Mathews, Sr., and Richard Bennett had returned to Virginia is corrected in the articles by Cook and Dorman cited in note 38.)

41. JHB, 106, 107.

42. Hening, Statutes, 1:372, 376, 402, 428, 431, 480, 498.

43. JHB, 108-109.

44. Ibid., 110.

45. Ibid.

46. Ibid.; Adventurers, 88; "Two John Smiths," WMQ, 1st ser., 23 (1914-1915):292-293; "Genealogy," VMHB 20 (1912):326-327; Nell Marion Nugent, Cavaliers and Pioneers: Abstracts of Virginia Land Patents and Grants (Richmond, 1934-1979), 1:219, 291, 306, 315; A Voyage to Virginia, By Colonel Norwood, in Peter Force, ed., Tracts and Other Papers, Relating Principally to the Origin, Settlement and Progress of the Colonies in North America . . . (Washington, D.C., 1836-1844), 3, no. 10. Norwood's continued connection with the colony and continued involvement with royalist efforts are discussed in P. H. Hardacre, "The Further Adventures of Henry Norwood," VMHB 67 (1959):272-274.

47. Hening, Statutes, 1:372.

48. Ibid., 500.

49. Ibid., 501-503.

50. Ibid., 502; OED, s.v., let.

51. Hening, Statutes, 1:502-503.

52. Ibid., 503-504.

53. Ibid., 504-505. The Assembly never was dissolved; the House of Burgesses adjourned itself (ibid., 493-494, 496-497).

54. Ibid., 515.

55. Ibid., 509-511.

56. Ibid., 511-512, 523-524.

57. Ibid., 372, 512.

EPILOGUE

1. U. S. Bureau of the Census, Historical Statistics of the United States: Colonial Times to 1970 (Washington, D.C., 1976), 1168; [Thomas Ludwell], "A Description of the Government of Virginia," VMHB 5 (1898):57.

2. Jeremiah Whittaker's sermon, 25 January 1643, is quoted in H. R. Trevor-Roper, "The General Crisis of the Seventeenth Century," in Trevor Aston, ed., Crisis in Europe 1560-1660 (London, 1965), 59. Baker's Chronicle is quoted in Godfrey Davies, Restoration of Charles II, 1658-1660 (San Marino, Calif., 1955), 83. The adage is quoted, ibid., 156.

3. John Frederick Dorman, "Governor Samuel Mathews, Jr.," VMHB 74 (1966):429-432; Hening, Statutes, 1:524; Nell Marion Nugent, Cavaliers and Pioneers: Abstracts of Virginia Land Patents and Grants (Richmond, 1934-1979), 1:391, 393; MCGC, 506.

4. Hening, Statutes, 1:517, 526-530.

5. Ibid., 503, 531; Peter Force, ed., "The Colonial History of Virginia," Southern Literary Messenger 11 (1845):1.

6. Hening, Statutes, 1:531.

7. Ibid., 530-531.

8. E. Millicent Sowerby, Catalogue of the Library of Thomas Jefferson (Washington, D.C., 1953), 2:239.

9. Force, "Colonial History," 2-3; Mary Patterson Clarke, Parliamentary Privilege in the American Colonies, Yale Historical Publications, Miscellany, 46 (New Haven and London, 1943), 75-78.

10. Force, "Colonial History," 2.

11. Ibid., 2-3.

12. Ibid., 3.

13. Ibid.; Hening, Statutes, 1:544.

14. Berkeley may have spoken to the House of Burgesses and the Council on the same day that the councillors signed the pledge of support, the 21st, or he may have waited until the 22d, the day on which the Council issued a land grant to Edmond Peters (Nugent, Cavaliers and Pioneers, 1:393). The speeches are printed in Force, "Colonial History," 1-2.

15. "Virginia in 1658-1662," VMHB 18 (1910):291-292; Force, "Colonial History," 3-5; Morton, Colonial Virginia, 188; Jon Kukla, ed., "Some Acts Not in Hening's Statutes: The Acts of Assembly, October 1660," VMHB 83 (1975):78, 94; York County Deeds, Orders, Wills, etc., No. 3, 1657-1662 (VSL), 243.

16. John Ogilbi [sic], America: Being the Latest and Most Accurate Description of the New World . . . (London, 1679), 197-198; Edward Arber and A. G. Bradley, eds., Travels and Works of Captain John Smith (Edinburgh, 1910), 526; Robert Gray, A Good Speed to Virginia (London, 1610); Hornbook of Virginia History, (2d ed., Richmond, 1965), 1.

SELECTED BIBLIOGRAPHY

Manuscript Repositories

British Library, London.

Library of Congress, Washington, D.C.

Manuscript Department and Rare Book Room, Alderman Library, University of Virginia, Charlottesville, Virginia.

Virginia Historical Society, Richmond, Virginia.

Virginia State Library, Richmond, Virginia.

Bibliographies

Haynes, Donald. Virginiana in the Printed Book Collections of the Virginia State Library. Richmond. 1975.

Swem, E. G., Jennings, John M., Servies, James A. A Selected Bibliography of Virginia, 1607-1699. Jamestown 350th Anniversary Historical Booklets. Williamsburg, 1957.

Vaughan, Alden T. The American Colonies in the Seventeenth Century. New York. 1971.

Printed Primary Sources

Arber, Edward, and Bradley, A. G., editors. Travels and Works of Captain John Smith. Edinburgh. 1910.

Bemiss, Samuel M., editor. The Three Charters of the Virginia Company of London; With Seven Related Documents: 1606-1621. Jamestown 350th Anniversary Historical Booklets. Williamsburg. 1957.

Billings, Warren M., editor. The Old Dominion in the Seventeenth Century: A Documentary History of Virginia, 1606-1689. Chapel Hill. 1975.

_____. "Some Acts Not in Hening's Statutes: The Acts of Assembly, April 1652, November 1652, and July 1653." Virginia Magazine of History and Biography (hereafter cited as VMHB) 83 (1975):22-76.

Breen, T. H., editor. "George Donne's 'Virginia Reviewed': A 1639 Plan to Reform Colonial Society." *William and Mary Quarterly* (hereafter cited as *WMQ*), 3d ser., 30 (1973):449-466.

British Public Record Office: History, Description, Record Groups, Finding Aids, and Materials for American History, with Special Reference to Virginia. Virginia State Library Publications No. 12. Richmond. 1960.

Brown, Alexander, compiler. *Genesis of the United States.* Boston and New York. 1890.

Fausz, J. Frederick, and Kukla, Jon, editors. "A Letter of Advice to the Governor of Virginia, 1624." *WMQ*, 3d ser. 39 (1977):104-129.

Flaherty, David H., editor. *For the Colony in Virginea Britannia Lawes Divine, Morall and Martial, etc.* compiled by William Strachey. Charlottesville. 1968.

Force, Peter, editor. "The Colonial History of Virginia." *Southern Literary Messenger* 11 (1845):1-2.

Gray, Robert. *A Good Speed to Virginia.* London. 1609.

Hening, William Waller, editor. *The Statutes at Large: Being a Collection of all the Laws of Virginia, from the First Session of the Legislature in the Year 1619. . . .* Richmond, Philadelphia, and New York. 1809-1823.

Kingsbury, Susan Myra, editor. *Records of the Virginia Company of London.* Washington, D.C. 1906-1935.

Lefroy, J. Henry, compiler. *Memorials of the Discovery and Early Settlement of the Bermudas or Somers Islands, 1515-1685.* London. 1877.

Leonard, Cynthia Miller, compiler. *The General Assembly of Virginia, July 30, 1619-January 11, 1978: A Bicentennial Register of Members.* Richmond. 1978.

Leonard, Sister Joan de Lourdes. "Operation Checkmate: The Birth and Death of a Virginia Blueprint for Progress, 1660-1676." *WMQ*, 3d ser., 24 (1967):44-74.

Massachusetts Historical Society, *Collections*, 4th ser., 9 (1871):81-149.

McIlwaine, Charles Howard, editor. *Political Works of James I.* Cambridge, Mass. 1918.

McIlwaine, Henry Read, editor. *Journals of the House of Burgesses of Virginia, 1619-1659/60*. Richmond. 1915.

_____. *Minutes of the Council and General Court of Colonial Virginia*. 2d ed. With supplementary appendixes, and preface by Jon Kukla. Richmond. 1979.

Newton, Arthur Percival, editor. "A New Plan to Govern Virginia, 1623." *American Historical Review* 19 (1914-1915):559-578.

Nugent, Nell Marion, compiler. *Cavaliers and Pioneers: Abstracts of Virginia Land Patents and Grants*. Richmond. 1934-1979.

Rolfe, John. *A True Relation of the State of Virginia Lefte by Sir Thomas Dale Knight in May Laste 1616*. Charlottesville. 1971.

Sowerby, E. Millicent. *Catalogue of the Library of Thomas Jefferson*. Washington, D.C. 1952-1959.

Stock, Leo Francis, editor. *Proceedings and Debates of the British Parliaments respecting North America*, vol. 1. Washington, D.C. 1924.

Strachey, William. "A True Reportory of the Wreck and Redemption of Sir Thomas Gates, Knight." In *A Voyage to Virginia in 1609*. Louis B. Wright, editor. Charlottesville. 1964.

_____. See also, Flaherty, above.

Van Schreeven, William J., and Reese, editors. *Proceedings of the General Assembly of Virginia, July 30-August 4, 1619*. Jamestown. 1969.

Virginia Magazine of History and Biography (1893-).

William and Mary Quarterly [title varies] (1892-).

Wyatt Manuscripts, earl of Romney's deposit, Loan Collection 15, British Library; extensive selections from which are in *WMQ*, 2d ser., volumes 7 and 8. See also Fausz and Kukla, above.

Secondary Works

Andrews, Charles McLean. *Colonial Period of American History*. New Haven and London. 1934-1940.

_____. British Committees, Commissions, and Councils of Trade and Plantations, 1622-1675. Johns Hopkins Studies in Historical and Political Science, 26. Baltimore. 1908.

Bailyn, Bernard. The Origin of American Politics. New York. 1968.

_____. "Politics and Social Structure in Virginia." In Seventeenth-Century America: Essays in Colonial History. James Morton Smith, editor. Chapel Hill. 1959.

Beer, George Louis. Origins of the British Colonial System, 1578-1660. New York. 1908.

Bemiss, Samuel M. Ancient Adventurers. Richmond. 1964.

Billings, Warren M. "Growth of Political Institutions in Virginia, 1634 to 1676." WMQ, 3d ser., 31 (1974): 225-242.

Breen, T. H. The Character of the Good Ruler: A Study of Puritan Political Ideas in New England, 1630-1730. New Haven and London. 1970.

_____. "Looking Out For Number One: Conflicting Cultural Values in Early Seventeenth-Century Virginia." South Atlantic Quarterly 78 (1979):342-360.

Brenner, Robert Paul. "Commercial Change and Political Conflict: The Merchant Community in Civil War London." Ph.D. diss., Princeton University. 1970.

Carson, Jane Dennison. "Sir William Berkeley, Governor of Virginia: A Study of Colonial Policy." Ph.D. diss., University of Virginia. 1951.

Clarke, Mary Patterson. Parliamentary Privilege in the American Colonies. Yale Historical Publications, Miscellany, 54. New Haven. 1943.

Craven, Wesley Frank. "And so the Form of Government Became Perfect. . . ." VMHB 77 (1969):131-145.

_____. Dissolution of the Virginia Company of London: The Failure of a Colonial Experiment. New York. 1932.

_____. "An Introduction to the History of Bermuda." WMQ, 2d ser., 17 (1937):176-215, 317-362, 437-465; 18 (1938):13-63.

_____. Southern Colonies in the Seventeenth Century, 1607-1689. In A History of the South, Wendell Holmes Stephenson and E. Merton Coulter, editors. Baton Rouge. 1949, 1970.

_____. White, Red, and Black: The Seventeenth-Century Virginian. Charlottesville. 1971.

Diamond, Sigmund. "From Organization to Society: Virginia in the Seventeenth Century." American Journal of Sociology 63 (1958):457-475.

Farnell, J. E. "The Navigation Act of 1651, the First Dutch War, and the London Merchant Community." Economic History Review, 2d ser., 16 (1963-1964):439-454.

Greene, Jack P. The Quest for Power: The Lower Houses of Assembly in the Southern Royal Colonies, 1689-1776. Chapel Hill. 1966.

Hecht, Irene W. D. "The Virginia Colony, 1607-1640: A Study in Frontier Growth." Ph.D. diss., University of Washington. 1969.

Hirst, Derek. Representative of the People? Voters and Voting in England under the Early Stuarts. Cambridge, London, New York, and Melbourne. 1975.

Jester, Annie Lash, and Hiden, Martha Woodruff. Adventurers of Purse and Person: Virginia 1607-1625. [Princeton.] 1956, 1964.

Jones, Howard Mumford. "Origins of the Colonial Idea in England." American Philosophical Society, Proceedings 85 (1942):448-465.

_____. O Strange New World: American Culture: The Formative Years. New York. 1952.

Kukla, Jon. "The Social Context of Institutional Development: Politics and Social Structure in Virginia, 1630-50." Paper read to the Ninety-fourth Annual Meeting of the American Historical Association, 29 December 1979.

_____. Preface to the Second Edition, H. R. McIlwaine, Legislative Journals of the Council of Colonial Virginia. 2d ed. Richmond. 1979.

_____. "Robert Beverley Assailed: Appellate Jurisdiction and the Problem of Bicameralism in Seventeenth-Century Virginia." VMHB 88 (1980):415-429.

_____. Speakers and Clerks of the Virginia House of Burgesses, 1643-1776. Richmond. 1981.

_____. "Some Acts Not in Hening's Statutes: The Acts of Assembly, October 1660." VMHB 83 (1975):77-97.

Kulikoff, Alan. "The Colonial Chesapeake: Seedbed of Antebellum Culture?" Journal of Southern History 45 (1979):513-540.

Levy, Babette M. "Early Puritanism in the Southern and Island Colonies." Proceedings of the American Antiquarian Society, n. s., 70. 1960.

Lucas, Paul R. "A Note on the Comparative Study of Politics in Mid-Eighteenth-Century Britain and Its American Colonies." WMQ, 3d ser., 28 (1971):301-309.

Miller, Perry. "Religion and Society in the Early Literature of Virginia," WMQ, 3d ser., 6 (1949):24-41.

Morgan, Edmund S. American Slavery--American Freedom: The Ordeal of Colonial Virginia. New York. 1975.

Morton, Richard L. Colonial Virginia. Chapel Hill. 1960.

Pole, J. R. Political Representation in England and the Origins of the American Republic. London. 1966.

_____. The Seventeenth Century: The Sources of Legislative Power. Jamestown Essays on Representation. Charlottesville. 1969.

Quinn, David B. "Sir Thomas Smith (1513-1577) and the Beginnings of English Colonial Theory." American Philosophical Society, Proceedings 89 (1945):543-560.

Rabb, Theodore, K. "The Early Life of Sir Edwin Sandys and Jacobean London." Ph.D. diss., Princeton University. 1961.

_____. Enterprise and Empire: Merchant and Gentry Investment in the Expansion of England, 1575-1630. Cambridge, Mass. 1967.

_____. "Sir Edwin Sandys and the Parliament of 1604." American Historical Review 69 (1963-1964):646-670.

_____. The Struggle for Stability in Early Modern Europe. New York. 1975.

Rainbolt, John C. From Prescription to Persuasion:
    Manipulation of Seventeenth Century Virginia Economy.
    Port Washington, N. Y. 1974.

Redlich, Josef. Procedure of the House of Commons: A
    Study of its History and Present Form. A. Ernest
    Steinthal, translator. London. 1908.

Rutman, Darrett B. "A Militant New World, 1607-1640. . . ."
    Ph.D. diss., University of Virginia. 1959.

_____. "The Virginia Company and Its Military Regime."
    In The Old Dominion: Essays for Thomas Perkins
    Abernethy, Darrett B. Rutman, editor. Charlottesville.
    1964.

Tate, Thad W., and Ammerman, David L., editors. The
    Chesapeake in the Seventeenth Century: Essays in
    Anglo-American Society. Chapel Hill. 1979.

Thornton, J. Mills, III. "The Thrusting Out of Governor
    Harvey: A Seventeenth-Century Rebellion." VMHB 76
    (1968):11-26.

Vaughan, Alden T. American Genesis: Captain John Smith and
    the Founding of Virginia. Boston and Toronto. 1975.

Washburn, Wilcomb E. Virginia Under Charles I and Cromwell,
    1625-1660. Jamestown 350th Anniversary Historical
    Booklets. Williamsburg. 1957.

Wight, Martin. Development of the Legislative Council,
    1606-1945. London. 1947.

Wright, Louis B. "Elizabethan Politics and Colonial
    Enterprise." North Carolina Historical Review
    32 (1955):254-269.

INDEX

Ames, Susie M., x
Amsterdam, 114; see also Dutch tobacco traders
Andrews, Charles McLean, x, xv-xvi
Andrews, Peter, 85
Antigua, 153
Arbitration, 172
Archer, Gabriel, 6
Argall, Samuel, 18, 61
Aristocracy, 97, 114, 115, 117, 122, 225
Aristotle, xxii-xxiii, 2, 5, 47-48, 97, 115, 117, 224-225
Atheism, 180
Authority, 150-151, 155, 165-169, 189, 198, 200-204, 207-209; see also Order
Bacon, Nathaniel, Sr., 202
Bacon's Rebellion, xv
Bailyn, Bernard, xviii-xx, 222-223
Baker, Sir Richard, 206
Baltimore, George Calvert, Lord, 33, 66, 82, 88, 95, 125, 158, 161, 190-192
Barbados, 153
Barbour, Philip, xiv
Beacons, 78
Beer, George Louis, xvi
Bennett, Edward, 77
Bennett, Richard, 38, 84, 117, 131, 154, 156, 158, 161, 163, 167-180, 190-192, 196
Bennett, Robert, 163
Berkeley, Sir John, 116
Berkeley, Sir William, xx, xxiii-xxiv, 10, 36, 38-39, 105-108, 111-119, 123-131, 133, 146, 149, 151, 157, 160, 169, 180, 197, 207-216
Berkeley Hundred, 21-22, 84
Bermuda, 10, 72, 76, 153
Bermuda Company, 51-52, 132
Bernard, William, 202
Beverley, Robert, 126

Bicameralism: xvii-xviii, xx-xxi; in Massachusetts, 37, 110, 119-122; in Virginia, 36-37, 110-119, 145, 165, 169, 212, 215, 241
Billings, Warren M., xvii, 138, 143
Blackman, Jeremy, 84
Bland, John, 85
Bloch, Marc, xi
Book of Common Prayer, 162
Booth, Sir George, 206
Boroughs, 23, 49
Bourne, Reuben, 76
Brazil, 172
Breen, T. H., 15
Bromley, George, 76
Bruce, Philip Alexander, x, xii
Buck, Richard, 11, 51
Buck, Benoni, 146
Burgess, 23-24, 37, 49
Burgesses, 141-145
Burgesses, House of, 37-39, 159; see also General Assembly; Speaker
Button, William, 83
Cade, Jack, 116
Caesar, Sir Julius, 54
Calvert, Leonard, 146
Capps, William, 17, 87
Carew, George, Baron Carew, 69
Carleton, Sir Dudley, 25
Carr, Lois Green, x
Carson, Jane E., xv
Carter, John, 201-202
Catholicism, 66, 158
Cattle, 78, 89
Chancery, 140
Charles I, 78, 123, 148, 151-152
Charles II, 39, 206, 211, 214-215
Chew, John, 115
Chicheley, Sir Henry, 197
Chichester, Arthur, Lord Chichester, 69

Chiles, Walter, 169-180
Civil War, 116, 148, 197
Claiborne, William, 29, 33, 36, 38, 82-89, 99, 117-118, 124-124-125, 131, 145, 154-158, 161-164, 167-180, 190-204
Clarke, Mary Patterson, 169
Clerks: of the House of Burgesses, 111, 167, 176; of the counties, 139-140; of the Council, 176; of the General Assembly, 111
Collingwood, R. G., xxi
Colony, 1
Committee, 56
Committee for Private Causes, 182, 189
Committees, 56-59, 80, 182-183, 189, 194
Commonwealth, 116
Commonwealth of England, Virginia's surrender to, 38, 149, 154-163, 171-172, 189
Community, xvii-xviii, 48-50, 73, 81-82, 99-104, 143, 148, 216
Conflict of interest, 177-179
Congregationalism, 164
Conquest, idea of, 234-235
Convention, xv
Corker, John, 111, 169, 176
Council, 44
Council of State, 4, 5, 11-13, 34, 38, 43-45, 87, 93-95, 104, 122, 150-153, 193-204, 212-216; legal powers of, 81
Council of War (1651), 160
Counties, xvii, 103-104, 109, 138-141
Court, General, 61
Courts: admiralty, 172, 175, 246-247; appellate, 59-63, 104, 144, 182, 189; county, 103-104, 138; circuits for, 140; monthly, 103
Craddock, Mathew, 84, 118
Cranshaw, William, 14

Craven, Wesley Frank, x, xii, xiv, 41, 47
Cromwell, Oliver, 160, 196-198, 201, 203, 207
Cromwell, Richard, 203, 207-208
Culpeper, Thomas, Baron Culpeper, 43
Curtis, Edmund, 154, 163
Custis family, 112A, 115
Dade, Francis, 197
Dale, Sir Thomas, 8, 11-13
Davis, Thomas, 53, 54
Davis, Richard Beale, x
Dawes, Abraham, 88
De La Warr, see West, Thomas
Debate, rules of, 185-186, 198
Declaration Against the Company (1642), 107, 114, 117
Dennis, Robert, 154
Dew, Thomas, 169, 197
Diamond, Sigmund, xviii
Digges, Edward, 38,
Digges, Edward, 158, 191, 196
Discovery (ship), 5
Ditchfield, Edward, 74-75
Domesticity, 32-33, 35
Donne, George, 34-35, 97
Dorset Commission, 87, 96
Drake, Sir Francis, 2
Dutch East India Company, 172
Dutch tobacco traders, 36, 86, 88, 98, 113, 117, 162-164, 170-171, 177
Elections, 48, 144, 183-184
Elliott, Anthony, 202
Ellison, Robert, 201
Engagement, the, 163
English, William, 90-91
Equality, 116; see also Order; Mixed government
Evelin, Robert, 29
Faction, xxii-xxiii, 34-37; alignments of, 112A-115
Fame of Virginia (ship), 171-176
Fauntleroy, Moore, 189
Febvre, Lucien, xi

Federalist, The, xxiii
Felgate, William, 85
Felgate, Tobias, 85
Ferrar, John, 85
Ferrar, Nicholas, 87, 91
Filmer, Robert, 225
Fiske, John, xiii
Fitzhugh, William, 182
Fletcher, George, 176, 178
Freeman, Bridges, 115
Garnett, Thomas, 60
Garwaie, Henry, 76
Gates, Sir Thomas, 7, 10-13, 29
General Assembly, created, 22-23, 43-64; confirmed, 73-79, 96, 132, 155; unicameral, 36, 51-54, 79-80, 97, 106, 154; bicameral, 36-37, 103, 106, 110-119, 145
Gerard, Sir Gilbert, 132
Gibbes, Thomas, 53, 57
Gilbert, Sir Humphrey, 2-3, 29
Gills, Stephen, 115
Glover, Richard, 114-115
Godspeed (ship), 5
Gosnold, Bartholomew, 6
Gourgainy, Edward, 57
Governor, 11-13, 22, 43-44, 93-95
Governor, 11-15, 167-169; military, 7
Governor's Land, 61
Grandison, Oliver St. John, Viscount, 69
Gray, Robert, 1-2
Green Spring, 157
Greene, Jack P., x, xv, 223
Gunnell, Edward, 175, 179
Hamor, Ralph, 27
Harmer, Ambrose, 146
Harris, William, 189
Harrison, Thomas, 242
Harvey, Sir John, xvi, 26, 34, 65-66, 112A, 147, 149; Thrusting Out of, 81-96, 236-237
Harwood, Thomas, 93, 146

Haselrig, Sir Arthur, 132
Hastings, William, Lord Hastings, 92
Hatcher, William, 181
Heath, Sir Robert, 72
Hecht, Irene, 20, 30-31
Henfield, Richard, 171-175
Hermaphrodites, English, 210
Hester, J. H., 132
Hiden, Margaret Woodruff, xi
Hill, Edward, 180-181, 145
Hinton, Sir Thomas, 33, 90
Hobbes, Thomas, xxi, 105
Hockaday, William, 178
Hoffer, Peter C., 236-237
Holte, Robert, 115
Hopeful Adventure (ship), 171-176
Hopewell (ship), 174
Horsey, Stephen, 174
Horsmenden, Warham, 201-202
House of Burgesses, 112; see also Burgess
House of Burgesses, 186-190, 194-204; see also Burgesses
House of Commons, 112
House of Commons, 190; see also Parliament
Huberd, Robert, 176, 180, 182
Hull, N. E. H., 236-237
Husband, Richard, 171-175
Indemnity, 162
Indentured servants, 19
Ingle, Richard, 125, 145
Ireland, plantations in, 2, 8, 26, 69, 72, 234-235
Jacob, Abraham, 76
Jamestown, founding of, 5-6
Jefferson, Thomas, xv, 209
Jennings, Abraham, 85
Jones, Sir William, 65-66
Judiciary, see courts
Juries, 104, 109, 120
Kammen, Michael, 184
Keayne, Robert, 120
Kemp, Richard, 93
Kendall, George, 6

Kent Island, 84, 125, 137
Lambert, John, 206
Land policy, 18-21, 23, 25, 86, 162
Land titles, 67-68, 70-71, 78 80-81; confirmed, 96-98
Laud, William, 26, 126
Lawes Divine, Morall and Martiall, xiv, 10
Lawrence, Henry, 203
Lawsuits, 102-103
Lawyers, 192
Lee, Richard, 115, 197
Leopoldus of Dunkirk (ship), 175-176
Levellers, 116
Levy, 182; see also Taxation
Littleton, Nathaniel, 172, 175
Lo stato, 9, 17-18; see also Machiavelli
Ludlow, George, 115
Ludwell, Thomas, 112A
Macaulay, Thomas Babington, xii-xiii
Machiavelli, Nicolo, xxiii, 9, 16, 48, 121, 227; see also Policy; Reason of state
Macock, Samuel, 50
Madison, James, xxiii
Magna Carta, 192-193
Major, Edward, 163, 177-178, 197
Majority, 177
Manchester, Lord, 132
Mandeville Commission, 69-71, 87
Marshart, Michael, 77
Martial law, 14, 22, 43, 91
Martiau, Nicholas, 91
Martin, John, 53-61, 74-76
Martin, Sir Richard, 54
Martin, Dorcas, 54
Maryland, 33, 86, 97, 145-146, 161, 190; founded, 66, 82, 94
Mathews, Samuel, Jr., (governor), 38, 158, 190-204
Mathews, Samuel, Sr., 32-33, 35-36, 82-92, 95, 99, 117,

Mathews, Samuel, Sr., continued, 131, 133-137, 149, 156, 161, 176, 190
Mathews-Claiborne faction, 76, 82-93, 97-99, 107, 112A-114, 117, 122-123, 151, 156-159, 161-164, 177, 190-204, 212
McIlwaine, Henry Read, x, xiii-xiv, 49, 165
Menard, Russell R., x-xi
Menefie, George, 32, 35, 84-85, 91-92
Menefie, Mary, 114
Merchant-planters, 31-36, 38; see also Mathews-Claiborne faction; Thompson, Maurice
Military regime, 4-5, 7-18; see also Martial law
Militia leaders, 8-9
Miller, Perry, v-vii, 224
Mixed government, 116, 120-121, 145, 157, 168-169, 215-216
Monck, George, 206
Monopoly, tobacco, 72, 74-79, 84, 98, 107, 114, 117
Morgan, Edmund S., xviii
Morton, Richard L., x, xvi, 191
Moryson, Francis, 197
Namier, Sir Lewis, xix
Navigation Act of 1650, 153, 171
Navigation Act of 1651, 83, 85-86, 123, 156, 158, 163, 170, 172
Nemattanow, 25
New Albion, 37
Newport, Christopher, 5
Niebuhr, Reinhold, xxiii
Northampton Protest, 173-174
Northumberland, see Percy
Norwood, Henry, 197
Oath of supremacy, 52
Oath of allegiance, 11, 126-131, 136, 155-156
Ogilby, John, 215
Opechancanough, 54, 62, 66, 99, 124-126, 129, 131

Order, ideas of, xvii, xxi-
    xxiv, 1, 11-12, 14-15, 28-29,
    45-46, 64, 115-116, 120-
    122, 123, 126-129, 148-153,
    155, 166, 181, 207-215, 224,
    225; see also Conquest
Orphans, 104, 140
Palisade, 32
Parishes, 130, represented by
    burgesses, 141-142
Parliament, 24, 37, 49, 52,
    55-57, 60, 84-85, 106, 110,
    118, 125, 132-137, 147,
    148, 155, 165-169, 171, 181
Parliamentary procedure, 184-
    186, 189, 198, 231
Peirce, William, 33, 89, 95, 117
Percy, George, 6, 10, 29
Percy, Algernon, earl of
    Northumberland, 132, 132
Pettus, Thomas, 202
Pierse, Thomas, 51
Plurality, 177
Plymouth Company, 4
Pocahontas, 18
Pole, J. R., xvii
Polentine, John, 57
Policy, ii, 16-17, 47-48; see
    also Machiavelli
Poole, Robert, interpreter,
    62-63
Popular sovereignty, 38-39,
    165-169, 190, 194-204,
    207-215
Population growth, 101-102,
    109, 138
Pory, John, 24, 29, 50-57, 59
Pott, Dr. John, 87, 90, 92
Pott, Francis, 90, 91, 93
Powell, Nathaniel, 50
Powell, William, 58, 60
Powhatan Uprising of 1622, 25,
    66
Powhatan, 18
Precedent, 92, 169, 177, 182-
    190, 193-194, 213; see also
    Records of the assembly

Price, Jenkin, 197
Privilege, parliamentary,
    181-189
Privy Council, 86, 89, 95, 116
Probate, 140
Profit, rates of, 31, 80
Protectorate, 215
Puritanism, 85, 126-131, 147
Pym, John, 132, 155
Quakers, 146
Quo warranto, 66-67, 98, 234
Rabb, Theodore K., 26
Raleigh, Sir Walter, 2
Ratcliffe, John, 6
Read, Abraham, 175, 179
Reade, George, 202
Reason of state, 164; see also
    Machiavelli; Policy
Records of the assembly, 39,
    183, 193, 199-203, 207, 209,
    213
Reform of 1618, 22-24, 42
Religion, 126-131, 133, 136-
    137, 180-181; see also
    Catholicism; Puritanism
Remonstrance (1642), 108-119
Representation, 141-145, 183-184
Rich, Robert, second earl of
    Warwick, 41, 84, 132-137,
    145, 149, 156
Rich, Nathaniel, 41
Richard III, 92
Rights of Englishmen, 162
Roanoke Island, 2-3
Robartes, Lord, 132
Robins, Obedience, 202
Robinson, Conway, 125, 191, 207
Rolfe, John, 18-20, 50, 60
Rotterdam, 171; see also Dutch
    tobacco traders
Royalists, 147, 149, 153, 159,
    165-169, 197
Royalty, 164, 215
Rutman, Darrett B., xiv
Sandys, Sir Edwin, xiv, 20, 29,
    27, 41-42, 65, 76
Sandys, George, 87, 99, 107

Saye and Sele, William Fiennes, Viscount, 132
Scarborough, Charles, 112A, 115
Scarborough, Edmund, 112A, 115, 146, 173-174
Sergeant of arms, 201
Shakespeare, William, 92
Sheriffs, 139
Sherman, Mrs. Richard, 120
Sibsey, John, 112
Smith, Captain John, xiv, 6, 10, 29, 215-216
Smith, John see Dade, Francis
Smythe, Sir Thomas, 20, 27, 41, 65
Southampton, see Wriothesley
Sovereignty, see Popular sovereignty; Order, ideas of
Spain, 22, 86
Speaker: in Assembly of 1619, 50-52; in Bermuda assembly, 51-52; in colonies, 110; of House of Commons, 51-52, 110; petition of, 177
Speaker of the House of Burgesses, 110-111, 114, 145-148, 167, 176-181, 185-186; election of, 169, 176-181
Spelman, Captain Henry, interpreter, 60, 62-63
Stacy, Robert, 53
Statecraft, 100, 212; see also Lo stato; Policy; Popular sovereignty, Reason of state
Stegg, Thomas, 36, 84, 110, 117, 118, 145, 154
Stephen, Richard, 90
Stone, Thomas, 84
Strachey, William, 10-11, 15, 29
Striker, Laura Polanyi, xiv
Susan Constant (ship), 5
Taxation, 78, 119, 161, 173-174, 182-183, 184, 193; poll tax, 193
Thompson, Maurice, 83-85, 88,

Thompson, Maurice, continued, 118, 170
Thornton, J. Mills, xvi
Thoroughgood family, 112A, 115
Thorpe, George, 29
Thucydides, xxi, 105
Tobacco, 19-23, 29-31, prices, 102; contract, 90, 98-99; see also Monopoly; Profit
Treason, 92, 152
Trinidad, 19
Tucker, William, 84, 88
Twine, John, 51
Tyler, Wat, 116
Utie, John, 83, 89, 92, 95
Vassall, Samuel, 85
Vicegerent, 12
Virginia Colonial Records Project, xii
Virginia Company, 2-4, 7, 19-21, 73-79, 132; 19-21; dissolved, xiv-xv, 27, 65-69; proposed revival, 83-84, 87-88, 98-99, 107
Walker, master of a ship, 89-90
Ward, Captain John, 53
Warwick, see Rich
Warwick Commission, 132, 137
Washburn, Wilcomb, x, xv-xviii
Washer, ensign, 57
Wertenbaker, Thomas Jefferson, x, xii-xiii
West, John, 83, 93, 95
West, Francis, 29
West, Thomas, baron De La Warr, 7-8, 10-22, 43-47, 96
Wharton, Philip, Baron Wharton, 132
Whitby, William, 176, 178
Whittaker, William 189
Willis, Francis, 202
Willoughby, Thomas, 145
Windebanke, Sir Francis, 90-91, 94
Wingfield, Edward Maria, 6-7
Winthrop, John, xxiii, 120

Wolstenholme, Sir John, 76, 83, 87, 89
Women, 32
Wormeley, Ralph, 115
Wraxall, Peter, 174
Wright, Louis Booker, x
Wriothesley, Henry, third earl of Southampton, 65
Wyatt, Sir Francis, 10, 17, 68, 77, 87, 96, 99, 105, 117, 146
Wyatt, George, 16
Yeardley, Argoll, 112A, 117, 172, 175
Yeardley, Francis, 155
Yeardley, Sir George, 23, 28, 40-59, 70, 96
Yeardley, Temperance Flowerdieu, 40
Yonge, Thomas, 89
Zouch, Sir John, 83, 87